After Colette

By the same author

NOVELS

The Women's House
Reasonable Doubts
Sisters by Rite
The Second Flowering of Emily Mountjoy
Greenyards
The Lord on Our Side
A Sort of Freedom
The Headmaster
The Tide Comes In
The Prevailing wind
Liam's Daughter

CHILDREN'S BOOKS

Between Two Worlds
Tug of War
Glad Rags
Rags and Riches
The Guilty Party
The Freedom Machine
The Winter Visitor
Strangers in the House
The Gooseberry
The File on Fraulein Berg
Snake Among the Sunflowers
The Clearance
The Resettling
The Pilgrimage
The Reunion
The Twelfth Day of July
Across the Barricades
Into Exile
A Proper Place
Hostages to Fortune

After Colette

Joan Lingard

SINCLAIR-STEVENSON

First published in Great Britain in 1993
by Sinclair-Stevenson
an imprint of Reed Consumer Books Ltd
Michelin House, 81 Fulham Road, London SW3 6RB
and Auckland, Melbourne, Singapore and Toronto

A CIP catalogue record for this book
is available from the British Library
ISBN 1 85619 471 X

Typeset by CentraCet, Cambridge
Printed and bound in Great Britain
by Cox & Wyman Ltd, Reading

For Francine and Iseabail
and in memory of Nancy Cole

Acknowledgement

The author and publisher are grateful
to Secker and Warburg for permission
to quote in English translation
from the works of Colette.

One

'For to dream, and then to enter into
reality, is only to change the position and
weight of a scruple.'

La Naissance du jour

The line to Paris is unusually bad. After an extra-loud crackle
during which I have made out little of the concierge's guttural,
rapid-fire response, I ask again:

'But when did you last see her, madame?'

'May, perhaps. Late May.'

It is now September.

'Can you try to think back, madame? Please! It's important.'

'Now wait, it's coming back! My mind was on other things,
when the telephone rang. You know how it is? She left on the
first of June!'

'You are sure?'

'It was my grandson Emil's birthday. He was four!'

'Already!' I murmur politely, then, 'Did you actually see her
leave?'

'Oh yes! A taxi pulled up, the driver asked for Madame
Bussac, I called her, and out she came carrying two suitcases.'

'You're sure? She was carrying *two* suitcases.'

'Yes, the cream and the red, the ones she normally took
when she was going on tour. The red was heavy and the
driver asked what she had in it. Rocks? Books, she said!'

'So you were under the impression that she was definitely
going *away* somewhere?'

1

'What else! You know what your cousin is like? She's always coming and going, isn't she? Like a gypsy.'

'Did she say where she was going?'

'No. I asked. Well, I made a little joke, you know. I said, "Where are you off to this time, Madame Bussac, gadding about?" But she did not say. I had the feeling that she was not sure.'

Strange to set off with two suitcases not knowing where you are going, but I do not spell this out to the concierge. She is surprised by little; during her long career she has encountered most vagaries of human behaviour. She has seen – or rather not seen – numerous midnight flits, when the apartments have been plundered, only the light bulbs left dangling, and the rent unpaid. In this instance the rent was up to date, for this I have already established, and nothing was taken that should not have been, and the flit happened in daylight, under her nose.

I ask if Amy seemed worried. Or anxious?

'I couldn't see her eyes. She was wearing dark glasses.'

'What else was she wearing?'

'Black. A skirt and top. She often wore black, didn't she? Easy colour to travel in, I suppose. Doesn't show the dirt. And sandals. It was a warm day. I had my door standing open and little Emil kept running in and out. Oh, and she was carrying her blue jacket over her arm.'

'Did you hear what she said to the taxi driver?'

'I think, Gare de l'Est.'

That night, I have a dream. Amy is advancing in a slow, dream-like way towards a long, low building walled with glass. The doors are gliding open to receive her. She stumbles, catching the toe of her scandal on an unseen protuberance, recovers her balance, raises her head for a brief moment to look up at the glittering sky, then moves on again. She goes through the yawning opening into the shadowy embrace of the interior. The doors close noiselessly behind her. She can no longer be seen.

*

I waken in the morning with my eyes feeling strained from the effort of trying to see her. I imagine that I can, behind the wall of glass: an ageing woman in black, carrying all her worldly goods in two battered suitcases, one dark red, the colour of blood, the other a yellowed cream. She is facing the door as if she would like to get out, but the automatic opening will not work. She puts down the suitcases and places the flat of her hands against the glass. I struggle to see if I can read the lines on her palms: the life line and the heart line. The glass is too dense. She is shut in behind that screen, mouthing words I cannot hear. Her mouth is squarish when she articulates. Is she asking for help? Is she saying goodbye? The image goes blank as if the glass has been wiped clean.

I phone her friends Marcel and Maxim, who live near the Luxembourg Garden.

It is Maxim who answers. They have not seen or heard of Amy, either, for three months. It's not like her, he admits; she's usually so good at sending postcards from her ports of call, or her little notes on blue paper. I have been away, I tell him, in Australia, for two months, and had expected, on my return, to find something from Amy in my pile of mail.

'But there was nothing?'

'Nothing.'

Maxim offers to contact the police, which he does, and rings back later to say that they were not overly interested in Amy's 'disappearance'.

'They said she was an adult and had left of her own free will. Did I suspect foul play? They rattled off some statistics about missing persons. But they did check their records. They had nothing on her.'

'Dead or alive?'

'Dead or alive.'

'Or anyone answering to her description?'

'Or anyone answering to her description.'

*

My next call is to Amy's bank in Paris. The manager, once I explain the situation and that I am a relative, her next-of-kin, is sympathetic.

'She always did live hand-to-mouth, didn't she? A precarious existence! I often wondered how she managed at all. Were there not other ways to earn a living? I used to ask her. How come at her age she had so *little*?'

He looks up her account and is able to tell me that on the thirty-first of May Amy drew out her entire balance, except for a hundred francs.

'So that was two thousand francs that she took. She wouldn't last long on that!'

And since then?

'Nothing. Nothing at all! No debits. No credits.'

'Going away for a while,' she had written to me, on the thirty-first of May. 'Don't worry if you don't hear for a week or two. Sorry to be so mysterious, but will explain everything when I'm next in touch. Je t'embrasse, et Jessie aussi, et toute la famille! — Amy.'

I read the note aloud, again, to my stepmother Jessie, though we both know it by heart already. We are sitting in Jessie's kitchen in front of a high-banked fire drinking gin, having begun on tea, and we are going over and over all the possible fates that might have befallen Amy.

'She might have met a fella,' says Jessie.

'At her age?'

'She's not *that* old. Mid-sixties isne old. No' these days.'

Jessie, who is eighty, still thinks of life in terms of pleasure, something to be seized in handfuls, from minute to minute, as and when opportunities present themselves. She may haved hung up her skates, at long last, where men are concerned, but she will linger in the street for a flirtatious interchange with a male neighbour, regardless of *his* age. She's known to be good for a laugh, hates wimps of either sex. She takes pleasure from her cigarettes and a drink. Wisps of smoke are curling now around the edges of her newly strawberryblonded head. As a girl and young woman – in the days before she married my father, who has been dead for many years – she enjoyed a reputation for being flighty. Nothing wrong with a bit of flight, she says. 'Might as well have a good time while the going's good. You get grounded soon enough.' When I feel low, I go and visit Jessie in the little flat where I grew up. In the same narrow street, a few doors along, lived Amy with her parents, her French mother and Scottish father, my father's brother. Jessie's company soothes me, helps to lower my level of nervous activity. And she still likes a bit of flight. Given any excuse, she'll put on her fine feathers and go out on a spree.

'There's life still in Amy,' says Jessie.

'Was.'

'C'mon!'

'Well, why hasn't she written?'

'Maybe she hasne had time. Maybe she's been having too good a time.'

I am sceptical. If Amy were alive, free, and in full possession of her senses, she would write, telephone, communicate somehow.

'She could have had a stroke, be lying in some hospital ward unable to speak or write – the worst fate of all!'

The ingredients for a number of horror stories have passed through my mind. I have seen Amy in the middle of a milling station crowd, arrested suddenly by a jagged, unseen pain as it zigzags through her chest like forked lightning . . . I have seen her in a quiet back street, a motor scooter coming around the corner, a hand outstretched . . . I have seen a man waiting in a deep shadow . . .

'Aye, but what about her suitcases?' demands Jessie. 'She'd have had her stuff in them, surely?' By 'stuff', she means Amy's publicity material, fliers, posters, scripts for her one-woman show. 'And her body?' Jessie's voice hushes. 'What about that?'

But we are aware, since we read newspapers, that bodies can be disposed of: they can be flung into quarries, weighted

5

and drowned in lakes, hacked into pieces, pushed into rubbish bins, burned in incinerators, buried in woods. We find it difficult to believe that Amy, whom we know and who has sat here in the kitchen beside us, could have suffered any of these bizarre fates. And we have excluded the idea of suicide, on the whole. Even when things were going badly for her, she remained intensely interested in life, in everything around her; she would enthuse over a crow-stepped gable against the darkening Edinburgh sky or a performance by a young group on the Festival Fringe, could be irritable if your enthusiasm did not match hers. 'What's the matter with you?' she'd say. 'You seem half asleep!'

'Mind you,' says Jessie, 'we're all capable of ending it, given that things are bad enough.'

I acknowledge that.

'You dinne think it's deliberate, do you? Her disappearing?'

'For what purpose? And to live on what?'

The more I churn over the facts – or lack of them – the more convinced I become that something must have happened to Amy; and if it has, then, at that moment, she was in some way separated from her identity.

Sunday morning, and the Edinburgh International Festival has just come to an end, for another year. With thoughts of Amy whirling around in my head, I go out and walk the deserted city streets. Last night the fireworks soared high above the castle battlements. It is time now for the clearing up to begin. Waste bins are overflowing with dead leaflets and programmes, greasy fish- and chip-wrappers, squashed beer cans, empty bottles, crumpled crisp bags, stained, lavatory-lid pizza plates. Posters advertising Orton and Othello, Pinter and Pirandello, song and dance, mime and music, poetry readings and post-modern films, all the fun of the fair, are looking blemished, from weather and defacement, but they've done their job, they've drawn attention; and now the props are being packed and the chairs stacked and the floors swept. I pass a group of students cramming luggage into the back of an old Ford transit van. They may have been doing a late-night revue, trying to repeat the successes of the legendary Oxford and Cambridge Revue groups of the fifties. They may have had only five or six people in the audience most nights. But who cares? They've had a good time, and they'll be back next year, if they haven't graduated and embarked on Real Life.

Amy was a well-known figure around the city at Festival-time. She looked so much like Colette that people who had ever seen photographs of the French writer would turn their heads and wonder.

She didn't travel in company in a transit van; she came alone, most years, though not the first (she had Pascal with her then), but latterly, always. She travelled as light as she could, with the two suitcases that contained all her personal possessions and stage effects. She didn't need too many props: a couple of hats and scarves, a vase for flowers, a lamp, a table and a velvet-covered chair. The furniture, she borrowed. She always put flowers on the table, country-garden ones for preference, in shades of blue, pink and mauve: cornflowers, dahlias, anemones, sweet peas.

She gave her first Edinburgh performance as Colette at the 1965 festival, in a small hall in the Dean Village, beside the Water of Leith, just off the West End. I hadn't known she was coming; at that stage in her life she was out of touch with us, and had been for twenty-one years. There'd been a big family row over an American airman, when she was nineteen, and then, a year later, in 1945, she'd gone to Paris to join her mother who'd absconded to France with her lover before the war. Our paternal grandmother, Granny Balfour, had ascribed Amy's going (and her dalliance with the Yank) to her inheritance of bad blood – on her mother's side, naturally.

I'd been browsing, in 1965, through the Fringe programme when my eye was caught by the word 'Colette'.

'Aimée Bussac as Colette,' I read. 'One-woman show, straight from Paris . . .'

I realized that my hand was trembling. I went at once to see

7

Jessie and my father, who was then still alive. 'Look!' I said. 'Aimée Bussac! It must be Cousin Amy!'

'Let's have a look!' My father put on his spectacles.

'Bussac,' repeated Jessie, trying out the word on her tongue. 'Wasn't that the name of Amy's mother's family?'

I knew for sure that it was. Amy's mother had inscribed her name on the books she'd left behind: Eugénie-Amélie Bussac Balfour.

'Then there was the Colette connection,' I said.

I went to the venue on the first day. The performance was due to begin at three. I got there fifteen minutes beforehand, earlier than I had intended. The door was open, and from the pavement I could see her sitting just inside the foyer, at a small table, with a tin cash box in front of her and a roll of what looked like pink cloakroom tickets. She was wearing a deep-blue blouse with full sleeves gathered into the wrists. (Blue was Colette's favourite colour, too.) Her thick hair was the colour of ripe chestnuts; in her youth it had been a dark, rippling red. I remembered my mother telling me that Amy looked rather like the woman in a Holman Hunt postcard that I had pinned on my bedroom wall – I was going through a Pre-Raphaelite phase at the time. Amy had her hair bobbed now, with a half-fringe obscuring part of her high forehead.

She lifted her head, and I saw that she was quite striking to look at, not beautiful exactly, but definitely arresting. Her eyes reflected her blouse. In other lights, when she was wearing different shades, they would seem aquamarine or turquoise. Her eyes gave me a jolt, brought back moments of childhood: Amy picking me up when I'd tripped and scuffed my knee, teaching me words in French, making me repeat them until I'd got them right, sitting on a bench in Inverleith Park telling me stories about the French childhoods of her mother and grandmother.

'Bonjour!' She smiled, without recognition. When she had last seen me I had been a child, only nine years old. I did not want to be recognized immediately; I needed a breathing space. I wanted to sit, incognito, at her show, and watch her perform. It might have been unfair of me to want to have this advantage over her, but I was not sure how she would receive me. The sight of her sitting at the door selling tickets had thrown me a little; I had not expected to encounter her so soon, face to face.

'Would you like a ticket for today's performance?'

'Please.' I handed over my money and she gave me a ticket and a roneoed programme.

'You're interested in Colette?'

I nodded.

Two Americans arrived then, and I moved into the hall to take a chair in the second row. The stage was a slightly raised dais, not much more than ten feet long, on which stood a deep-rose velvet-covered chair and a round mahogany table draped with a lace cloth. A young man, dark, with melancholy eyes – most certainly French – was arranging pink and mauve dahlias in a vase. A lamp with an oyster-coloured shade, a small pile of books, a decanter of clear liquid – water, presumably – and a glass were the only other props. The crystal decanter and the furniture had been lent by a local antiques shop, to whom grateful thanks were expressed in the programme. There were a few notes on the performer: where she lived now, where she had played, where her maternal mother and grandmother had been born. They did not say where she herself had been born. Her Scottish inheritance was unacknowledged. At the foot, it said: 'Stage manager – Pascal Audry.'

The American couple came in and seated themselves with some fuss in the middle of the front row. After they had stashed their folded-up plastic mackintoshes and cameras under their seats, the woman proceeded to read the programme aloud to the man. 'It says she played Colette in New York, at the Gotham Book Mart.' 'For goodness' sake!' 'She's toured widely throughout the US and Canada.' 'We could've seen her back home.' 'We didn't though, did we, Gord? She lives in Paris, France.' 'Guess that's what you'd expect, isn't it, her being Colette?'

On the dais, the stage manager, satisfied with his flower arrangement and the tilt of the lampshade, stepped down, gave us – the Americans and myself – a covert, assessing look, and went out into the foyer.

Soon afterwards, a couple of Frenchwomen arrived, talking volubly and knowledgeably about Colette, then came a young man who might have been Dutch and did turn out to be (he'd seen Amy perform in The Hague), followed by a bearded student in sandals and jeans with a girl in a long, floor-sweeping, granny-print dress. (Sixties, flower power.) We, the audience, were spread out over three or four rows. We waited. The Frenchwomen fell silent. The steady buzz of West End traffic reached us, punctuated by the squeal of tyres and the blare of horns. The flower-power couple held hands and smiled at one another. The Dutchman made a gravel-sound at the back of his throat. It was seven minutes past three. Perhaps Amy had taken stage fright, had fled up Bell's Brae, hand in hand with Pascal, and left us sitting here with our expectations. Then we heard the outside door closing. It squeaked, and they seemed to be having trouble with the bolt. We listened to it scrabbling about as they tried to direct it into its slot. Someone swore softly in French. The American half rose from his seat, as if he thought he should go and help – he looked the kind and helpful type who doesn't like to sit still when another person, particularly a woman, is in trouble. I was also poised to move and then the tap of Amy's feet came towards us and we relaxed back on to our hard chairs.

She came in, followed by Pascal, who was carrying the cash box. The amount they'd taken would scarcely cover the rent. Pascal sat down at the end of the back row. I could not resist turning slightly in my seat to take a quick glance at him. His eyes were directed towards the front, at Amy. There was anxiety in his look, and something else. Affection? Adoration? Love? All three? He must have been about twenty-four or

-five then. And she was forty. Though that of course did not rule out an attachment. (I could not but be conscious of *Chéri*.)

I, too, was anxious for Amy. There was a vulnerability about her that tended to make people feel concerned for her, made them put out a hand in case she was about to trip. She, however, seemed composed, although she told me afterwards that she had been exceedingly nervous. She always was before performances.

She stepped up on to the shallow platform. Her movements were fluid, elegant; there was no awkwardness, no hesitation in the way that her foot adjusted to the change of elevation. She kept her head up, her back straight; she did not look down. Then, taking her time, she bowed to us and said, 'Bonjour!' The American murmured, 'Bonjour!' in return, and she smiled at him. She then began, in English mostly, slipping in a few French words here and there for flavour, but using to a large extent the actual words of Colette, to build up a picture, scene by scene, of the long and varied life of the writer. I thought her performance brilliant: she seemed to have got into the skin of her character, to have her gestures, or ones that convinced, as well as — most importantly of all, perhaps — a voice that rang true. But then her maternal mother and grandmother had come from the same Burgundian village as Colette.

Two

> No doubt I told you of a country of
> wonders, where the savour of the air
> intoxicates? . . . Don't believe it! Don't go
> there: you will search in vain.
>
> *Jours gris*

The first scene was played out on a raw January day in 1873, in Saint-Sauveur-en-Puisaye, a village of no great architectural distinction, with narrow, unpaved streets, set in a countryside of woods and meadows, and low, rolling hills.

Daylight is dwindling. Gas lamps glow softly in the dusk. Midway down the steep rue de l'Hospice one comes to the rue des Gros Bonnets, which runs off at right-angles. At the intersection of the streets stand two women, huddled in shawls, well placed to observe both houses: the large, lofty one with the formal, rather stern façade and double flight of stone steps in the rue de l'Hospice, and the other in the rue des Gros Bonnets, smaller, less imposing, sitting level with the street.

The women's voices rise and fall and mingle with the wind. They have heard that Madame Colette is in trouble. She has been labouring for two nights and three days, but the child, it seems, does not want to be born. One of the watchers knows of a woman in Saint-Fargeau who was unable to eject her baby – it had monstrously wide shoulders (like her husband), and was stuck, half in, half out. Not even the combined efforts of the midwife and doctor were enough to pull it free.

'Her screams were terrible, God rest her soul.' The woman makes a vague movement with her hand over her chest.

Neither mother nor child survived the ordeal. 'She'd been carrying the baby too high. Like Madame Colette.'

'They say children carried so high are reluctant to leave their mothers.'

Their heads whip round as the door of the house in the rue des Gros Bonnets opens and Mathilde, younger sister of Madame Grenot, appears, clutching her coat round her thin body. She looks like a frightened rabbit. The women call over to her.

'Has she started?'

'Yes. And it's coming fast. I'm going for the midwife.'

Mathilde slides past and goes scuttling up the steps of the Colette house to ring the bell. The shrill sound echoes in the street. It is Captain Colette himself who opens the door. He stands on the step leaning on his stick, his empty right trouser leg pinned up behind him. He's quite a man, this Jules-Joseph Colette, a former Captain in the First Zouave Infantry and a Chevalier de la Légion d'honneur. He lost his leg at the battle of Marignan during the wars of the Second Empire. When the emperor came to ask after him, Captain Colette said, 'Mother and child are doing fine,' the child being his left leg. He'd wrapped it in a towel.

Even in the poor light, the women can see that the expression on the Captain's face is grave. He'll have no jaunty greeting to toss at them today. He's tugging at the underside of his beard with his free hand. He says a few words in response to Mathilde, which the watchers fail to catch, then he turns back into the house, hunched over his stick. The door closes behind him.

Back comes Mathilde, running, almost slipping on the steps, forgetting to keep hold of her coat. Its tails fly out in the wind like black wings behind her.

'She can't be spared,' she gasps as she goes past.

Madame Colette *must* be in a bad way. And this her fourth ... Now if it was her first, like Madame Grenot ... No one has heard of any trouble at Madame Colette's previous confinements.

As Mathilde reaches her sister's house the door swings inward, and out on to the pavement steps her brother-in-law, Monsieur Grenot, rubbing his hands as if he has just done a good day's work. An unusual smile lights up his narrow face.

'A girl!' he shouts across to the two women. 'With a good pair of lungs. Slipped out as if she'd been buttered. No trouble at all!'

And so was born, on 28 January 1873, Berthe-Amélie Grenot, grandmother of Amy. A few hours later, when the watchers had given up and gone home and the street outside was dark and deserted, Sidonie-Gabrielle Colette, half-strangled and blue, emerged into the world. For a moment the midwife and servant in attendance thought the baby dead. Everything in the room had gone eerily silent and cold. The fire had died; they had forgotten to replenish it. But the mother, exhausted though she was, knew there was life in her child.

I first heard the story of the births of Amy's grandmother Berthe Grenot and her friend Gabrielle Colette when I was a young child. Amy told it so often that I came to feel as if it were Amy and I who had stood on the corners of the rue de l'Hospice and the rue des Gros Bonnets, with the wind nipping our ankles and the cold creeping up through the soles of our shoes to numb our legs. Long before I ever went to Saint-Sauveur myself, I had an image in my mind of the façades of the two houses and of the two fathers coming out onto their doorsteps; the one anguished, with an eventful history of his own behind him, the other a boring post office clerk and jubilant. When I did finally go, I had a strong feeling of déjà vu. If Mathilde had appeared with coat-tails flying I would have known her face, and that of Monsieur Grenot, and the expression on it when he opened the door to announce the birth of his daughter.

Two dramas played out at the same time. But there was no question as to which interested – inspired – us more. Yet Amy had always seemed proud, as if her grandmother was the one who had been handed the greater role.

*

Amy drew a map of the streets in the back of my drawing book. She inked in the streets in black, marked the houses with a red cross and coloured their gardens green, leaving me to crayon in the flowers. (Loads of red and pink, Amy instructed; to please Sido, Colette's mother, for those were her favourite colours when it came to flowers.) I walked often in my imagination down the rue de L'Hospice and along the rue des Gros Bonnets. I walked in the wake of the nuns as they went to and from the hospice, their long dark skirts trailing in the dirt. Their wide white bonnets went out in front of me, like sails.

'Sido called the rue des Gros Bonnets the rue des Soeurs,' said Amy. 'Sido was very important in Colette's life.'

How could a mother not be important in a child's life? I wondered.

My map showed the rue des Vignes running behind the rue de l'Hospice. A high wall crowned with trailing vines guarded the back of the Colette maison, so that from the roadway it was impossible to see into their secret garden, even when standing on tiptoe, Amy reported. As a child, on holiday in Saint-Sauveur, long after the Colettes had left the village, she had scrambled up the wall and lain draped along the top like a cat, peering down through the branches, trying to see what her grandmother had seen, when she was her age.

To the young Berthe Grenot, the Colette garden appeared enchanted. On the occasional summer afternoons that she was invited in to taste its pleasures, time seemed to stand still. It was as if she heard it click off with the closing of the gate behind her. She would wait there for a moment and listen. Sounds were soft: the buzz of insects, the lazy cluck of a hen in the farmyard on the other side of the wall, the sigh of the breeze in the topmost branches of the massive old lilac trees. Ancient twin firs looked over the garden. Apricots ripened on the wall. Hydrangeas, pelargoniums and roses bloomed, as did a profusion of geraniums, foxgloves and red-hot pokers.

Madame Colette, in her wide-brimmed, burnt-straw hat held down by its brown taffeta ribbon, might be collecting green walnuts from the walnut tree, dropping them one by one into her apron. In the long grass Gabrielle's half-brothers, Achille and Léopold, might lie face downward, propped on their elbows, between which would rest a book. The Colettes were known in the village as great readers. The boys would not notice the new arrival, who was treading gently so not to ruffle the peace of this green and golden world. Berthe did not like it when other children were invited in to play, as they sometimes were on Thursdays. Then hoarse voices split the silence, hobnailed boots bruised the grass, black pinafores made ugly blots against the green, skipping ropes whirred, and arguments broke out.

On days when Gabrielle felt indolent, she would summon Berthe to the small stone-flagged terrace at the back of the house that trapped the sun. A worn iron trellis, sagging in the middle and mantled with wistaria and bignonia, provided dappled shade. Gabrielle would lie in the hammock and dreamily swing to and fro, not speaking, lids half closed over her clear blue-green eyes, her pointed little chin raised in the air. Berthe, fingering her own, was aware of its roundness. She was happy, though, not to talk; to be there was enough. She would hug her knees close in to her body and she, too, would dream.

More often, Gabrielle and Berthe would play together in the grounds of the nearby ruined twelfth-century chateau or in the woods on the edge of Saint-Sauveur. They played together when Berthe could escape from the sticky clutches of her younger brothers and sisters. Six were born after her, putting a strain on the post-office clerk's meagre purse and the energy and patience of his wife. Berthe was expected to assume the role of 'little mother'.

'We can't take *them* with us,' Colette would declare, and off she would fly, pigtails bouncing on her sturdy shoulders, down the rue des Vignes, past the church on the corner, towards open country and freedom. She was allowed to roam the countryside for hours at a time, after Madame Colette had listed her restrictions. 'Don't go near the Petit-Moulin fields – they're flooded! Don't go towards Thury – gypsies are encamped there!' Once out of sight, Gabrielle would disregard the warnings. She would return muddied, with mouth stained from wild strawberries and spindleberries, knees and elbows scraped and rents in her pinafore, to be only mildly scolded, if at all. She would proffer a bouquet of blond grasses and mauve meadow safron. When Berthe came home late she was cuffed about the ear, not because her mother had been worrying about her but because she had been unavailable to run errands, hang out the washing, or change the baby when he'd soiled himself.

'Those Colettes!' said Berthe's mother. 'They're not like other people. Who do they think they are? As for Madame – she's got a slate loose, if you ask me! And water's got in through the crack. They say she can sit for half a day watching an insect that any normal person would squash underfoot. And she listens to the wind – the wind, can you imagine! She claims she can predict the weather.'

It was true: Berthe had seen her listen, had heard her say, 'It's raining over Moutiers,' or, 'It's going to freeze, the cat's dancing.'

Gabrielle's mother was fond of animals, great and small. She never turned away a stray. She brought her dog Moffino to church. He was well behaved, she maintained; he got up and down with the rest of the congregation. Why shouldn't an animal have as much right as a human to enter God's holy place? She and the old curé quarrelled when he objected to Moffino barking during the elevation. Madame Colette retaliated. Of course Moffino would bark. Hadn't she trained him to raise his voice whenever he heard a bell?

So Berthe, the child, saw Madame Colette as an easy-going mother who allowed her daughter a great deal of freedom, who made few demands on her, who did not fuss and carp and spread a choking net of anxiety around her. Later – and

17

by then a grandmother herself – reading *La Maison de Claudine*, Berthe came to see that this picture was not only incomplete but largely inaccurate. Almost inevitably so, since a child's view is limited, and adults are practised in concealment. Underneath, it seems that Madame Colette was eaten up with anxiety for Gabrielle, had feared even that she might be kidnapped. She would leave her bed to go and stand in the doorway of her room and watch her sleep.

Gabrielle was the last born in her family. Her mother called her 'Minet-Chéri', and her father 'Bel-Gazou', which in the Burgundian dialect means 'pretty warbler'. Berthe did not expect anyone to call her pretty but she longed for a nickname, for something softer than her own harsh-sounding given name. Berthe Grenot. She hated the way it grated between her teeth. And Berthe could be neither shortened nor lengthened. Who would want Berthine! 'Change your name completely!' said Gabrielle. 'I would, if I were you. Call yourself Alphonsine. That would be more romantic. Or Grenadine.' Berthe thought she might like to be called Eugénie. She confided her desire diffidently. Gabrielle was shocked. 'You can't be called *that*!' 'Why not?' 'It's an empress's name.' Berthe knew that was not Gabrielle's real objection. Madame Colette's given names were Adèle-Eugénie-Sidonie. Did Gabrielle think that if Berthe were to take part of her mother's name she might take a part of her mother, too? Berthe did not ask the question, would not have been able to then, could only sense it. No more was said of her changing her name. But when she came to have a daughter of her own (who was to become the mother of Amy) she called her Eugénie.

'My mother carried me high,' Gabrielle liked to say, with pride. 'That meant I was close to her heart.'

Berthe's mother carried all her babies low; they pulled her forward and downward. Her ankles swelled. Blue-black veins bulged in her heavy thighs. She walked with legs apart and feet splayed. When her time drew near she supported her sagging burden with cupped hands. Her temper shortened. Berthe, ears stinging from quick cuffs, thought that if only her

18

mother had managed to carry her high she might have been closer to her heart.

One day, Berthe, when climbing the back wall of the rue des Vignes, lost her footing and tumbled, striking her forehead as she landed. For a few seconds she was concussed. Opening her eyes, she saw the top of the big fir tree wavering against the blue of the sky, then felt herself being gathered up by Madame Colette's strong, comforting arms, and held in her ample lap. Gabrielle's mother bade her daughter fetch a basin of warm water and a cloth. 'Quickly now, Minet-Chéri! Don't just stand there!' When the water came she gently bathed Berthe's grazed forehead. 'Am I hurting, Berthe, my child?' Berthe shook her head. She did not wish to speak, to break the spell that encased her. Gabrielle stood, feet planted wide, bottom lip protruding, eyes looking fiercely on from under lowered lids. 'I don't think she's hurt much, Maman.' 'How can you say that, Minet-Chéri? Can't you see how her temple is swelling?' Berthe was loath to surrender the warm lap, and the encircling arms.

Lying there, entranced, she could imagine what it would be like to be Madame Colette's child. And perhaps she really was. Perhaps she and Gabrielle were twins, and Madame Colette – *their* mother – had given her to the Grenots to be suckled, temporarily, on account of Gabrielle being puny at birth and in need of extra care; and when the time had come to hand her, Berthe, back, her foster family had been unable to part with her. That night, in bed, Berthe told her sister Jeanne that she and Gabrielle were twins, that Madame Colette was her real mother. In the morning Jeanne told their mother, who boxed her eldest daughter's ears until they stung, and her head reeled, and stars pranced before her eyes.

'Lies, lies, filthy lies! They spill out of your mouth like vomit! Don't you know who you are? You're Berthe Grenot, do you hear? – Berthe Grenot! And *don't – you – forget – it!*'

*

Berthe, once her ears had cooled and her tears dried, went back to day-dreaming. She carried the Colette garden over into her night dreams in the lumpy bed that she shared with her two small sisters. If they rolled on top of her and broke her sleep she would get up and go to the open window, lean on the sill and gaze out at the Colette house across the way. After the marriage of her half-sister Juliette, Gabrielle was given her pretty bedroom at the front on the first floor. It had pearly-grey wallpaper sprinkled with cornflowers. Berthe imagined Gabrielle lying curled like a question mark in the white lace-curtained bed, the moonlight raking in through the open window and touching her long, rippling, chestnut-coloured hair, making her look like a princess in a fairytale. Sometime, surely, a handsome prince would come and bear her away on his dashing white horse. Perhaps two princes would come, and they would gallop off together, she and Gabrielle, two sisters who would never be parted.

The garden behind the house would now be dark, with dense, ink-black shadows under the trees, which could only deepen its enchantment.

In the hall in the Dean Village, at the 1965 Festival, Aimée Bussac, alias Colette, is leading us along the rue des Gros Bonnets, into the rue du Bourg Gelé, the route the young Gabrielle took to school. We see her walking with her friend Berthe in their black smocks, carrying bottles of lemonade on summer mornings, boxes of live coals in winter for foot-warmers. Gabrielle's warmer, made of forged iron, is by far the prettiest in the class and weighs as much as a full suitcase. Gabrielle huffs and puffs but she carries it proudly. It can be useful in the playground, as a shield or an offensive weapon. Both girls are wearing clogs, which on chilly days ring out on the frosted road. They walk close together and they chatter. The sky above is black, with a waning moon throwing down a shaft of light on the path in front of them. They must reach school by seven in order to sweep out the rooms, carry logs in from the shed and light the cold stove.

The makeshift school building where the girls receive their elementary education is old and dilapidated, and far from healthy; the air in the closed-up classrooms turns foul by midday, compounded as it is of stinging smoke from the stove, carbon-dioxide fumes from the foot-warmers and the smell of unwashed children. In the afternoons the pupils often doze off. 'A rough paradise', Colette called it.

At recess Gabrielle and Berthe come tumbling out into the playground to play marbles and hopscotch, wage war with their warmers, fight with their fists, scream at the tops of their voices, climb trees with little regard for modesty. They are a wild, unruly lot and cause their poor, unqualified teacher, Mademoiselle Veillard, much distress. In the classroom, too, before the fumes bring on drowsiness, exuberance spills out of them. They clatter around in their wooden shoes, delighting in the noise; they push and shove one another; they giggle, gossip round the stove and eat everything they can get their teeth on, from the lead in their pencils to blotting paper, erasers, pieces of cloth, cigarette paper. At times Mademoiselle Veillard comes close to weeping. She is incapable of disciplining these children from rough peasant homes. Gabrielle comes from a better-off background, her brothers and sister were sent to boarding school in Auxerre. But it is known that Captain Colette is having financial difficulties; he is inept when it comes to managing money, he's made some poor investments, and is being forced to sell part of their farm. Gabrielle insists that she is being kept at home not for financial reasons but because her mother cannot bear to part with her.

'You know that is true, don't you, Berthe? That my mother would shrivel up and die if I were to be sent away?'

Mademoiselle Veillard does not survive; she is replaced by Mademoiselle Terrain, who in years to come will achieve the dubious distinction of being the model for the schoolteacher in *Claudine à l'école*. In vain does she protest that she has done none of the scandalous things attributed to the fictitious Mademoiselle Sergent in the book. But it would take a lot to convince the villagers that she is not Mademoiselle Sergent, just as it would be difficult to convince them that Colette herself is not Claudine.

Amy – Colette – looks directly at us, her audience. 'Are you imagining that I'm portraying myself? Have patience: this is only my model.'

As Gabrielle and Berthe came into their teens, they became less boisterous in class; they put away marbles, climbed trees only occasionally, sat now at break-time on two stone benches outside the school, their belts tightened to emphasize the smallness of their waists, their hair twisted into makeshift chignons or bobbing with ringlets. They stole horsehair and stuffed it along with rags of cotton or wool into bags to make bustles, so that their skirts were shorter at the back than at the front. They sprinkled violet scent on their handkerchiefs. They sat on the benches alongside the other girls, giggling and chattering like a row of songbirds on a wire, their bright eyes watchful for passing salesmen, soldiers home on leave, notary clerks going about their business. Few men could resist slowing their steps or even stopping. The girls would then shriek and try to push one another off the bench.

Sometimes, after school, Berthe would go home with Gabrielle and they'd heat tongs over a little spirit-lamp and corkscrew the ends of each other's hair, wrapping them first in tissue papers that smelled of vanilla. They loved the scent of vanilla and would close their eyes to inhale it. Smells were more powerful when you closed your eyes, said Gabrielle. They'd eat wholemeal bread with cream cheese and pink onions, and talk about boys and sex and having babies – what else? Gabrielle had read a description of childbirth in a novel of Zola's which had terrified her. 'It was all blood and tearing! But my mother says the pain passes and that one forgets.' It was not what Berthe's mother said. Gabrielle's mother had told her it was a marvellous thing to have a child. 'She says Zola has no business to poke his nose into things like child-birth! It's a woman's affair and the men should stay away.' The girls reread the passage in Zola, though, and shuddered at the thought of the tearing. They talked of the things they might do if they did not marry and bear children: go to Paris and Brussels, travel in Italy, cross the Atlantic in an ocean liner, see the Statue of Liberty. Berthe had a desperate yearning to go to Paris; she longed to see the fine buildings and walk in the Bois de Boulogne.

'Do you think I shall ever get to Paris, Gabri?' she asked.

'Why not? If you want to *enough*, you can do it. As for myself, I shall probably stay in Saint-Sauveur for the rest of my life. I am just a country girl! How could I ever leave the *woods*, Berthe? And my garden? The big fir trees? The old lilac? They're my friends, they've watched over me since I could crawl. They'd miss me! They might sicken and die. And so might I.'

When Berthe was sixteen, André Bussac, the baker's son, began to pay her attention. He was a handsome lad with delicate features and blond hair that fell engagingly over his forehead; and he had a slow smile. He detained Berthe in the boulangerie, held her loaves of bread against his floury chest while he paid her pretty compliments, brought a blush to her cheeks.

'Don't let him sweet-talk you, Berthe!' warned Gabrielle. 'What future would you have with a baker? You don't want to spend your whole life washing clothes and scrubbing floors like your mother, do you? You want to go to Paris some day, don't you? Do you think *bakers* go to Paris?'

On fine spring evenings, which were just beginning to lengthen into summer, Berthe and André would meet and go walking in the woods. He would take her hand as they put the confines of the village behind them, and once inside the screen of the trees he would slide his arm around her soft waist. He allowed his hand to rest on the top of her bustle. In the wood it was almost dark. The trees had assumed weird shapes. If Berthe had not been able to feel the warm, comforting arm of André around her she might have been afraid. Their feet crackled on fallen twigs. A bird squawked and swooped through the branches overhead. The earth smelt new and raw. André would lean in close to Berthe to inhale her scent. He liked the violet perfume that she wore. He whispered in her ear, sending little shivers down her spine, making her shoulder twitch and come up to meet her ear.

'Be careful!' said Gabrielle. 'You know what he wants from you! Remember that a few moments of pleasure – if you could call it that! – might end in a lifetime of drudgery! It has been the fate of too many women. It shall certainly never be mine! And don't smile at me like that, Berthe, like a cat that has lapped up the cream! You *haven't*, have you?'

'Of course not!' said Berthe, and turned away so that she could continue to smile.

At the end of the summer term in 1889, the pupils in the top class went to Auxerre to sit for their upper school diplomas. They set off with hilarity and excitement, travelling first by coach and then by train. Some of the girls, like Berthe, had never been to Auxerre, the town on the hill overlooking the Yonne, with its magnificent cathedral and golden abbey church. Gabrielle knew it well, having often accompanied her mother there on her three-monthly shopping trips, when they would set off at two in the morning in their blue-lined victoria. She was able to point out the landmarks as soon as they appeared.

The pupils stayed in a hotel, crammed into rooms like dormitories.

'How is one to sleep peacefully here?' demanded Gabrielle, who was used to sleeping alone. 'We shall be fit for nothing in the morning, let alone our final exams!'

They had to rise at five. Berthe got out of bed looking as if her face had been floured. She stood in her nightgown, holding a hand to the base of her neck. Gabrielle moved towards her, alarmed.

'Berthe, are you all right? You look as if you have a fishbone stuck in your throat.'

Berthe retched, and ran with arms outstretched for the

enamelled wash-basin on the dresser. Bending over it, holding back her soft brown hair from her temples with both hands, she was violently and convulsively sick. The other girls froze in the midst of dressing, petticoats half on, stockings pulled up to the knee. The stench of Berthe's vomit filled the room. For a moment there was silence, then Gabrielle spoke.

'Berthe – you can't be! You *can't*!' Her eyes were wide with horror.

Gabrielle returned triumphantly to Saint-Sauveur, knowing that she had given a good account of herself. She received high marks. Berthe, who had not managed to attend all the exams and had had to flee the room in the middle of solfège and sight-reading, received a bare pass in spelling and dictation, writing and arithmetic. Anything she had ever known about history or geography had fled her mind, which was otherwise preoccupied.

'You will never escape the village now!' said Gabrielle. 'You will never go to Paris. You will spend your life on your knees.'

But Berthe was not despondent, for she was fond of André and, unlike Gabrielle, she wished more than anything else to escape her mother's house.

'We're going to have to leave this house?' Gabrielle stared at her mother. '*Our* house? You can't mean it! You can't!'

Panic rose in Gabrielle and seized her by the throat like a fox snatching a stoat; she felt she was about to choke on her own blood. The taste in her mouth was metallic. There must be some mistake. Her mother must have a fever. She waited for her mother to say that it was a mistake, a joke, a perverse thought that had entered her head in a moment of madness. Of course they were not going! But her mother did not speak, and Gabrielle read resignation in her face. Gabrielle had known, like everyone else, that their fortunes had been declining, that her father had been a poor manager of their estates, that everything he had ever touched had shrunk. For

25

a moment she wanted to upbraid her mother, but she knew what she would say. 'That was his province; I had mine.'

Her mother was telling her the house was to be leased and that they were to go and live with her brother Achille, who was now a doctor, in Châtillon. Until they found a little house of their own.

A little house. In Châtillon-sur-Loing, seventy kilometres away in the Loiret. Gabrielle needed air.

She ran into the hall and, wrenching open the front door, stumbled out on to the top step. She grasped the wrought-iron rail and let her body lean forward. She stared down the narrow, familiar little street where she had spent all seventeen years of her life. Every detail was familiar, each crack in the road was known to her.

Lifting her hands she saw that the rail had left deep gouge marks in the soft pink undersides of her fingers.

Amy unclenches her hands and, letting the fingers unfurl, like petals loosening in warmth, turns them towards the audience in an encompassing gesture, as if to say, '*You* understand what she felt, what *I* feel, don't you?' Her fingers have left deep gouge marks where they have bitten into the palm. She is staring at them. Her vulnerability, her sense of loss, is palpable; I feel I could almost reach out and touch it. I marvel at her courage, facing an audience, playing out such a gamut of emotion, exposing herself. Difficult enough to be a writer, but at least at the point of creation one is alone, shut away, with the light illuminating the page, and not one's face.

As I sit staring at her hands, an echo of recognition comes to me, and then the memory . . .

Amy is sitting at the table in the kitchen of her father's house. Normally so lively, so mercurial, talking volubly, gesturing freely, her glossy, dark-red head bobbing, catching the light, today she sits motionless, as if carved out of stone. There is a terrible silence and stillness in the house. I, a small child, having arrived in the midst of this drama unexpectedly, stand trapped in the doorway, unable to advance or retreat. I realize that something terrible is happening to my cousin. I sense that her life will never be the same. She has just unclenched her hands. They lie on the table top, splayed, helpless. Her father is facing her across the table, his right hand a huge, white plaster-of-Paris fist. He has broken the knuckles of this hand on a man's jaw. He has told his daughter how this came to be: how he surprised her mother, cavorting like an animal, in the King's Park, behind the ruined chapel of St Margaret, with a man. A Frenchman. He never cared for the French, which might seem odd in one who took a French wife. But, as his mother would have told you, he was not himself when he made the commitment.

On that dour afternoon I watch as George Balfour raises his dazzling fist. He tells his daughter that her mother has gone and will never return.

In the kitchen of her father's house, Amy closes her own hands up tight.

The Colettes' furniture was advertised for sale and sold, under the auctioneer's hammer, to the highest bidders. Gabrielle stood shivering in the hallway, horrified, as their everyday possessions were carted off. Her mother's love seat. Her father's armchair. A commode with a bombé front. The big, four-doored, figured mahogany bookcase. Their books. Volumes of Musset and Voltaire, Goethe and Schiller — she was allowed to keep her Balzac. Their pots and pans went. When she saw her walnut bed go past, shouldered by two brawny, aproned men, and then her old Norman armoire, and after that her little ink-stained mahogany desk, she became hysterical and had to be comforted by her mother, who rocked her as she had done when she was a small child.

'They're only *things*, Minet-Chéri. We still have one another.'

But the sale marked Gabrielle for life. In her writing she constantly denounces the need for possessions, warns against becoming attached to them. The auction marked the end of the first part of her life; it closed the gate on her earthly paradise and pitched her out into a different world. No longer securely rooted, she became nomadic. 'I belong to a country that I have left,' she wrote many years later.

Out in the street the villagers gawked, enjoying the spectacle of the Colettes' downfall. Gabrielle saw them from an upstairs window. She hated those women, the ones with the hamster-like mouths and the greedy eyes. 'We must never become like *them*,' she and Berthe had always said. They must not become women who existed only in kitchens, who waited on street corners for drama to erupt in other people's houses. And now Berthe, at seventeen, was a wife and mother and the walls had closed in around her, cutting off her dreams of Paris, while she, Gabrielle, who had never wanted to go, was leaving. The pain inside her was like a burning fire that threatened to spread into every part of her body and consume it. It was like going through the birth trauma again. Saint-Sauveur had always held her high, close to its heart, just as her mother's womb had done. She did not want to be forced down another long tunnel and out into the cold unknown.

She turned away from the window and ran down the stairs, dodging the removal men. She fled across the garden, where the air was heavy with the smells of summer, scrambled up the back wall for the last time and dropped down into the rue des Vignes. Her hands were scuffed. She dusted them on the back of her skirt and stood for a moment with her eyes closed, her fingers clenched together in front of her. She would not cry, she would *not*. She found tears as distasteful as vomiting. She hated the way they bloated her face and distorted it, and made her look ugly. Berthe cried easily. She had cried in the hotel room at Auxerre, after she'd been sick. When tears spilled down Berthe's soft, peach-like cheeks, Gabrielle glanced away.

At the top of the street she came into the rue de la Roche, where the Bussacs had their boulangerie. André was serving in the shop. She heard his voice through the open doorway. 'Bonjour, madame! Comment ça va? Ça va bien?' All day he would say the same things and listen to the women's troubles. 'How are your veins, Madame Perreau? And your palpitations, Madame Doucet — I hope they are not keeping you awake?' André Bussac was polite, he was kind, he was decent. But unexciting. Life with such a man would stifle a woman as surely as any pillow placed upon her face.

Gabrielle said a quick 'Bonjour!' and went through the shop and up the stair to the Bussacs' apartment. 'Berthe!' she called. 'It's me — Gabri.' She found her old friend in the cramped little kitchen. There was only one other room, in which the Bussacs, man, wife and child, all slept. The thought made Gabrielle feel claustrophobic. If ever she married, she would make sure she had a room of her own. Berthe was sitting in a low nursing chair, feeding her baby, Robert. She had wanted a girl.

Gabrielle pulled up a chair to face her.

'It's terrible, Berthe, what is happening to our house . . .'

Berthe listened and nodded and murmured soft words of sympathy and the baby slurped and burped and Berthe smoothed the top of his hair with her hand and Gabrielle talked and talked until she ran dry. She sat back. She sighed. She raised up the thick heavy curtain of her hair to air her head. Today, it was giving her a headache. Mademoiselle Terrain used to say she should have it cut, that it was unhealthy to have hair reaching to your feet. Her mother had nurtured her daughter's hair since she was born. She called it her pride and joy.

The cheap clock on the wall ticked sharply. A cart rattled past in the street. The baby was breathing through half-open lips. His mouth had slipped off Berthe's huge brownish-pink nipple and his head had fallen to one side. Gabrielle averted her eyes from the sight of the nipple. How could Berthe bear to have her body distorted so? A dribble of milk ran down the baby's chin. The room was warm and smelled of baby and Berthe's milk. Berthe's finger came slyly up and stroked the boy's cheek. Her eyes were on him and not Gabrielle. Gabrielle sighed again.

'What will you do, Gabri?' Berthe looked up now. 'Do you think you might find a job in Châtillon?'

Gabrielle shrugged. What could she do? There were not many jobs that a poor country girl could get other than clerking in the post office or the railway, or working as a salesgirl in a shop. All of those options were out of the question for her! Could Berthe see her selling stockings to fat women? And she had elected not to go to the teachers' training college, as some of the girls in their class had done. They would have to spend three miserable years there, and what would their lives be at the end of it? They'd be shackled to some beastly little school full of beastly little children from seven in the morning until five at night and be ridden by some ghastly harridan of a headmistress. And then they might have a slimy little man like Deputy-Mayor Merlou sniffing round them looking for favours. And all for seventy-five francs a month! Laundresses earned as much. Better to be a laundress, declared Gabrielle; at least you could dream while you worked. Sheets and pillowcases would not expect to own your body and soul.

The only other option open to a girl was marriage.

'I expect you will meet someone handsome in Châtillon,' said Berthe.

Henri Gauthier-Villars, alias Willy, writer, journalist, humorist and music critic, was thirteen years older than Gabrielle Colette and came from a well-connected, orthodox family. Willy himself was anything but orthodox. He has been variously described as a ladies' man, highly sexed, a man of the world, a libertine, sophisticated, complex, subtle, egoistic, charming, witty, irresistible, one of the most putrid wrecks of the belle époque, excellent company, an entertaining conversationalist, with a flair for lying and shocking people and an acid tongue that was quick to denigrate. People could not be indifferent to him. In appearance he was small, stout and balding, with pale-blue eyes and a heavily moustached, fattish face. His voice was on the coarse side. Colette, long after they had separated and he had died, described him as being not so much large as swollen, with a powerful skull and protuberant eyes and a rather shapeless nose between pendulous cheeks. He was reputed to look like Edward the Seventh but she thought the resemblance closer to Queen Victoria. Presumably, though, when she married him she saw him in a different light.

'So why did I marry him?' Amy, alias Gabrielle, asks us.

For a moment I think the American in the front row is going to answer, then he remembers himself. We can all see the reasons against Gabrielle's marriage to Willy, but also several in favour of it. He is not boring, and Gabrielle's boredom threshold is low. He is a man of letters (though less successful than she knows at this point), and a man of the world; his father owns a publishing house in Paris; he lives in *Paris*, knows Marcel Schwob, Paul Verlaine, Claude Debussy, Rémy de Gourmont, Camille Flammarion, Anatole France ... Gabrielle lives in Châtillon-sur-Loing in the provinces with her parents in a nondescript little house. Her most exciting activity is to accompany her brother Achille, who is a doctor, on his rounds.

'I have few opportunities to meet interesting bachelors and I am at an age when I am ripe for marriage!' Gabrielle, as we are coming to realize, is a sensual young woman, and highly sexed herself.

Madame Grenot went to visit her eldest daughter. Berthe was now the mother of three sons.

'Did you hear that your friend Gabrielle Colette has got herself betrothed to that journalist from Paris? The one who is always involved in scandals. They say that his father and Captain Colette served together in the army. They say also that he is old and fat and a roué. Un vrai libertin!'

Berthe shrugged. 'Gabrielle said he was a man of letters.'

'Letters! Pah! Money, more like. Those Colettes always were ones to get above themselves. So she wrote to you?' Madame Grenot glanced about, as if she might be shown the letter.

31

Berthe made no move. In the crib the baby, Louis, slept; André had taken the two older children, Robert and Alain, downstairs to the boulangerie to play.

'You have a good man there,' said Madame Grenot, in a tone that suggested Berthe did not deserve him. 'Could you imagine your father looking after any of the little ones?'

Madame Grenot was with child again. It was her eleventh pregnancy. Eight of the children had survived.

'But he's like all other men, your André' – she nodded towards the crib – 'when it comes down to it. They pleasure themselves, and we women pay for it.'

After her mother had gone, Berthe took Gabrielle's letter from her apron pocket.

'He both attracts and repels me,' her friend had written. 'I want to marry him and yet I want to remain as I am, untouched, *me*. Can you understand, Berthe?'

Berthe thought that she could.

'Tell me what it was like,' Gabrielle had demanded, when they were in Auxerre to take their exams, 'the first time you lay with André.'

'I can't tell you. I don't know what it was like. It just happened.'

Hearing André's step on the stair, Berthe quickly thrust the letter back into her pocket.

There was talk in Paris, too, as well as Saint-Sauveur. The gossip columnists enjoyed themselves hugely and when the popular daily *Gil Blas* issued advice in its columns to the 'pretty owner of two incredible golden plaits' in Châtillon, recommending that she withhold her kisses from a well-known Paris wit until she had his ring on her finger, Willy challenged the editor, Lefebvre, to a duel. Willy was an experienced dueller and managed to wound Lefebvre in the stomach, thus creating a few more column inches for the journalists. Many thought that he would never actually *marry* this little girl from the provinces. A flirtation was all very well, but marriage? Who could imagine Willy married, anyway?

But, on 22 April 1893 at 7.15 a.m., Willy sent a telegram from Paris to the mayor of Châtillon-sur-Loing: 'Publiez les bans Gauthier-Villars – Colette. Salutations empressées. Gauthier-Villars.'

On 15 May 1893, Sidonie-Gabrielle Colette and Henri Gauthier-Villars were quietly married in the sixteenth-century church of St Peter and St Paul in Châtillon, in the presence of the Colette family, the maid of honour, two best men (Parisian friends of the groom), a local timber merchant, and his wife and daughter who were to act as witnesses. The Gauthier-Villars parents did not attend; they would have preferred their son to marry an heiress and had made their own selection. At the ceremony the bridal couple received a simple benediction. There was no nuptial mass. The bride wore a white muslin dress sprigged with flowers and a blue ribbon tied round her forehead, 'à la Vigée-Lebrun', as her mother described it. Madame Colette herself was stiff in a black faille dress trimmed with jet. The colour of mourning. Her face was stiff also, in an effort to conceal its sadness; she was losing her beloved daughter. The image of her mother's face would accompany Gabrielle the next morning as she journeyed on the train to Paris with three 'completely unknown' men, and swell her heart with pain.

The wedding day was unseasonably hot. A hazy, amateur photograph shows the little procession struggling across the village square towards the church. They look as if they are pushing through waves of warm air.

The heat made Gabrielle feel languid. The day dragged. The men talked, batted literary puns around. The wedding feast was rich and heavy. They ate sea pike with a sauce mousseline and, to follow, bastions de Savoie, a moulded almond pudding topped with pink spun sugar. Gabrielle drank champagne and for a few seconds dozed off, her head fallen back against her chair, anxiously watched over by her mother. Willy made the observation that his bride looked a little like Beatrice Cenci in the Barberini Palace.

His friend Paul Veber disagreed. 'With her red carnations,' he said, 'she looks more like a stabbed dove.'

We are in Paris now, in the rue Jacob. The year is 1894. The mood changes in our Edinburgh hall and we straighten up in response to the lifting of Amy's head. Oh là là! it's the belle époque, the heyday of the Moulin Rouge, the Casino and the Folies!

In the evening Willy and Gabrielle set forth, creatures of the night, dressed in their finery. 'You should see me in my plumed hats and dangling earrings!' They go to concerts and the theatre and the music-hall. They eat and drink in cafés and hear the gossip of Paris. Their marriage is still attracting much attention. 'The gay dog of high Parisian society has actually *married* the little savage from Burgundy! I have had to get used to people staring. Some say I look like a little fox being led about on a string by Willy! He jokes that I look so young he is afraid he might be arrested in the street for the corruption of a minor.'

The salons are the great thing. They're run mostly by women, amazing, beautiful, well-born women who love to entertain writers, musicians, artists. They vie with one another to snare the most prestigious people. Gabrielle meets the poets Catulle Mendès and Paul Valéry, and two younger writers called André Gide and Jean Cocteau, whom she finds interesting. She thinks that she and Monsieur Cocteau could become friends. 'He has a most sensitive, appealing face. Then there is a young writer with an exceedingly soft voice and soulful eyes by the name of Marcel Proust.'

And then, late at night, the Willys go to the offices of *L'Echo de Paris* so that he can correct his copy for the next day's edition. He is fastidious about this and will not hurry. Gabrielle sits on a chair and droops with fatigue, but Willy is a night owl. They go to the Brasserie Gambrinus, foggy with cigar smoke, where men with thick beards make bets about the amount of beer they can drink, or to the Café d'Harcourt in the Latin quarter, which young prostitutes frequent. Gabrielle prefers the prostitutes to the bearded men. In the small hours of the morning, as the sky is lightening over the rooftops of the city, they climb into a cab and make their weary way back to the rue Jacob.

Mornings are different: solitary and grey. Willy goes off about his business around Paris, leaving his young wife in their third-floor, rear apartment which, being sited between two courtyards, gets no sun at any time of the day or year. Gabrielle longs to be able to step out into a garden at dawn. 'Can you imagine me living without woods and ponds? Can you imagine me living without *sun*?'

She hates this street of faceless apartment buildings with its ground-floor shops, situated between the boulevard Saint-Germain and the river. The street narrows, as if out of spite, just as you reach their part. If she leans out of the back window she can see the old red tiled roofs in the rue Visconti, which remind her of Burgundy and home.

One of Gabrielle's greatest pleasures is her cat. She is the most beautiful angora that you ever saw and her name is Kiki-la-Doucette. She comforts Gabrielle and helps lighten her days in the gloomy flat. When her mistress is sad Kiki rubs her face against hers and purrs into her ear and makes her shiver with delight. She gives her petits pois in a dish and the cat eats them delicately, like a real lady, one by one. Like her mistress, she sees no reason to rush. They have nowhere to go. They lie on the sofa and Gabrielle eats sweets and reads by the light of an oil lamp. The salamander stove gives off poisonous fumes that penetrate her brain. She is growing thin. She sometimes wonders if she could summon enough energy to scale the back wall into the rue des Vignes.

Gabrielle wrote to Berthe about her life in Paris. Berthe kept the letters and passed them on to her daughter Eugénie, who, in turn, passed them to her daughter Amy, though that is not strictly true, for Eugénie was forced to leave them behind when she ran away with her lover. After Amy herself went

35

away, the letters, along with Eugénie's books, came into my mother's keeping, and later into mine.

Berthe meant to write back to Gabrielle but her children occupied her from morning till night and took all the energy that she had, which she did not resent, knowing it was the way with children. Robert was a particularly wild child from whom she scarcely dared lift her eyes. 'He'll be trouble later,' predicted Madame Grenot, whose last pregnancy had resulted in a stillbirth.

Berthe no longer imagined that she was the daughter of Madame Colette; she had put away such childish thoughts. But the longings still remained, even if they were submerged most of the time under a welter of domestic chores. Sometimes, though, in the middle of the night, sitting by the stove nursing Louis, when all was silent except for the sound of André snoring on the bed behind her, these yearnings would surface, and she would write to Gabrielle in her head, saying things she would not have said aloud or set down on paper . . .

I love André, and the children, but every now and then I long to leave them all behind – yes, to escape! We could meet and run off together, Gabri! Where would we go? South? To the Mediterranean? To Provence, perhaps – I would like that. We could go and find that mill near Arles where Alphonse Daudet lived with his owl and wrote his letters. Do you remember how you used to recite to me the story of Monsieur Seguin and his pretty little goat Blanquette? The one who wanted freedom so desperately that she was willing to risk being eaten by the wolf. So sad that she had to die in the morning. I so much wanted her to live. I thought Monsieur Daudet should have let her live. But you always said that the important thing was that she had fought off the wolf until dawn and had had her night of freedom on the mountain.

Amy told me the story of Monsieur Seguin's goat when I was a child. I loved the charming, light-footed Blanquette, couldn't understand why she'd had to go to the mountain.

'But, Amy, Monsieur Seguin was kind to her!'

'Sometimes the mountain is irresistible,' said Amy, who had a look on her face that I did not like.

I cried when Blanquette was finally eaten by the wolf.

'If I could have such a night,' said Amy, 'I would willingly die, too!'

Now, at the time of her disappearance, her words come back to me, though she must have been only sixteen or seventeen years old when she spoke them. It was a romantic notion, the sentiment of someone young, who did not take the idea of death seriously. By the time she came into her sixties she would not have supported the idea. Or would she? I realise that I'm not sure. It's not like Amy, Jessie and I keep saying, she wouldn't do this or that; it would be out of character. But how well do we really know her? I am trying to find out, to put together the pieces that made up her life and brought her to a point when she was capable of vanishing, seemingly without trace.

'Don't die, Amy!' I pleaded, then, all those years ago.

Seeing my distress she said she had no intention of tangling with a wolf on a mountain, and promised to live for ever.

Three

Proclaim your liberty, I tell you! It's the
custom. Every time a door is opened, you
must run, jump, twist yourself into half
circles and cry out.

Toby-Chien to Kiki-la-Doucette in
Dialogues de bêtes

It is the summer of 1895. Gabrielle has brought her husband
on a visit to Saint-Sauveur. They are staying at the school,
enjoying the hospitality of the headmistress, Olympe Terrain,
who will greatly regret her invitation after the publication of
Claudine à l'école.

Willy had long wanted to see the youthful haunts of his
young wife. They walked in the woods and in the grounds of
the old ruined castle. They were seen strolling along the dusty
country roads, the short-legged, corpulent man in his tightly
buttoned suit, with his waxed moustaches, and Gabrielle in
her Parisian dress, twirling a parasol over her newly-shorn
head. Yes, she had cut her hair.

The Gauthier-Villarses came to call on the Bussacs. Berthe
had given birth to a daughter only a few weeks before. The
baby was nursing at her breast when the visitors arrived
unannounced; André was downstairs in the boulangerie. The
three older children were scrabbling around on the floor. Their
hands were dirty and Georges' nose needed wiping.

Berthe got up, flustered, and the baby slid off her breast,
leaving it exposed. It was large and creamy-white and veined
in blue. Milk dripped from the engorged nipple. Berthe saw
that Willy saw these things, too, and that his eyes were
lingering. Hurriedly she tried to push the breast back into its

bodice, but the baby was screaming and Willy was saying, 'Please do not stop on our account,' so she pulled up the child's head and let its mouth re-engage. The noise stopped.

'Please, do sit down.' With her free hand Berthe lifted some clothes from the chairs and made room.

Willy sat on the edge of his chair, his stomach bulging as he leaned forward, openly watching the baby feed. Berthe was glad that André had not come up with the visitors; she knew he would not like this man from Paris. When she had read parts of Gabrielle's letters aloud to him, he had snorted and said that such people led immoral lives. He had heard about the Moulin Rouge and the Folies: they were sinful places.

Berthe offered damson wine. Gabrielle got up and poured it into the little green-tinged glasses on the table.

'So you've cut your hair, Gabri!'

Gabrielle's hand went to her nape. 'I was very ill last year.'

'I'm sorry.'

'A votre santé!' Willy raised his glass to Berthe.

'Yes, I went into a decline. The doctor advised me to cut my hair – he said it was sapping my strength. And I must say I feel the better for it. My head is lighter.' The short bobbed hair with the thick fringe made Gabrielle's face look even more triangular and fox-like. She had changed, apart from the hair; she was not what Berthe thought of as 'a woman of the world' exactly, but she was no longer a Burgundian village girl, either.

'And your mother? How did she take it?'

'As if someone had died,' interjected Willy.

'You are unfair to her, Willy! After all, she'd spent twenty years caring for it! But it was done before she came, and when she saw how low I was I think my hair was the least of her worries. They thought I might not make it. My mother nursed me back to life.'

'Madame Colette blamed Paris.' Willy smiled, a smile that Berthe did not like. 'And me. I think she thought *I* was sapping her energy.'

'And you, Berthe,' Gabrielle put in quickly, 'you have four children now. Four in five years!'

'You have certainly not been idle,' murmured Willy.

Berthe blushed, aware of the innuendo, but conscious also of how dull her life must seem to people who passed their lives in the cafés, theatres and literary salons of Paris. Once she used to like to read herself – Gabrielle had lent her books – but now, if she were to take up a book at night, her head would begin to nod before she reached the end of the first paragraph.

'And this one is a girl?'

'I am pleased to have a daughter.'

'What is her name?'

'Eugénie. Eugénie-Amélie,' said Berthe defensively.

'Ah – *Eugénie*!'

'I have always liked the name.'

'I, too,' said Gabrielle.

Willy lit a fat cigar and puffed a stream of thick blue smoke into the room. 'Berthe, tell me about your schooldays.'

'Schooldays?' Berthe looked at Gabrielle for help.

Her friend laughed. 'Oh, he is obsessed with our schooldays.'

Berthe could not understand why. Everyone went to school, didn't they? Theirs had been nothing out of the ordinary, except to them.

'What did you do together?' asked Willy, bringing his face close to Berthe's and the baby's. He reeked of cigars and his protuberant eyes were bloodshot. He was quite ugly, thought Berthe; she would not care to be his wife and lie with him.

'You girls – did you caress one another?' Willy's voice was hoarse and his breathing irregular.

'Leave her alone!' commanded Gabrielle. She turned to Berthe. 'He has been tormenting poor Mademoiselle Terrain also. He has got her quite confused.'

At that moment Berthe's sister Jeanne put her head round the door and would have withdrawn when she saw the guests, but Berthe asked her to take the three little ones across the road to play in the castle grounds for an hour. Louis was becoming fretful and Robert and Georges were fighting over the possession of a tin whistle. Berthe could see that child's play did not amuse Monsieur Willy.

Jeanne removed the children, and Gabrielle suggested that her husband himself should go for a walk.

'Ah, you want to recall girlish memories, is that it?' He heaved himself out of the low chair. 'Far be it for me to come between you.'

They listened to his heavy footsteps descending the stair. He whistled softly as he went. The baby Eugénie continued to suck.

Gabrielle threw off her shoulder shawl. 'So many babies, Berthe!' She shook her head. 'Distending your body. Eating you up. Don't you mind?' Her own waist was slender, compressed by a wide leather belt.

'Sometimes.' Of course there were times when Berthe longed for a different life. That was why she had kept Gabrielle's letters. 'And you, Gabri?' she asked. 'Will you have children?'

'Some day, perhaps. I, too, should like a daughter. But Willy is not a family man.'

'Your life would not allow for children. It is too Bohemian.'

'Do you remember how we used to fancy the Bohemian life? But do you know, Berthe, it doesn't suit me, not at all. It exhausts me. I find some of the people I meet interesting, but those salons and those hostesses are so artificial! Sometimes, when I'm sitting on a satin brocade chair sipping champagne beside some raddled old nincompoop, I nod as if I'm listening, but in truth I'm thinking of the woods of Saint-Sauveur – and the garden!'

They were both silent at the thought of the garden.

'And Monsieur Willy?' Berthe ventured. 'Are you . . . are you happy with him?'

'Happy? Who knows what that is? I find him stimulating.'

'He seems – talented?'

'Oh, very. He's not faithful, of course.'

'No?' Berthe was shocked, though she tried not to show it.

'He has several mistresses that I know of. Oh yes! His sexual appetite is *immense*. Like all his other appetites. I caught him with one woman – not *in flagrante*, but doing her accounts, of all things! Perhaps that bothered me more. Made it seem more serious. *Domestic*, almost. Her name is Charlotte Kincler and she's quite small, and not particularly pretty, but she has a certain je ne sais quoi! Or perhaps I do know what it is! She has many conquests to her name, at any rate. She is quite a character. She came from a poor home in Montmartre and runs a herb shop now. We have become friends, or at least close acquaintances, shall we say.'

'But don't you hate her?'

'I've learned a great deal from her – about tolerance and survival. I have come to admire her. She was brought up in a hard school.'

'But don't you mind about your *husband*, Gabri? When he is unfaithful to you?'

'Oh yes, I mind! I mind very much. I want to go away and die. I'm a jealous woman.' Gabrielle's eyes glowed. 'I feel I could be quite violent if I gave way to it. When I lie at night alone in our big cold bed waiting for him to return, thinking about him with another woman, I plan to kill him. But when he does come in and calls out, "What, not asleep yet?" my resolve crumbles into dust!'

The baby had fallen asleep. Berthe gently lifted her from her breast and pulled her bodice across, mindful that Monsieur Willy might return. She had felt his eyes at work, peeling the bodice back from her other breast, sliding her dress down over her hips, and then she had seen them shift to the old sagging bed in the corner where she and André slept. Willy had intended her to see him; he had engaged her eyes until she'd looked away, a fiery heat welling up from her neck into her face.

'I have never before met a man like your husband.'

'Neither had I.'

'Why is he so interested in our schooldays?'

'He wants me to write my memoirs.'

'But why?'

'He thinks they could be titillating, especially to older men. There is a great fad in Paris for older men to take young girls as mistresses. The Libertine and the Innocent go hand in hand! Willy is always trying to think of different ways to make books. That's what he does – he *makes* books, he doesn't write them, or not much of them. He's a good editor, though, and he can inspire people. He gets hold of an idea and then finds someone to write it.'

'And publishes it under his own name?'

'Oh yes, under the name of Willy! He loves the sight of his name in print. And anything to make money, Berthe. Anything at all! "Money's short!" *That* is his constant cry.'

Claudine à l'école was not published until 1900, Amy tells us, five years after the idea was first conceived by Willy. When Gabrielle had written the first draft, he had looked at it and tossed it aside, deciding that he had been wrong after all, there was nothing saleable in the memoirs of a village schoolgirl. She was happy to accept his verdict. She had no burning desire to write. She went back to fondling Kiki-la-Doucette on the sofa and reading other people's work. A couple of years later, clearing out his desk, Willy came upon the manuscript and decided that he had been mistaken. It just needed a bit of 'tarting up', a little work on the attachments between the adolescents themselves and the teachers, on the sexual attachments . . .

'Come on, Gabrielle – we haven't a sou!'

He kept her hard at work, locking her in her room each day until she had produced a certain number of pages. There is some debate about how much Willy actually contributed to the manuscript, but Colette herself said that it was written entirely in her own hand, though with another, very small handwriting adding a pun here and there, changing a word, delivering a reprimand. It seems likely that she learned something from his interference, for always afterwards she wrote and rewrote, seldom satisfied. Her prose, which reads with such fluency, did not flow straight from her pen in its perfected state.

The novel was published by Ollendorf of Paris (it was a copy of this edition that Amy inherited from her mother Eugénie) under the signature 'Willy'. On the cover Claudine sits on top of a desk looking, in a red cloak and yellow clogs, like an angelic version of little Red Riding Hood. The depiction amused Gabrielle. Amy holds up the book for us to see, and we crane our necks; it is not her mother's copy – that is on my bookshelf. I reflect that I shall have to give Amy her books back, now that she has returned.

Willy wrote, in a rather coy preface, that he had received the manuscript from an anonymous donor. In public he patted his wife's head and said how precious she was and how much she shared with him. Reviews mentioned the novel's spiciness, scandal was hinted at, by Willy as well as others; he was an excellent self-publicist, more than willing to draw attention to himself, no matter if that attention was vitriolic (any publicity is better than none), and to provide fuel for the gossip columnists' fires. He had no need of publicity managers, dump bins, authors' tours and bookshop signings. The book sold forty thousand copies in two months.

Willy became famous. 'Only God' wrote Sacha Guitry, 'and perhaps Alfred Dreyfus are more famous than Willy these days.' Willy became if not rich, then solvent. He set his wife to work on a sequel. She acquiesced. She might, one supposes, have refused, for a writer can be locked in a room but not made to write. But there was a certain perverse streak in Colette that would have enabled her to enjoy, to some degree, the mystification surrounding the authorship of *Claudine*, and to relish the anonymity; and the exploitation of her talents by Willy may have been yet another facet in their far-from-straightforward sexual relationship.

The next three years saw the publication of *Claudine à Paris*, *Claudine en ménage* and *Claudine s'en va*. All appeared under Willy's name, although it was generally known that the author was, in fact, his young wife Gabrielle.

In later life she was critical of the books, which by then had been reissued under her own name. They were written between the ages of twenty-three and twenty-nine; they were part of her apprenticeship.

'My name is Claudine,' read Berthe, fixing her elbows on the table on either side of the book, ready to push it under the pile of mending should she hear a foot on the outside stair. The boys were at school and Eugénie was playing with her doll – whose name was Gabrielle – crooning to it, rocking it gently in her arms. She was a pretty child with soft blonde hair who lived much of the time in the land of make-believe; she preferred to play with her dolls than the village children. André said she spent too much time hanging around her mother's skirts. He was downstairs in the bakery.

Eugénie was their last-born surviving child. In the meantime Berthe had had two miscarriages and one stillbirth, and the doctor had said that it would be unwise for her to conceive again. So far she had been lucky. And if she were not, she would go for help to a woman in the rue du Bourg Gelé. This might be a sin in the eyes of the church, but if she were to die her children would be left motherless and her husband without support, which in her eyes would be an even greater sin.

Her sister Jeanne had bought the Claudine book in Auxerre. People had been talking about it for months and Berthe had been eager to read it. Jeanne had read parts of it herself and been scandalized. The schoolteacher, Mademoiselle Sergent, was depicted as a libertine. Quite unsuitable as a person having young girls in her care, especially when they were at such impressionable ages. Mademoiselle Sergent was conducting affairs with the school inspector *and* another mistress! As for the girls themselves . . . 'We were never like that!' Jeanne had said indignantly. 'And poor Mademoiselle Terrain! She hardly dares show herself in the street.' The permanent blush that had spread across the teacher's face was like a birthmark.

Berthe read on; the fire dwindled; Eugénie fell asleep with her doll cradled in her arms; André came up the stairs unheard. Flustered, Berthe pushed the book under a heap of socks and stood up, looking about her, trying to remember where she was and what she should be doing. She had been quite lost in the village of Montigny with Claudine and her friends.

André was irritable. The fire was almost out, the place was in a muddle, and where was his lunch? His annoyance led to a bout of coughing. His lungs were bad – it was the flour that irritated them. Since his health had deteriorated, so had his temper. He smiled less now and was impatient often with the women in the shop when they gossiped and cluttered the floor space.

'I was mending.' Quickly Berthe went to resurrect the fire, to put on potatoes that were now going to take an age to boil. André slumped down at the table, his left arm sprawled close to the mending. She cooked anxiously, an eye on André's outflung arm. He did not find the book, not that day.

It puzzled Berthe, this novel by Gabrielle's husband. So much rang true, *was* true, whilst others parts were false and gave the wrong impression of their school. But then it was not their school exactly, was it? It was one imagined by Willy – or Gabrielle? – and Claudine was *not* Gabrielle, though Berthe could see much of her friend in the character.

She dropped the hot lid of the potato pot, and it narrowly missed Eugénie's foot. The child wakened from her dream and began to cry.

'What are you doing today?' demanded André. 'Your head seems to be up in the sky.'

'I am sorry, André,' murmured Berthe.

She read part of the book every day, under cover. Most of the time she was careful, but losing herself on another occasion she again failed to hear the approach of her husband, who caught her in the act.

She looked up guiltily into his face.

'What book is that?'

He knew before he lifted it. 'Why are you reading such filth, Berthe?'

'It's not filth! You haven't read it, how can you know?'

'I've heard about it and that is enough! It is about the people of Saint-Sauveur, and perhaps about *you*, too.'

'No it is not, André. Why don't you read it? Look – try, please!'

She opened the book at the first page, held it open in front of him. He began to read, very slowly, his lips moving a little, though he did not speak aloud. He was not very good at reading, not as good as she was; he always said he had little need of it.

'You see, André, it's about a place called Montigny, a place that does not exist. Montigny-en-Fresnois, above the Thaize. The Thaize does not exist, either; it says so.'

'But it says that the houses tumble from the top of the hill to the bottom of the valley.' André's voice stumbled as he coped with the words. 'And there is a squat, ivy-covered Saracen tower *and* a ruined château!' That seemed to clinch it for him; he closed the book at once and, putting it under his arm, made for the door.

'Where are you going?'

'To burn it.'

She ran after him down the stairs and stood in the doorway of the bakery, watching while he put the book on a long shovel and pushed it into the red-hot fire that heated his ovens. The pages, in those first few brief moments of conflagration, when they were turning yellow and orange and purple and blue, appeared quite glorious, then they curled and began to blacken and give off grey, putrid smoke. The burning did not matter too much, for *Claudine à l'école* survives – as do most books that are burnt – and is still alive; and Jeanne was able to buy another copy in Auxerre, the copy that was eventually to travel to Edinburgh, Scotland, with Eugénie.

André's cough continued to worsen. The nights were bad; there were times when it seemed impossible for his chest to be at peace. He sat propped against pillows, wheezing, struggling for breath, while Berthe hovered round with steaming kettles. The doctor prescribed sedatives and talked of sending him to the hospital in Auxerre, but André said it was only a cough and he could not leave the boulangerie.

He died in February 1902, aged thirty-five, leaving his widow with four children under the age of twelve. His brother inherited the bakery. He, too, had a family of four children, and another coming. He said that the bakery could not support more than one houseful of mouths, which could not be denied. André's family was allowed to remain in the flat above the shop and given free bread. Berthe took in laundry. Now her kitchen was thick with steam and smelled of boiling soapsuds as well as bread during the days, and in the evenings, more peacefully, of warm ironing.

The years that followed were hard. Louis, who had never been strong, developed a cough like his father's and died of tuberculosis. Robert ran wild and got into trouble, with local farmers and the fathers of young girls. Eugénie remained quiet and dreamy and stayed close by her mother's side. Berthe's rounded face thinned, her ankles swelled and her hands became red and coarse, but every night when the children had finally gone to bed, no matter how tired she was, she would read by the light of the old oil lamp on the kitchen table. After the death of her husband she had taken up the habit of reading again. The sight of her book waiting on the window-sill for night encouraged her through the day. She read each of Gabrielle's books as they came out – after the publication of the four *Claudine*s her friend had let it be known that it was she who was the author. And in 1904 she published *Dialogues de bêtes* under the name of Colette Willy, a *nom de plume* she was to use until 1923, when she dropped the 'Willy' and became solely 'Colette'.

Berthe liked to reminisce about Gabrielle and the long, unhurried days of their childhood, when she was doing her ironing in the evening and she and Eugénie were on their own together, with the shutters closed and the lamp lit. The girl would be curled up in a chair, cheeks rosy from the fire, a book in her lap. They would talk about Paris, too. 'Can we go sometime, Maman?' 'Sometime, yes, perhaps. But it's expensive.' '*Please*. We could stay with Aunt Yvonne.' Berthe's youngest sister, Yvonne, had married a Parisian, Giles Lebrun. He was a coach-builder and they lived in a small apartment on the northern edge of Montmartre.

After the death of Louis, Yvonne sent money to Berthe and Eugénie for their fares to Paris. It would do Berthe good, she wrote, to get away from Saint-Sauveur for a while.

'Write to Gabrielle, Maman!' begged Eugénie. 'Tell her we're coming to Paris! Ask if we can come and visit her!'

'Oh no, I couldn't possibly do that! I haven't seen her for such a long time – not since you were a baby. I don't even have her address any more.'

That could be got from Madame Colette, said Eugénie; they could write to her at Châtillon-sur-Loing. 'I'll write, Maman!' She wrote the letter to Colette, too. Berthe wondered at her daughter's determination; normally content to drift along, she had become suddenly and intensely alive. She waited every day for the postman, and when Colette's letter arrived, she pounced on it and opened it eagerly.

'She says we're to come!' she announced triumphantly.

Two days after they arrived in Paris, Berthe and Eugénie set out to visit Colette. They found the traffic on the boulevards alarming.

'Come on,' urged Eugénie, 'we must get across.' They had reached the Arc de Triomphe, where they were in danger of being becalmed. Eugénie was afraid that her mother might use the traffic as an excuse to turn back. 'Right, Maman! *Now!*'

They dodged a carriage, allowed an automobile to pass, and broke into a little jog-trot, with Eugénie going cantering out in front like a young colt, head held high, blue ribbons flying, and made it, finally, to the other side. Berthe was out of breath and she felt hot and damp under the too-tight arms of her old navy-blue moiré silk dress. Laundry work broadened the shoulders.

The avenue de l'Impératrice stretched away in front of them, long and wide and tree-lined, leading to the Bois de Boulogne.

'Look at all the people, Maman! Look how dressed up they are!' Eugénie smoothed down her own skirt. How shabby her blue cotton dress looked now, and her chenille jacket which her mother had worn when she was a girl. And her mother, under her ancient navy-blue dress, was wearing laced-up working boots! 'We must look like country bumpkins.'

They were passed by fine ladies towing little dogs on leads in their wake. They would be going to walk the dogs in the Bois. Eugénie kept step with them in her head. Artists and writers met in the Bois; they picnicked out of hampers, drank wine, reclined on their elbows and talked about Art. Aunt Yvonne's husband had been telling Eugénie about the attractions of Paris the evening before.

A little way down the avenue, a crescent swept round on the left, elevated above the road. Go with the curve, Uncle Giles had told them, showing them on the map, and they would come upon the rue de Villejust. When they reached it, they stopped while Eugénie consulted yet again the piece of creased blue paper in her pocket, even though the address was imprinted on her mind. She nodded. 'We want number forty-four.' They turned into it.

'I hope she has remembered.' Berthe resettled her old navy straw hat on her head, trying to push wisps of damp straying hair up under it. 'She must be busy, with so many things to do. People to see.' Important people, she meant.

'Why shouldn't she remember? Look – she has written the date and the time on her letter! Eleven o'clock.'

'But it's been twelve years . . . Perhaps it was not a good idea, after all.'

'Of *course* it was a good idea!' Eugénie opened the black wrought-iron gate and led the way into a shady courtyard planted with chestnut trees and bordered with forget-me-nots and pink campion. It was quiet after the hectic activity of the avenue. Berthe glanced nervously at the windows that over-looked them.

'Are you looking for someone?'

Startled, they glanced round. A woman – the concierge, they presumed – was advancing towards them. A battery of keys swung from her waist. They were conscious of her eyes raking them from head to foot. She probably thinks we are looking for work, thought Eugénie, or begging!

'Yes, for Madame Willy,' Eugénie said, lifting her head to return the woman's stare. 'Madame *Colette* Willy. She is expecting us.'

The concierge sniffed. 'That's her door over there.' She stood her ground.

Eugénie pulled the bell before her mother could change her mind at the very last moment.

The door opened almost immediately, and out onto the step came a woman holding an English bulldog in her arms. The triangular face and pointed chin and the amused look in the eyes could not be mistaken. This woman looked forceful and vigorous, and years younger than Eugénie's own mother.

'Welcome!' said Colette, setting down the dog (who was not amused and began to yelp) to embrace her guests. 'Come in, come in! I am so pleased to see you. You bring with you a whiff of sweet Burgundian air.'

Eugénie gave her mother a triumphant backward look as they followed Colette into her salon. The room, which was on the street side of the apartment, was filled with yellow sunshine.

'What a lovely room!' Eugénie whirled around, holding out her arms as if to enfold it. She liked the lightness of the room and the absence of heavy furniture and she liked the books and paintings and the posy of violets in the little earthenware pot and the mauve crystal lamp etched with lilac flowers – how beautiful *that* was! – and the exquisite glass paperweights. She liked, too, their hostess's white cambric blouse with its colourful embroidery and the wide belt which held in her waist but did not strangle it and the soft leather sandals on her feet. Her thick springy hair was cut in a short bob.

'Yes, I am fond of my room, even though the walls are as thin as cardboard. The American owner – whom I have never set eyes on – is contemplating tearing it down and putting up luxury apartments in its place. That is Paris for you!'

Colette squatted, letting her hand work over the back of the dog's thick neck, stroking him into submission. His eyes bulged at her with adoration. She swept him back into her arms.

Eugénie advanced to take a closer look. 'Is he Toby-Chien?' They were now regarding one another eyeball to eyeball, she and the dog. He did not blink under her scrutiny.

'Don't tell me you've *read Dialogues de bêtes*!'

'Six times. I thought it was marvellous. And terribly funny.'

'I'm glad. How nice to find someone who has *read* one's book!'

'Millions must.'

'One often doubts that, Eugénie. People tend not to *speak* to you about it. Grown-ups are odd, don't you think?'

They smiled, and their eyes engaged. Colette looked across at Berthe, who was sitting stiffly on a chair, the fingers of her red roughened hands interlocked on top of her lap.

'Your daughter has grown up to be a real beauty, old friend. What a graceful way she has of holding her head! Am I making you blush, child? A tender blush always helps to lend enchantment. She resembles her father, don't you think, Berthe?'

'So people say.'

'Though I see something of you in there, too – the expression in the eyes? A little faraway look, perhaps? So, Berthe, have you read my *Dialogues*? Oh, that is an unfair question! One should never ask that.'

'But I have read it,' Berthe replied. 'I've read all your books,' she added, in order to avoid giving an opinion on the one in question. (She had thought it silly, a cat and a dog talking to one another, and much preferred the Claudine stories.)

Colette sat down on the floor with Toby-Chien. 'So how do you like my room, Berthe?'

'Is it not expensive, so near the Bois?'

'Only seventeen hundred francs – not bad for Paris. It's cheap because it is on the ground floor. That's regarded as rather a comedown, you know! Oh yes! The young and fashionable like to live higher up. The elderly favour these apartments – they can sit by the window and temper their loneliness a little by watching the world go by. I like to listen to the horses' feet as they trot past with their riders on their way to the Bois. And then there are the carriages, which have to slow down before coming to the corner. I can open my window and fondle the horses' ears!'

'But *you* are not lonely!' Eugénie was indignant. 'Or elderly.'

'No, I am not lonely – though I see many fewer people than when I was married – nor, as you say, elderly, not yet! We have a little while to go before we face the grave, wouldn't you say, Berthe? Thirty-four is not *so* old. What age are you now, Eugénie? I've lost track – time passes so quickly.'

'Twelve. I'm in my thirteenth year.'

'I expect you would rather be in your thirtieth? Twelve is a magical age, though, isn't it, Berthe? On the brink!' Berthe lifted her shoulders in a slight shrug. Colette sprang up in one smooth, lithe movement. 'Now then, I'm going to make you some hot chocolate. Do you like chocolate, Eugénie?'

'Very much!'

Colette heated the milk in a copper pan over a little spirit stove. She served the chocolate in fine blue-and-white cups.

'See how the chocolate looks almost mauve in colour.' She nodded at the swirling liquid as she passed the cups round.

'You like mauve and lilac, don't you?' said Eugénie.

'I do.'

'So do I!'

They smiled again at one another, as if they shared a secret.

'I cannot see that it looks mauve-coloured.' Berthe stared down into her cup. 'It looks chocolate-coloured to me.'

Eugénie sipped her chocolate slowly, to make it last. She had never tasted anything so delicious. Colette began to recall old times and Berthe joined in, hesitantly at first, then her awkwardness eased and after a while her face became flushed and the two women were laughing together. They were recalling the terrible way they used to torment poor old Mademoiselle Veillard in elementary school. 'We were so cruel to her. Your mother used to spit erasers at her, Eugénie. Can you believe that? Ah yes, those days were good days!' Colette sighed. 'Innocent and carefree.'

'But she wouldn't want to come back, would she?' asked Eugénie. 'To the village?'

'No, probably not. Going back is seldom an option. Don't be in a hurry to lose your innocence, Eugénie!'

Eugénie smiled. She did not feel innocent: her mother would be surprised at some of her thoughts.

The women went on now to talk about their losses; both had known grief. Colette commiserated with Berthe over the deaths of her husband and son, Berthe with Colette over the death of her father, the Captain, who had died two years before, in 1905.

'And your mother, Gabri – how has she taken it?'

'Badly! She misses him – he worshipped her, of course. Now *that*'s a real love story. Not all of us can be so fortunate.' Colette's voice had become sad. Toby-Chien eyed his mistress anxiously, and she consciously changed mood. 'Wouldn't it be nice to have a husband who adored you? You must look for one, Eugénie!'

Eugénie sipped another droplet of her sweet chocolate, letting it roll on her tongue, and thought for the first time about a husband. It would be a long time yet before she took one, but when she did she would make sure he was not a village baker!

'I am sorry, Gabri, about – ' Berthe hesitated.

'*My* husband?' Colette finished for her. 'Oh well, my marriage was bound to end sooner or later. Would you believe it, though, Berthe, but in the last years, whilst I was dreaming of escape – for I have always been dreaming of escape, like you, eh? – that man of mine was trying to work out a way of showing *me* the door, my own door! My vanity was wounded, of course, even though I hadn't really wanted to keep him. How that man made me suffer! And still does. Or tries to, by spreading slander about me. It's not easy, going out into the world as a woman on your own. Though you are one, too, Berthe, are you not?'

'But I don't go out into the world.'

A woman on your own, thought Eugénie. She liked the ring of the words. How she would love to live in an apartment like this, surrounded by flowers and books, and listen to the carriages swinging past as they went on their way to the Bois, to be free! Seated by the window, on the edge of the room, she felt drowsy and half-hypnotized by the fragrance of the chocolate, the heat of the sun coming through the glass and the murmur of the two women's voices. She wanted the afternoon to stay still and never end.

'And how will you live, Gabri?' asked Berthe. 'Can you earn enough from your books?'

'No, not yet, and that creature Willy has seen to it that I don't get much from my Claudine books. So I am going to try to earn my living as a music-hall performer. I shall play in music-halls and at private receptions.'

'You'll perform in *music-halls*?'

'I *have*! I've played in the Moulin Rouge.'

'The Moulin Rouge!'

'Let me show you the poster!'

They all three huddled over the poster. 'MOULIN ROUGE', it said at the top, and then, beneath:

?YSSIM?

et

COLETTE WILLY

dans

REVE D'EGYPTE
PANTOMIME
de Mme la Marquise de Morny

The first performance had been on January the third that year.

The visitors stared at the poster, uncertain what to make of it. Berthe shifted uncomfortably on her seat. Eugénie pointed at '?YSSIM?'

'Oh, that is just a private joke.' Colette smiled, and laid the poster aside.

'It sounds exciting,' said Eugénie, 'being a music-hall performer. Will you play only in Paris?'

'No, I plan to tour the provinces as well. One must, to survive. Though I doubt if I'll come to Auxerre. That might be too close to home!' Colette laughed, a deep-throated laugh that increased Berthe's feeling of disquiet. 'I might cause a riot.'

The front-door bell cut across Colette's laughter. She excused herself and went to answer it.

They heard a woman's voice and then Colette saying, 'Missy!' She had left the sitting-room door a little ajar. The two women were whispering and laughing softly. Eugénie left her chair and went to look at the bookshelves. Her mother's back had stiffened again, and she was staring down into her lap as if it might be unwise to look too closely into the room.

Eugénie took down *Claudine à l'école*.

'Put that book down, Eugénie! You are too young to read it.'

Eugénie did not say that she already had. It had been passed around amongst the girls in her class.

The door reopened and Colette returned, followed by the new arrival. Eugénie frowned with confusion. She heard quite clearly Colette call her friend 'Missy', yet here was a man with fattish cheeks in a hard black hat, black coat and vest and checked trousers. He was smoking a cigar.

56

He removed his hat to show black cropped hair. He bowed to them, his dark, incandescent eyes fastening on Eugénie.

'This is my friend the Marquise de Morny, who wishes to meet you. Missy, my old Burgundian friends: Berthe and her daughter Eugénie!'

Berthe fumbled as she reached for the marquise's hand. The *marquise*. A woman, then. But she looked exactly like a man. Berthe glanced anxiously at her daughter, whose colour was high.

Eugénie extended her hand freely, dipping her knees into a slight curtsey as she said, 'Enchantée!'

'What a delightful child! And please call me Missy – everyone does. It's a pleasure to meet old friends of Colette's from Saint-Sauveur. It sounds like a heaven on earth, that place.' She was still looking at Eugénie.

'I should prefer to live in Paris.'

Colette and Missy laughed. Berthe did not. The marquise draped an arm around Colette's shoulder and began gently, unconsciously almost, to stroke the back of the other woman's neck, her fingers penetrating deep into her thick hair. Colette's neck arched a little like a cat's, and they turned inward to smile at one another. At Colette's feet, the bulldog gave a low growl.

'Do you play in music-hall too, Missy?' asked Eugénie, feeling bold.

'We performed in the Moulin Rouge together in a little drama called *Rêve d'Egypte*.'

'So you are ?YSSIM?!' Eugénie crowed as she spelled out the letters. She clapped her hands. 'Do you get it, Maman?'

Berthe did not reply. Her face looked frozen.

'Colette played a mummy whom I awaken from her sleep!' said the marquise. 'Oh, là, it caused quite a stir! We were hit by a hail of orange peel and other unpleasant objects.' The memory of it did not seem to disturb either her or Colette.

Eugénie put her hands over her cheeks, which were scalding hot.

'Well, I must run along!' Missy slapped Colette's hip, bowed to the other two and said to Eugénie that when next she was in Paris she must come and visit her. 'Don't forget – the rue Georges-Ville. Number two. It's not far from here, only a step.'

Colette saw the marquise out. The room had changed in the last few minutes, and not just because of the smell of cigar smoke. Eugénie's eyes moved restlessly over the titles of the books. She let her fingers trail listlessly along their spines. She did not look at her mother.

'Missy has some interesting forebears,' said Colette, when she returned. 'She is the niece of Napoleon the Third.'

'My goodness!' gulped Eugénie.

'And the great-granddaughter of the Empress Joséphine.'

'We must be going,' said Berthe, rising to her feet. 'Yvonne will wonder if we've got lost.'

Colette took a copy of *La Vie Parisienne* from a shelf. 'Since you like reading, this might interest you, Eugénie. I have a story in it.' She flipped the journal open and, taking up a pen, dipped it into the ink-pot and scrawled under the byline, 'A ma petite amie Eugénie, affectueusement, Colette Willy.'

'Oh, thank you!' Holding the magazine open between her hands, Eugénie read aloud the title. '*Les Vrilles de la vigne*. Thank you *very* much!'

Colette and Toby-Chien escorted them to the door. The dog looked smugly out at them from the crook of his mistress's arm. He knew that they were leaving, he was staying.

'Come again!' said Colette. 'It has been wonderful to see you both.'

Eugénie looked back to wave. Colette returned the salutation. Berthe did not look round. She walked with quick steps through the courtyard and out into the street.

On the swaying omnibus going back to Montmartre, Eugénie read the story of '*Les Vrilles de la vigne*'. She read with eyes racing along the lines, oblivious to the other passengers pressing against them and the streets of Paris through which the omnibus was passing.

They alighted from the bus. As they were walking up the

hill to the Lebruns' apartment, Berthe asked, 'What was it about – that story?'

'A nightingale. Yes, a nightingale! Who used to sing in the daytime and sleep all night until, one night, when it was fast asleep, the tendrils of a vine snaked up and wound itself about the bird's feet.'

'I have never heard of such a thing happening!'

'When the nightingale woke up, it found it was imprisoned. It had to struggle desperately to wrench itself free. It damaged itself with all the wrenching, of course – that was part of the price it had to pay. For the rest of that spring, and for ever afterwards, the nightingale swore that it would never again let itself fall asleep while the vine's tendrils were growing. So it kept itself awake by singing all night.'

She has forgotten that I am with her, thought Berthe, as she puffed up the steep incline behind her daughter, who had gone streaking ahead. She thinks that it is easy to sing all night.

In April, 1909, Eugénie went to Auxerre to spend a few days with her Aunt Jeanne. Since she was now almost fourteen she was allowed to travel alone on the train.

Her aunt was waiting for her on the platform with her two small daughters. Eugénie leapt out before the train had quite shuddered to a halt, her long blond hair swirling around her shoulders, unrestrained by any ribbon.

'Careful!' cried her aunt.

Eugénie hugged her mother's sister and swept her cousins up into the air to be kissed. Jeanne, straightening her hat which had been knocked slightly askew, saw that her niece was growing into a most attractive young woman.

On their way out through the station they waved to Pierre Dufour, Jeanne's husband; he was at work in the ticket office. He was employed as a railway clerk. Outside in the street, cabs waited.

'Let's ride home!' said Jeanne, infected by her niece's gaiety.

'Can we?' Eugénie looked over her shoulder; Pierre was not known for his open-handedness.

'Please!' cried the children. They wanted the cab with the chestnut roan.

'It is quite a long walk,' said Jeanne. The station was out of town, on the other side of the river from the medieval quarter where the Dufours lived. 'And the children are tired,' she added, justifying the expense.

They climbed into the cab of the children's choosing, the driver flipped his whip in the air, and they were off.

As they approached the bridge over the Yonne, Eugénie leant out of the window almost from the waist so that her aunt had to put out a protective hand, ready to restrain her if need be. The girl had an impetuosity and intensity about her which Jeanne did not remember Berthe having at the same age. But who knows? Perhaps Berthe had had it inside, had not let it out?

Eugénie loved this moment of arriving in Auxerre, when the old gothic cathedral of Saint-Etienne came into view, sitting on its pinnacle, topping the medieval roofs that sprawled down to the quays below. And then, to the right of the cathedral, there was the honey-golden abbey church of Saint-Germain. 'Tu as bon vin, bonne eau, bon pain, Aussi tu as le corps de Saint-Germain!' The jingle ran through her head. She loved the Yonne here, too, where it was wide and placid yet held promise of adventure in its boats and barges. Life on a barge could be exciting. As they swept round into the quai, a young bargee came out on to the deck of his boat. He had a red cravate knotted round his neck and his shirt was open, revealing a chest as brown as mahogany. He looked up and, catching her eye, smiled broadly. She smiled in return. Allowing herself to take a quick glance backward she saw that he was standing still, watching them go. Her heart sang.

The cab turned up a narrow winding street to the Dufours' house. When they came inside, Jeanne said to Eugénie, 'I have a surprise for you! Guess who is coming to Auxerre next week!'

'I can't!'

'Colette Willy!'

'*Colette Willy?*'

'She is playing here in Auxerre, at the old Salle de Comédie. She is playing in *Claudine*.'

'She said she would probably never come to Auxerre!'

'Well, she *is* coming! I promise you it's true, and I have bought tickets for us.'

All week Eugénie went round in a dream. She couldn't believe it – she was going to see Colette Willy again, see her perform! She walked along the quai but saw no sign of the bargee with the red scarf; he must have sailed for some other town. She did not envy him now; she thought Auxerre the most beautiful place in the world. After Paris, of course. That went without saying!

On the day of the performance she was so excited she could hardly eat. She was too thin as it was, said Pierre, she must eat; you could see the salt-cellars in her neck. He was to look after the children while his wife and Eugénie went to the theatre.

'Does her mother know that you're taking her to this thing tonight?' he asked Jeanne. He did not approve of Colette Willy: he had made that clear to Eugénie. 'She is not a respectable woman,' he told her. He is such a petit bourgeois, thought Eugénie, while listening demurely. And such a bore. Each evening, when he came in from work, he told them about the people who had tried to cheat the railway and how he personally had foiled them. There is one thing, thought Eugénie, I shall never marry a bore. It may be that I shall marry a bargee, and he might even knock me about a bit, but at least it won't be boring.

'It's a play we're going to, Pierre,' protested Jeanne, 'not a music-hall.'

'I saw her arriving at the station this morning.'

'You saw Madame Willy?' Eugénie sat up straight. 'Is that true?' She could not bear the thought that *he* would have seen her first.

61

'She looked nothing special to me.' Pierre pushed a forkful of mutton stew into his mouth. Gravy clung to the edges of his droopy moustache and Eugénie had to look away. 'Quite ordinary, I thought. Drab, Tired, too, washed-out looking. The lot of them did.'

'I expect you'd look like that yourself if you were on tour.' Eugénie spoke with such fierceness that her aunt was worried. Jeanne quickly lifted the casserole dish and served her husband another helping. 'They have to travel from place to place and face new audiences every evening,' said Eugénie. Colour swamped her cheeks.

'What do *you* know about going on tour?'

'I can imagine it,' said Eugénie loftily, and left the table, taking her plate with its half-eaten food to the sink.

The Dufours lived only ten to fifteen minutes' walk from the theatre but Jeanne and Eugénie set off early, at the girl's insistence. There could well be crowds, she said, and it wasn't a very big theatre, was it? It would be terrible to miss the opening. She could not bear it if they were to miss even five seconds. 'Wait for me!' Jeanne had to plead. Her niece seemed to be flying along the pavement on winged feet.

The old red-brick theatre had previously been an ancient chapel, and still looked like one from the outside, with its rounded arch windows. People were always complaining about its lack of comfort, said Jeanne – the benches had no backs, the corridors were narrow and ill-lit, the heating was inadequate, and in winter your feet froze. They were agitating to have a new theatre built. But Eugénie thought it perfect. Their seats were in the front row; only the orchestra pit separated them from the stage – and from the star of the evening, when she appeared. The auditorium, as it filled, buzzed with anticipation; the musicians tuned up; the audience verged on rowdiness. Eugénie fretted lest they would continue their conversations and their silly laughter during the play. Some of the men looked and sounded so *coarse*. She shut her ears to their comments. To think that *they* were going to ogle a woman like Colette Willy! But when the curtain rose and Colette Willy, alias Gabrielle Colette, alias Claudine, was revealed, the noise died and the house became still.

Afterwards everyone agreed that Colette Willy's performance had been superb. She had played Claudine with passion and tenderness.

Eugénie sat on in her seat as the audience made its way noisily out into the street. She seemed to be in a trance.

'We must go.' Her aunt touched her on the shoulder. 'They'll be sweeping us up with the cigar wrappers.'

Eugénie came to life. 'Let's go round and see her, Tante Jeanne!'

'See her? Backstage? Oh no, I don't think – '

'Why not? Why shouldn't we go? She's a friend of Maman's.'

Eugénie was already on her feet. She led the way out of the theatre round to the stage door. She would not listen to the objections or entreaties of her aunt, who hurried after her, afraid to let her out of her sight. 'Madame Willy is a very old friend of my mother's,' Eugénie told the burly man at the door who would have barred their way. 'They were at school together. In Saint-Sauveur. My mother was part of the Claudine group.'

They were allowed to pass. He came with them to the corridor to point the way to the dressing rooms.

The corridor was dimly lit. A thin-looking young woman with a fox tippet slung around her neck, smelling strongly of cheap perfume, squeezed past them murmuring, 'Excusez-moi!' Her lips appeared dark and garish in the weak light and her eyes sunken into the deep pools of their sockets, unlike the fox's which protruded with a saucy glint.

When they found the door marked 'Colette Willy', Eugénie did not hesitate. She knocked, and immediately a voice within said, 'Entrez!' *Her* voice. Eugénie reached for the handle, and it was only then that her aunt saw her falter for a second.

The girl squared up and opened the door.

'I'm Eugénie,' she said. 'Do you remember me? Eugénie Bussac.'

'Eugénie!' Colette rose from her stool at the mirror to come forward and take the girl's hands. 'Can it really be you? You've grown so tall! And so beautiful.' She looked past Eugénie, and frowned. 'And can it be – ?'

'Jeanne. Jeanne Grenot, that was – Berthe's sister.'

Colette brought them in and closed the door. The room, with its dirty floor and yellowing walls, looked seedy to Jeanne's eyes, though not to Eugénie's: she saw only the greasepaints spread out in front of the mirror and the costumes hanging on the rail and the colourful figure of Colette wrapped in a blue satin kimono patterned with small green and red fans. Her eyes, rimmed with kohl, reflected the blue of her gown.

'Look at me – I'm like a clown! With my greasepaint half on and half off. You don't mind if I carry on?'

'Please,' said Eugénie, who seemed now to have lost her tongue, though soon refound it as Colette, re-seating herself on the stool, creaming her face, pouting at her reflection in the glass, began to talk and draw them out. She wanted to know everything that was happening in Saint-Sauveur.

When a quarter of an hour had passed, a man with a cigarette hanging from his lower lip put his head round the door and asked Colette if she was going to take all night. He was waiting to lock up.

'Five minutes! That is all!'

Eugénie and her aunt stood up.

'Are you still living in the rue de Villejust?' asked Eugénie.

'No, I was evicted, alas. They're building luxury apartments. I have moved a bit further north and east, to the rue Saint-Sénoch – I am always on the move. I think I must have gypsy blood in me!'

'Come, Eugénie!' Jeanne had put her gloves back on and was restraightening her hat, ready for the street and the return to her family. 'We must not keep Gabri any longer.'

Colette embraced her visitors in turn and thanked them for

coming to see her show – and her. 'How good it is to see familiar faces!'

'Where do you go now?' asked Eugénie wistfully.

'South. To Avignon, Marseilles, Nîmes . . . Would you like me to send you picture postcards from some of these places?'

On stage, in Edinburgh, Amy is continuing to take us beyond the confines of the Dean Village; we are on tour with Colette and her troupe in the provinces of France. We lounge around a station somewhere in mid-France on a sultry morning waiting for the train to come and carry us on to our next destination. There is the under-manager, unshaven, fag-end stuck to his lower lip, and the senior lead with his matted, badly dyed beard, a line of orange make-up staining the collar of his soiled shirt, and the peroxide-haired ingénue yawning with fatigue, displaying the large tonsils in her thin throat. And now, sauntering along the platform, comes the grande coquette sporting three black ostrich plumes in her hat, her tan-coloured bloomers spilling over the tops of her cloth boots; she is proud of her Bourbon profile and fancies that she resembles Sarah Bernhardt. But she is dying to sit down; she complains that her legs are pressing into her body.

And what of Colette? How does she see herself?

She is in no better shape, she claims. We are invited to look at her hair, observe how lacklustre it is. And can we see the deep shadows underneath her eyes? 'And just look at the way the limp lapels of my tailor-made, chestnut-brown costume rise and fall with every listless step I take! I look like a moulting bird or a discouraged beetle battered by spring rains.'

Life on tour certainly does not resemble a picnic in the Bois, sitting under the trees drinking wine and talking about Art. They visit Auxerre, Dijon, Avignon, Nîmes, Toulouse, Montpellier, Pau, Bayonne, Bordeaux . . . They have little time for sightseeing. They might snatch a walk in the Jardins de la Fontaine in Nîmes or visit the temple of Diana or take a few minutes to admire the Pope's Palace in Avignon, but mostly what they see are seedy backstage dressing rooms and equally seedy digs.

Amy is playing out this part with extra feeling, it seems to me. The life of a touring performer cannot have changed so very much.

Colette goes to Toulon, the birthplace of her father, the Zouave captain. The townspeople are aware of the connection. 'The house is full and they give me a tremendous reception. "Vive Colette!" they shout.'

Next morning, she will rise at dawn, travel, arrive in a new place, check in to her digs, rehearse, perform, sleep, depart the following morning, and begin again.

'I lead the life of a vagabond,' says Amy, alias Colette.

'Avignon, Nîmes, Toulouse, Bayonne, Pau . . .' Eugénie whispered the names to herself. Magical names, conjuring up images of Roman arenas and popes' palaces and a spangled sea glittering under a southern sun. She felt the heat of the sun on her face, smelt thyme and lavender. She kept the postcards in her 'special box' where she hoarded other treasures, such as the copy of *La Vie Parisienne* that Colette had inscribed for her. Her mother did not like to see her 'dreaming' over the postcards, as she called it; Eugénie would wait until Berthe went out to deliver her laundry, then she would take the cards from their box and reread the messages written in the strong, flowing handwriting.

'Marseilles: My room looks down on the Canebière – this broad boulevard which runs like a river through the city and teems with people and traffic night and day. When I have a half-hour to spare, I like to sit at a pavement café, drink a citron pressé or a café crème, depending on the day, and watch the people pass. I like to look at their faces and imagine their lives. The most ordinary people have stories in them, Eugénie.'

'What are you doing, child?'

Startled, Eugénie lifted her head and the postcards cascaded from her lap on to the floor. Her mother was standing in the doorway, laundry basket parked against her angled hip. Her face was blotchy and red, as if it had been brushed by stinging nettles, and her eyes were angry. Hurriedly the girl scooped up the cards and thrust them back into the box. Her mother had an equable temper most of the time, but sometimes Eugénie worried that she might burn her box, as she had one day threatened to do.

Four

What a difference there is between being a
girl and a woman!

Mes Apprentissages

Eugénie left school when she was sixteen and took a clerking
job in the post office, having sworn that she would never join
the snivelling band of clerks grinding away under dim lights,
their shoulders hunched, fingers stained blue-black below the
second joint, eyes watery from poring over columns of figures
in ledger books. Robert and Alain had gone to work in
Bordeaux and Dijon respectively and sent money home only
occasionally. 'You have to be sensible, Eugénie,' her mother
told her. 'Any job is better than no job.'

'What if I were to become a . . . harlot?'

'It is only desperation that drives women to that.' Berthe
carried on with her laundry.

Eugénie went back to her book (*Claudine à Paris*, which she
was reading for the fourth time), though, unusually for her,
she found that she could not concentrate. Her mother
upbraided her at times for reading so much. 'It's good to read,'
she would say. 'You know I've nothing against books – I read
myself – but it is not good to read all the time. Remember
Juliette Colette, that poor demented sister of Gabrielle's who
had her head stuck in romances night and day when she was
your age! Remember what happened to her!' Colette's half-
sister had committed suicide in 1908, so it was widely thought,
even though her doctor husband had claimed it was a heart

attack. 'You should be out and about with all the other young people on these fine evenings. There's plenty of time to sit in the house when you're married and settled down.'

Married and settled down. What a deadly ring those words have for one who is dreaming of escape! They made Eugénie feel as if a potato had settled, whole, in the pit of her stomach.

She sat beside the open window smelling the evening air. There seemed to be a scent of jasmine on the breeze, though there were no jasmine bushes close by. Did her mother not realize that she felt desperate at times? Though she had of course no intention of becoming a common whore, for she had read enough novels to know that their lives were seldom amusing. Now, a courtesan might be different. Une femme du monde running a salon where wits and artistes of the day would gather. But for that she would need un homme du monde to keep her, and there was little opportunity to meet one of those in Saint-Sauveur. There was little opportunity for anything in Saint-Sauveur. Gabrielle Colette had been fortunate to meet a man of letters in Châtillon-sur-Loing.

'You would not say that if you had seen him,' said her mother, slapping a wet sheet in the air. 'Take the other end, Eugénie – come on, make yourself useful! It does no harm to know how to fold a sheet.'

Eugénie started to walk out with the watchmaker's son, Jean-Paul, who was good-looking and good-natured and on the lookout for a wife. Not that she had any thoughts of marrying him. She chose his company out of boredom. A girl does feel restless on sunny summer evenings; she did not need her mother to tell her that.

She was careful, though, to see to it that they skirted the edges of the woods; she did not succumb to his pleading to take the paths that would lead in amongst the trees. In the shelter of the wall in the rue des Vignes, as the shadows were deepening, she allowed him to kiss her cheek and then her mouth, but when he began to crush it and writhe against her she pushed him away. He stood there looking hot and flustered and *stupid*. Yes, stupid. Especially with his mouth hanging half open, panting like a farm dog.

'You could do worse than to marry a watchmaker,' her mother told her.

'Such as a baker?'

'At least watchmaking doesn't harm the lungs.'

'Only the eyes. Do you see how his father peers?'

'You will lose him if you're not careful.'

Eugénie lifted one shoulder in a shrug. It was a gesture that infuriated her mother.

Jean-Paul took to courting Marie-Louise, a pretty, talkative girl with a plump face, who had been a friend of Eugénie's since their elementary schooldays. Eugénie saw Jean-Paul and Marie-Louise vanishing into the woods together. They became betrothed.

'I told you, didn't I?' said her mother.

Eugénie said that she would dance at their wedding.

She read Colette Willy's *L'Ingénue libertine* and wondered if she, like the heroine Minne, might not develop a passion for a ruffian from the underworld, but again there would be little chance of encountering one in the alleyways of Saint-Sauveur. Crime here was of the pettiest kind: the theft of a loaf of bread or, at the most, a chicken. No one had any imagination in this place! At times Eugénie felt as feverish as Minne.

She read *La Vagabonde* and longed for a life on the road, as a performing artiste, travelling from place to place, treading the boards of small provincial theatres, coming at the end, triumphantly, into Paris. She was not so silly as to think that it would be roses all the way: she was realistic, in spite of her dreams. But who would want roses all the way? The smell would suffocate you. She wanted to live. To the full. That was all. Was that too much to expect? She was not sure. She wanted a lover. An interesting, charming lover who would appreciate and admire her, not a slobbery-mouthed, pimple-necked, hot-handed youth.

*

War came, and reached even as far as Saint-Sauveur. Trumpets sounded and young men struggled into stiff khaki uniforms. Berthe developed cramps in the lower part of her abdomen and at night tossed in the big sagging bed whilst murmuring the names of her sons. Robert and Alain went off to fight the Boche, as did Jean-Paul, who had by now married Marie-Louise and was the father of a baby boy. Eugénie and Marie-Louise saw the men off at the railway station. Two of them were not to return.

In 1915, Eugénie took the train to Auxerre and offered herself as a nursing auxiliary. At the hospital she met a man, a doctor called Claude Laroche, and they fell in love. But, as is sometimes the way with romantic attachments, they had a misunderstanding, and fell out, if not of love, then of sympathy for one another. They backed off. Their disagreement lay between them like a deep trench. Shortly afterwards, he was transferred to another hospital closer to the Front.

Eugénie said little to anyone about this period in her life; it was her way when she was emotionally hurt, as it was to be her daughter Amy's, in her turn.

In May 1917, following the break-up of her romance and the death of Alain on the Aisne (Jean-Paul died at Verdun), Eugénie asked to be sent to the Front; and it was there, in a field hospital, in late November, as she worked her way along the cramped rows of hospital beds on which agonized men tossed and moaned, that she encountered George Balfour from Edinburgh.

He had been badly wounded at the Allied battle for Cambrai; he had head and leg injuries, and was suffering from the effects of gassing. He'd behaved gallantly, his commanding officer told Eugénie; he'd pulled back a wounded comrade under heavy artillery fire. It was thought he would be decorated. He was not expected to live.

As Eugénie reached George's cot, he held out his hand to her. He held it palm upward, in a gesture of supplication. She

71

laid her hand gently on top of his, and his fingers closed over hers and held on to them. His clutch felt like that of a drowning man who knows that he is about to go under but is determined to hang on until the last second. George hung on to Eugénie. When she brought a drink of water or a damp cloth to cool his raging brow, out would come his hand. His eyes, a keen, pale blue, stared at her. She thought sometimes that he stared through and past her, into space. Seeing men with legs blown off, faces blasted away, heads with gaping holes? Or did he see his home back in Scotland, his family, his mother? In good health he would have been a handsome man: well-built, with thick, sandy-red hair. He flinched but uttered no sound when she dressed his appalling, suppurating wounds. His right leg was in a bad way. Gangrene was a threat; the surgeon kept a close watch. For weeks George hovered between life and death. He coughed up thick yellow gobs of phlegm into a rag, while Eugénie held his head. He made sounds at the back of his throat that sounded like muted machine-gun fire. He held his hands over his ears. He sang snatches of a song about the Siegfried Line. 'We're going to hang out our washing . . .'

George Balfour, as his family back in Scotland well knew, was a stubborn man who would seldom give quarter. His attitude did not vary when it came to fighting for his life. He lived. He kept his leg. He called Eugénie an angel, he on whose lips no one had ever heard endearments, not even his own mother, the person to whom he was most attached, and always would be. But then war is not a normal time, and neither is the slow recovery from near-mortal illness.

'You're an angel, Eugénie,' he said. He pronounced it U-Jeanie and made no effort to get it right, even though she tried to coach him and after they'd been married a year he dropped the 'U' and called her simply 'Jeanie'. 'You brought me back from the gates of Hell,' he said.

He spoke English, naturally, and she French. 'Edinburgh,' he said, thumping himself in the chest. 'Scotland.' 'Mais oui, Ecosse! Très jolie. Les montagnes. Les lacs.' Their eyes engaged, and she smiled. 'Washing on line,' she said. (She hated washing: the smells, the steam, the leaden weight of it when wet.) He nodded, pleased with her. 'Hang out your washing,' he said. Thus proceeded their courtship.

The noise of artillery fire was gradually receding, the front line moving steadily eastward. It was said that the tide had turned, though there was still strength left yet in the German military machine and a few surprises, too, and the allied troops were weary. The daily tally of the dead was spirit-breaking. The wounded talked of going home.

'Marry me, U-Jeanie,' said George, the week before he was due to be sent home to convalesce. 'Come back with me to Scotland!'

They became engaged. Over the fourth finger of Eugénie's hand George slid his gold signet ring, bought in Hamilton and Inches, the Princes Street jeweller, by his parents for his twenty-first birthday. (His mother was to have a fit when he came back and told her he'd given it to a *French* girl, and a Roman Catholic!) The ring was engraved with his initials on the back: GWB. George William Balfour.

Eugénie was unable to accompany George back to Edinburgh; she had to work until the war ended and arrangements could be made for her to follow. The fighting dragged on throughout most of 1918. The couple kept in touch with short weekly letters. They each wrote in their own language. Eugénie had help in translating hers; George did not bother. As long as he saw his name at the top and hers at the bottom, that was all that he needed. Fond though he was of his mother, he closed his ears to her arguments against his bride-in-waiting. He had given his word, and he would keep it.

Their marriage was arranged to take place in the Church of Scotland, in St Vincent Street in Edinburgh, in March 1919. Eugénie was uncertain about the nature of the Church of Scotland, though she knew that it was not part of the Church of Rome, but she was going through a period of disbelief at the time so did not mind much what it was. Berthe liked no aspect of the whole business – she had lost a son to the war, now she was losing her only daughter, and she had not even set eyes on this Scottish man! – but there was nothing she could do about it. From her teens onward, Eugénie had been wayward and impulsive and determined to be different. At times Berthe was inclined to blame the influence of Gabrielle Colette, though she would dismiss that notion briskly. Surely one afternoon in Paris could not influence a life? She knew of course that Eugénie had spent much time when she was younger reading Colette's books, but then so had she herself, and here she still was, a widow with swollen legs living in Saint-Sauveur, a laundress. This was her real life, the other was fiction, and she knew better than to confuse them.

In February, en route for Scotland, Eugénie stopped off in Paris for a few days with her Aunt Yvonne and Uncle Giles.

'You waited a long time to come back,' said Yvonne.

'I never thought it would be so long. But there was the war.'

'Ah, the war,' said Odile, Giles' sister. 'Let's hope there's never another. Enough French blood has been spilt. Your mother must have suffered greatly over the loss of Alain? She's never been back, either.'

'Berthe never really took to Paris, did she?' observed Yvonne.

'Perhaps not. She hasn't been out of Saint-Sauveur for years,' said Eugénie, 'except to visit Aunt Jeanne a couple of times in Auxerre.'

They were sitting in the kitchen, Eugénie, Yvonne and Odile. The day was dark and wet, and although it was only three o'clock in the afternoon they had lit the lamp. They sat close to the stove, their feet resting on the hearth. Steam rose from Odile's stockings, for she had just walked through the rain to come here. A stack of flesh-coloured stays lay heaped on a chair. Yvonne was a corsetière. Her shoulders were strong from pulling hard on the tapes and her knees puffy from kneeling. She was making Eugénie a pair of stays for a wedding present, decorating them around the top and bottom with tiny blue satin roses. Blue for luck, she said. And men liked blue, she added, with a sly look at her niece, who did not respond.

They were drinking hot chocolate. Eugénie gazed into the swirling mauve-coloured liquid.

'When I was here with Mother we went to visit Colette Willy. Do you remember, Yvonne?'

'Colette Willy!' exclaimed Odile. 'What a woman! Talk about lovers and scandals!' She sounded admiring rather than censorious. 'We went to see her once at the Moulin Rouge, didn't we, Yvonne? Treated ourselves. She did one turn dressed as a cat. She made a marvellous cat. She looked like one, moved like one! That was a few years ago. She's given all that up, of course, now that she's a baroness, the Baronne de Jouvenel, and gone up in the world. Although I think she still uses the name Colette Willy for her books.'

'She does,' said Eugénie. She had been reading *Les Heures longues*, a collection of Colette's journalism, on the train. She was taking with her to Edinburgh all her Colette books, as well as her box of postcards. It was some years since she had received a card from Colette.

'The Baron's the editor of *Le Matin*,' said Odile, who worked as a cleaner at the newspaper's offices. 'She's been made literary editor. His family is wealthy – they have an estate in the Corrèze. He's involved in politics, too.'

'An influential man,' said Yvonne.

'They've got a daughter,' said Odile. 'Must be five or six years old now.'

'Somehow I've never thought of Colette as a mother,' said Eugénie.

'She probably has a nursemaid. They say the marriage is tempestuous. He's quite the ladies' man – doesn't always treat them well, either, from what I hear. Walked out on his first wife, went to buy matches, never came back! I expect he still has mistresses.'

'What man does not?' commented Yvonne.

Eugénie looked at her. 'Not Uncle Giles?'

The other two women laughed. 'No, not him! He wouldn't have the time, or the energy.'

'Or the money,' added Odile.

'How true! No, for mistresses, I'm talking about the bourgeoisie.'

'You must see that your handsome Scotsman does not take a mistress, Eugénie,' said Odile. Eugénie had shown them a photograph of George in his full regimental dress, taken before he was wounded in battle. They'd asked her if he wore his kilt when he was at home. She had been unable to answer. She had only ever seen him in a nightshirt. That had amused the women, who had made ribald remarks. She's never seen her fiancé with trousers on! He might have to take them off before she recognized him!

'I don't think that George would take a mistress. Besides, he is not a bourgeois.' Eugénie shrugged. 'At least, I don't think so.'

'What is his work?' asked Odile.

'He's a soldier,' Yvonne answered for her niece.

'But he must have another occupation. It's not wartime now.'

'He is an official in the Co-operative Society,' said Eugénie.

'Ah, a petit bourgeois!'

But Eugénie's thoughts had stayed with her mother's old schoolfriend. 'Colette Willy – have you ever seen her, Odile? Apart from at the Moulin Rouge?'

'No, not I! How would I, on my knees scrubbing in the early hours of the morning!'

Eugénie looked away from their lamplit circle for a moment, out at the curtain of rain falling on the other side of the window. 'I should like to see her again. I'd like to let her know that I'm going away. If I wrote a letter, would you leave it at the office for her, Odile?'

'I suppose I could. But she probably won't answer. She's famous.'

Colette replied on a single sheet of blue notepaper. 'Please *do* come. I should love to see you before you set off for your new country. I am living now in Auteuil, in a little house close to the Bois on the boulevard Suchet, no. 69. You can take the Métro or the no. 16 bus.'

It was a long way from the northern side of Montmartre to the Bois de Boulogne. Eugénie took the bus so that she would see more of the city. She loved Paris. She loved its wide boulevards and its squares and parks. She loved the feel and smell of it. This was only her second visit, yet it felt like home. 'Why go to Scotland, then?' her aunt had asked. 'It's a cold country, so they say. He must be some man, this Scottish soldier, to tempt you away from your own?'

The house on the boulevard Suchet was quite small and low. Across the road there was a copse and, beyond that, the Bois. Eugénie was admitted by a young housemaid with a sallow complexion and rather protruding eyes. As the maid was helping the visitor off with her wet coat, Colette herself came down the stairs. She was in her mid-forties now and had aged a little, which was only to be expected, but she still showed the same energy and vigour that she had twelve years before. Eugénie thought her beautiful in her peacock-blue dress, with her eyes shadowed in matching colour and lined with kohl.

She welcomed Eugénie warmly, fussed over her. 'My goodness, you're soaking wet, child! Take off your shoes. Pauline, dry the coat and shoes in the kitchen. Come upstairs, Eugénie, we'll sit in my little boudoir. You won't mind clutter, will you?'

Eugénie loved the clutter: the desk piled high with papers, books on the floor, on shelves – books everywhere – and crystal glass paperweights on ledges and vases filled with violets. And there was the lilac crystal lamp. The objects looked so familiar; they had stayed long in her memory. Her nervousness began to leave her. On the bus she had wondered if she'd had a cheek to write and invite herself; she had lost the confidence of the twelve-year-old leading her mother down the avenue de l'Impératrice to the rue de Villejust.

'Pauline despairs of my untidiness! She has to rescue me. I keep losing things – my watch, my pen. She finds them. I don't know what I should do without her. She is a country girl, from the Corrèze – she suits me. We understand one another. Pull up your chair, Eugénie, let us sit close to the fire. It's a nasty February day out there.'

Eugénie glanced up at the photograph of the young girl on the mantelpiece.

'That's my daughter Colette! Doesn't she look sturdy and cheerful? We call her Bel-Gazou.'

'Pretty warbler!'

'You know your Burgundian!'

'Is she here, in Paris?'

'No, she stays most of the time on the Jouvenel estate in the country with her English nanny, Miss Draper, a rather fearsome, grumpy woman.' Colette laughed the deep-throated laugh that was another of Eugénie's memories. 'But Bel-Gazou likes Miss Draper. And neither of them cares for Paris. I can't say that I blame them. What child would want to live in the city when she could have woods to play in?'

Pauline brought in hot chocolate and Eugénie smiled. Colette remembered, too, how they had drunk it in the rue de Villejust, surprising her visitor.

'Oh yes, I remember that day very well! You looked so eager, like a young bird hovering on the edge of the nest, fluttering its wings, but knowing it is not yet strong enough to embark on a solo flight.'

Eugénie blushed and laughed.

'And now you are about to be married, to leave your village, your mother – a whole way of life.'

'You did it, too.'

'That is true.'

'I know you didn't like Paris at first, but you got used to it, didn't you? You don't regret coming here now, do you?' There was a note of urgency in Eugénie's voice. Last night, lying in her narrow, warm bed in the Lebruns' kitchen recess, listening to the sounds of the street below – a man calling to a woman, a woman calling to a cat, sounds she could distinguish, voices she could understand – a surge of panic had washed through her and left her trembling.

'Regrets are a waste of time, Eugénie. It's a well-worn cliché. Are you having cold feet? It's understandable. It's a leap in the dark, isn't it? To go and live with a strange man, sleep in his bed, eat at his table, have him ask about your thoughts. It is an enormous intrusion. Tell me about him. Is he handsome?'

'Quite. He's different from any other man that I've known. He is from Scotland – I told you in my letter.'

'Is it that he is a foreigner?'

'I'm not sure. No, I don't think so. You see, I've seen him when he was at rock bottom, helpless, in terrible pain. Then it doesn't matter whether someone is Scots or French.'

'Ah yes, but that is how the romance of war can deceive us! We think the details are of no importance. But what will he be like when he is at full strength, on his own territory, calling the tunes? Oh, don't listen to a crusty old married woman like me! I shouldn't be speaking to you in this way. Try to be happy, Eugénie. It's as good a way of being wise as any other.'

Colette got up and went to a side-table. She lifted from it a glass paperweight and held it in the palm of her hand. Eugénie left her chair to come and look.

'Hold it. Take it under the lamp.'

The weight felt smooth and heavy in Eugénie's hand. Gazing down into the dome of glass she saw a five-petalled white flower rimmed with green leaves on a midnight-blue ground.

'It's absolutely beautiful. It's perfect. I have never seen anything so perfect.'

'Keep it!' said Colette. 'Take it as a wedding present!'

The Baccarat paperweight sat on the Balfours' dresser between a douce china shepherdess and a delft plate with a picture of a Clyde steamer bearing the inscription *Greetings from Rothesay*. It sat there in the kitchen-living-room of their flat in St Stephen Street long after Eugénie ran off and left George Balfour. I remember wanting to handle it as a child and being told by Amy to hold it carefully, with two hands, as it was very precious. I used to think it was like a precious stone on a par with diamonds, its price beyond rubies, with magical properties. Whichever way you twisted and turned it, it looked different. It had hidden, unreachable depths. Rub it, and a genie might appear! If I closed my eyes hard enough and for long enough and then opened them quickly I saw one, rising in front of me, like a gentle spiral of white, green and blue smoke.

It might seem surprising that George Balfour did not banish the paperweight from his house along with every other trace of Eugénie after she left, but perhaps even he hesitated to maltreat an object which everyone else in the family and the street (apart from his mother) thought was something special. He might have been worried that if he dashed it to the ground he'd be visited by ten years' bad luck. He had enough to be going on with.

His mother had warned him against this marriage from the beginning, hadn't she? She'd known no good could come of marrying a foreigner. The wedding photographs show them posed on the steep grey steps of St Stephen's church in the usual stilted way of the time, unsmiling, so that one can see this is serious business they're embarked upon. There is no question of snapping the groom stealing a sly kiss from his bride. Eugénie is wearing a stiff white taffeta dress; her veil is back and has been caught by the fierce Edinburgh wind. Her chin is lifted. The day looks cold and grey. George and his best man, James, his younger brother (and my father-to-be), are both kilted and sporraned. Their knees rise sturdily out of thick socks. Eugénie's best maid, Agnes, sister of George and James, is holding her bouquet out in front of her bosom as if it were a grenade. She looks ready to throw it and cut and run. (Aunt Nan, as she was known, often looked as if she were handling a grenade. She was a little simple: or that is how she was perceived. She never married, though she came home once to announce that she was engaged to Tam the tinker, who came round at intervals to grind their knives. Her mother told her not to be daft and Tam not to bother coming to their door again, they would grind their own knives and, what was more, they knew how to use them!) To one side stand the groom's parents, his mother in a stout black serge coat and black hat, her black-gloved hands clasped over her stomach, dwarfing his father in tight suit and spats. The bride has no relatives present.

I have the photograph amongst my mother's memorabilia. She was a guest at the wedding, along with her friend Bunty MacFarlane, Jessie's older sister.

'She's a right bonny lass,' said my mother to Bunty as they stood in the street waiting for the photographs to be taken. Neither of them had seen the bride's face before she'd thrown back her veil and come walking down the aisle on her husband's arm; there had been none of the usual showing-of-the-present affairs beforehand with cups of tea and nips of sherry. Eugénie had arrived from France only two days previously and been kept closeted in the Balfours' flat.

'Puir thing! Imagine getting merrit into thon crowd! Nan's the only decent yin among them. But then she's a bit saft in the heid.'

'James is no so bad.'

'Aye, mebbe no, though he's ower fond of the lasses.'

My mother protested.

'You ken fine he is, Janet. He'll settle one of these days, likely. It's a wonder he didne bring a bride back from the war like George. She might have been a mermaid!' (My father was in the Navy during the war, had served with HMS *Hood* and been torpedoed.) Bunty laughed, a bit over-loudly, as she was wont to do, and attracted a few looks of censure. 'Any road, with a mither like yon the sons havne a chance. Nor would their wives, so just you tak' my word for it! There's plenty other fish in the sea than Jamie Balfour!'

The reception was held at St Cuthbert's function suite in Fountainbridge. St Cuthbert was to play a large part in Eugénie's life. One of her early misunderstandings was in thinking that it had something to do with a religious body; it was my mother who put her right and explained that it was the Co-operative society of Edinburgh, and all-important in the Balfour family's lives. George was a clerk in the main office at Fountainbridge, James worked in the engineering workshops in Hamilton Place alongside his father, and Nan served in the bakery. All the family's shopping was done at St Cuthbert's in Hamilton Place, a block away from St Stephen Street and parallel to it. There you could buy your groceries, butcher meat, fruit and vegetables, boots and shoes, hats, dresses, pots and pans and scrubbing brushes, pins and needles, aspirins and laxatives, even your furniture. There was no need to go past it, as Granny Balfour told her daughter-in-law. And besides, you got the 'divi'. 'The dividend,' she had to repeat, thinking this French girl was slow on the uptake. Don't tell her George had married a dummy, to boot! Eugénie, walking one day in Princes Street Gardens, enjoying the tranquil swards of green grass and the blossoming flowers and the sight of the fairytale castle high above her, crossed the road on her way back and went into Jenners' department store, where she purchased a pair of silk stockings. Unfortunately she was seen by a neighbour, so word went back and Eugénie, on her return, was delivered a stern lecture. (It was as well that the 'silk' part of it was not also reported, as that would have compounded the sin.) Eugénie felt as if she had acted like a traitor.

George introduced his bride to my mother and Bunty at the reception.

'My wife, U-Jeanie. U-Jeanie, these here are Janet Geddes and Bunty MacFarlane.'

Eugénie smiled and held out her hand. My mother met her direct look and smiled in return. They took to one another straight away.

'She needed a friend, I can tell you!' said my mother. 'At the reception everyone talked across her, as if she didn't exist. Except for Nan. But then you know Nan – half the time even we don't know what she's on about.'

Eugénie and George went to Rothesay for their honeymoon and brought back a plate.

'Ve*rrr*y cold,' said Eugénie to my mother, hunching her shoulders and shivering. She often used her body to communicate. It had been a bit blustery, George admitted, but bracing, and he'd prefer that any day to too much sun. Sun brought him out in a rash. And they'd had good value for their money at their Bed and Breakfast. Black pudding or white pudding every morning, a stack of fried bread, and two eggs if you wanted them. He'd been a bit annoyed with Eugénie for not eating more. A piece of toast had done her at breakfast. He hadn't been able to get her to realize that he had to pay for the food, whether she ate it or not. And she'd asked for hot chocolate! Whoever heard of anyone drinking cocoa for their breakfast?

George and James went one night a week with their father to a lodge meeting. The Orange Lodge. George kept his bowler hat and sash on the top shelf of the wardrobe. Eugénie was expected to brush the hard black hat. What was this *orange* lodge? she asked my mother, who replied evasively. She found it difficult to explain that it was an order which had been founded to protect the property of Protestants against Catholic attack following the Battle of the Boyne in 1690. After all, Eugénie might no longer be a practising Catholic but everyone knew she had been born one, and my mother was inclined to go along with Granny Balfour on this point: once an RC, always an RC. My mother said merely, 'It's a men's club. The orange bit comes from Holland.'

She took to dropping in on Eugénie on Lodge nights; they'd sit by the big black kitchen range with the curtains drawn and drink cocoa and she'd teach Eugénie words and phrases in English. I thought it was a pity Eugénie did not teach my mother French in return, but they probably saw no point in it. It was not a language that was often heard on the streets of Edinburgh.

They had many a good laugh on these evenings, said my

83

mother. Eugénie was willing to try and didn't mind if she made a few howlers. As she said, 'I have to speak. Silence is hard. Like fog.'

They were laughing one evening when Granny Balfour opened the door and came in without knocking. She had her own key. They stopped laughing at once.

'Well, Janet, and how're you the night?'

'Fine, thanks, Mrs Balfour.'

George's mother nodded at her daughter-in-law, then her eyes raked the kitchen, stopping at the draining board, where the tea dishes sat washed but not dried. She sniffed.

'She's a bit lazy, if ye ask me,' she remarked to my mother.

'It's my fault, I interrupted her. She was doing the dishes when I came in.'

Granny Balfour went over to the gas cooker. 'That's not ower clean, either. There's a skim of grease on it. You can aye tell a woman's character by the state of her cooker. And the bunker could do with a bit scrub. Has she never heard o' bleach? Mebbe they dinne hae it in France. They tell me it's a richt dirty place. I've tellt Geordie he'll need to keep after her. My sons are used tae a kitchen wi' a flair clean enough to eat aff. Nae man likes livin' in a midden.'

'I don't think it's a midden, Mrs Balfour.' My mother would have spoken softly; she was a gentle woman. I never knew her to have an argument in her life, except for the one disastrous one with Amy, which would prove to be the last time she ever saw her. Everyone in the street liked my mother, even Granny Balfour.

'I've been doing what I can to help her, takin' her to the steamie and the like, but it's some job! I was trying to teach her to mak' mince the ither day. She didne want to put the Bisto in! I think she's a bit thrawn, doesne want to learn. Whit Geordie had to go and marry a Frenchie for, I dinna ken.'

'There's nothing new about Scotland having links with France. There was the Auld Alliance.'

'Whit in the name's that? Is that whit you've been learning aboot at the night school?' But Granny Balfour was impressed in spite of herself. She said that my mother was a right smart lass.

'Way back in the Middle Ages,' said my mother, 'Scotland and France banded together, to help protect themselves against English aggression.'

'And where did that get us, tell me!'

'Then there was Mary Queen of Scots – '

'Her! She caused a bellyload of trouble, that yin! Ended by getting her heid chapped aff! Auld Alliance or no, to my mind George would have been better aff marrying a guid Scots lass like yersel'. I think he must've got hit on the heid wi' a bit shrapnel.'

'She saved his life, Mrs Balfour.'

'Aye, weel.' George's mother did not seem totally to believe that. No doubt she thought he could have made it on his own.

Meanwhile Eugénie sat by the stove, her cup clenched between her hands, the colour mounting high into her cheekbones. For a long time she found it difficult to make out anything of what her mother-in-law said; her accent (West Lothian rather than Edinburgh) was the broadest in the family. Once Eugénie got the hang of the English language, she and George had many a row about his mother being allowed to walk in any time she chose. Eugénie demanded he ask for the key back; he refused. Why didn't she walk out? By the time she might have thought about it, she was pregnant. And where could she have gone? Back to Saint-Sauveur, where her mother lived in semi-poverty? There was a limit to the number of sheets Berthe could launder to keep her daughter and a grandchild.

It was when Eugénie was about five months pregnant that she was seen coming out of the Roman Catholic cathedral. There was an unholy row. It was Nan who unwittingly spilled the beans. She said when they were having their tea, 'I saw U-Jeanie coming out of yon big kirk at the top of Leith Walk the day.'

Her mother put down her knife and fork. 'Whit big kirk?'

'That yin by the roundabout. Before you cross ower to Picardy Place. It's got a lot of steps at the front.'

Her mother looked at her father. He nodded. He laid down his knife and fork. They got up, leaving Nan to gape in bewilderment, and their oatmealed herring to congeal on their plates.

They marched straight along the street to George's house, where they, too, were in the middle of their tea. High tea, as Eugénie had learned to call it. She and George had finished their plates of stew and were now embarked on the afters. George had a half-eaten drop scone spread with lemon curd in his hand when his parents pushed open the kitchen door.

'We're wanting a word with you, George.'

He dropped the scone, curd-side down, and pushed back his chair. A little shiver of fear ran up Eugénie's spine. The Balfours retired to the lobby but Eugénie, her ear pressed against the door, heard and understood enough to realize what was going on. She caught the key words 'Rome', 'disgrace', 'shame'. By this time my mother had explained to her that members of the Orange Lodge feared and hated the Church of Rome. George's parents withdrew, leaving him to deal with the matter.

He came back into the room in a fearful temper.

'Why can I not go to my church?' asked Eugénie. 'I go to pray and light a candle for the baby. What can be the harm?'

'You bloody well won't light Fenian candles for my son!' Inflamed by the vision, George struck his wife across the face with the back of his hand. She tried to run out of the flat, to go to my mother's house round the corner, but he pulled her back and pushed her into the bedroom. 'Leave that room and I'll bloody kill you!'

Next day her face was swollen from crying and her eye almost closed with a bruise which, over the next few days, was to flower and change into myriad colours of purple, mustard and maroon. A beauty spot, Granny Balfour called it. 'That'll learn her a lesson and let her ken who's boss in the hoose.' She was the undisputed boss in hers, as everybody well knew, and if her husband had ever tried to hit her she would have knocked him backward with the flat of her hand. George had inherited his shoulders from her, not his father. She was a miner's daughter from West Lothian, had known hard times and thought Edinburgh folk were 'softies'. 'A wee bit blaw and they keel ower on to their knees.' Grandfather Balfour was a mild man who would give any ground in order to have a quiet life. I never knew him; he was to die of peritonitis the year before I was born.

During the nineteen years of her marriage Eugénie suffered regularly at the hands of her husband. When his temper came up, he let fly. He couldn't seem to help it, she said. Perhaps it was the result of his war injuries? She tried to think so: it helped ease her anguish. And she had been a witness to his suffering. Usually, a few hours later, he'd mutter that he was sorry, he hadn't meant to hurt her, and since she thought that was probably true she forgave him. She believed in the forgiveness of sins, if it was accompanied by repentance. After each bout she'd come to my mother, who'd comfort her and bathe her face. My grandmother-to-be, Granny Geddes, thought George Balfour a dreadful man. 'The likes of him should be locked up!' Others in the street, including not a few of the women, thought that if a man didn't rule the roost in his own coop he was no more than a mouse.

'And whit lassie wants a moose in her bed?' demanded Bunty MacFarlane.

'Don't talk so daft, Bunty!' said my mother. 'How'd you like to get beaten up?'

'It mightne be sae bad. If he was guid in ither ways.'

Bunty had a reputation for being a bit fast and when a navy came into Leith she was off down to the docks with the other girls, though not my mother. Bunty said there was something about a uniform.

Eugénie's first child, a boy, was born prematurely at six months and survived for only two hours. George was taking the loss of his son hard, his mother reported up and down the street. She implied that if it had been a Scottish womb that had carried the child he would have gone to full term and been delivered safely.

'It's his wife you should be thinking of,' said Granny Geddes, sending her home with a flea in her ear. After that the two women were cool with one another and when eventually my father declared his intention of marrying my mother, Granny Balfour warned him against her mother. 'It's no her mother I'm marrying!' he retorted. He was less under *his* mother's thumb than his brother.

Eugénie lost two more babies through miscarriage. Granny Balfour said she despaired of her daughter-in-law. George was kind to her, though, Eugénie said, after the loss of each child; his sorrow softened him. On the third occasion he cried and they clung to one another helplessly. Would they ever get a live bairn? he asked.

In the spring of 1925, Eugénie was pregnant again, and had passed the seven-month mark. She had lain in bed from the tenth to the thirtieth week. Now the doctor said she should be all right; that even if she were to start now, the child should survive. Go carefully, George cautioned her, don't walk more than you have to. But the doctor said exercise would do her good. George wouldn't let her lift as much as the kettle off the range. He carried down the buckets and brought up the coal from the cellar in the basement area. You'd have to look far before you'd find a better husband, said his mother in the St Cuthbert emporia along Hamilton Place and the steamie in Henderson Row. She turned the handle of the big mangle with extra vigour. 'He willne even let her dae her ain washin' – I've to dae it fer her!' She flipped the damp sheets up into the air, sending a draught through the steamie.

On weekend afternoons Eugénie and my mother went out walking, which suited George well enough. On Saturday he went to the football at Tynecastle, wearing his maroon and white Hearts scarf, and on Sundays slept after his midday dinner. Eugénie loved the Botanic Garden at all times of year, even in winter when the trees were stripped bare and ice crackled at the edges of the duck pond. She could spend hours underneath the palms in the hothouses. They stayed so long in the tropical heat that they'd emerge in a slight swoon, which would soon be dispelled by the sharp east wind. Sometimes they walked along by the Water of Leith, through to the Dean Village. Eugénie found she was growing fond of Edinburgh. It had taken her a while – six years, after all! – but there were many things about it that she enjoyed. Though she still felt a stranger.

'They will never take me for their own. Except you, Janet!' Eugénie squeezed my mother's arm.

On weekdays, when my mother was at work (she was a book-keeper at St Cuthbert's head office), Eugénie took the tram across Princes Street, up the Mound, as far as the High Street. She would then walk down the hill to the Cowgate, to St Patrick's RC church, where she attended mass. She could rely on going there unseen by members of the Balfour family: the Old Town was out of their orbit and that of most of her Stockbridge neighbours. Princes Street divided the city like a broad river.

As her time drew near she went daily to St Patrick's to pray for the safe delivery of a healthy child. George had promised that if this baby were to thrive and grow well she could take him home when he was six months old to show to her mother. She had not been back to Burgundy since her marriage. They had not had the money to pay for her fare. Times were hard; many men in the street were out of work. A number of them had gone on the big hunger march to London just before Christmas in 1922. She and Janet had seen them gathered at the Mound. All those desperate men; what a pitiful sight they had been! They were lucky, for George had always been in work, but his wage did not go far.

She found that she was thinking more about France again, as she had in the early days of her marriage. After that first terrible year, when she had been on the brink of running away many times, she had deliberately shifted her mind from thinking about it too much. 'You'll have to give Scotland a chance, Eugénie,' Janet had said to her, and she'd thought, yes, Janet was right, and so she'd tried. She had continued to write regularly to her mother and Aunt Yvonne in Paris, and both wrote back short but informative letters, which Eugénie hoarded and reread. Uncle Giles's sister Odile would write, too, when she had news of Colette.

In the autumn of 1921, Berthe had written to say that her old friend had been back on a visit to Saint-Sauveur. 'She told our neighbour old Monsieur Blum that she is going to write a book about her childhood. Not a novel, it seems, but a book about her real life. Unfortunately I was away in Auxerre, visiting Jeanne – the first time in years – so I missed her. She had her young stepson with her, Bertrand de Jouvenel, the Baron's son.'

A letter had come from Yvonne, dated 14 December 1921: 'Odile and I went to see *Chéri* at the Théâtre Michel yesterday evening, and who should be playing the part of Léa but Colette herself! It was the hundredth performance, apparently. She was marvellous! You would have so enjoyed seeing her, Eugénie. We spoke about you afterwards, Odile and I, when we went to drink a glass of marc in a café on the boulevard. It is not often we have such a night out!

'It broke my heart at the end, though, when Chéri leaves her. You remember how she is watching him from the window and he stops and she thinks he is going to turn back? But he doesn't – he walks on! The agony of it! I felt my insides ache for her.'

Odile wrote to Eugénie when Colette's marriage to the baron broke up at the end of 1923. 'Hardly a surprise. But they say he left without a word when she was away on a lecture tour. He went into their house on the boulevard Suchet and removed all his clothes! Men! Cowards, all of them. Maybe not Giles – Yvonne says not. They are still as happy as a couple of lovebirds, those two. And you – how are you and your gallant Scotsman?

'I heard that Baron de Jouvenel was planning to marry some rich society woman, a member of the Dreyfus family. I know nothing of your friend Colette Willy, where she is or with whom – if anyone. But a woman like her will surely not stay on her own for long.'

And then, not long afterwards, another letter: 'I have some more news for you. And it is causing much gossip here, I can tell you! They say that Colette Willy is having an affair with Baron de Jouvenel's son, Bertrand. And he is *thirty* years younger than Colette! She must have something, that woman. I doubt if any young man would have me, not with scrubbing hands like mine!'

Odile and Yvonne had sent Eugénie each of Colette's books as they came out. During her spell in bed she passed the long hours in reading. Before George came in from work she would stow the books away in the kist, underneath the blankets. He knew of their existence; she did not try to deceive him, wished merely not to exacerbate his irritation. He was suspicious of the books, as if he thought they might take her away from him. It was the fact that they were in French, she thought, and he could make nothing of the language.

On the last day of April, Eugénie went into labour. A taxicab took her with George and my mother – who was now her sister-in-law, having married James Balfour earlier in the year – to the New Hospital at Abbeyhill. The following morning, after many troubled hours of labour, Eugénie was safely delivered of a baby girl. The doctor said that she'd never have another child.

'She's right bonny, Jeanie,' said George, when he was allowed into the ward to see his wife and daughter. Eugénie was sitting against a bank of pillows, her face the colour of the sheets, holding the bundle in her arms.

'You don't mind that it's not a boy, George?'

'I quite fancy having a lassie. And she's alive, isn't she?'

Eugénie nodded.

'We'll need to think of a name for her.'

Eugénie had already thought of one. George had not, since he'd chosen a boy's name: William.

'We could cry her Williamina.' He was only half joking. 'Ina for short.'

'I want to call her Gabrielle-Amélie, George.'

'*What? Gabrielle!* We canne give her a mouthful like that! You're off your head, woman! Imagine her at the Stockbridge School and the bairns crying her that in the playground!'

'I want to, I *want* to!'

He thought she might go into hysterics or do something bad to the baby. He knew she'd had a rough time and that not all women could be like his mother, who'd given birth and got up to get her man's tea two hours afterwards. To calm his wife, he said, 'Oh, all right then!'

When he went to the Register Office he put the child's name down as 'Amelia'. 'How could we cry her Gabrielle?' he said to my father. 'Yon's a French name, and a pape's name.' He did not tell Eugénie, nor did anyone else. She never saw the birth certificate, never thought to ask. And when the time came for the christening at St Stephen's, George told her that the minister couldn't cope with a name like Gabrielle so they'd just have 'Amélie' for the service. The minister pronounced it 'Amelia', of course, and the family soon shortened it to Amy.

George kept his promise; he put by money for Eugénie's fare to France from his weekly wage. At the end of November Eugéne took her child to Saint-Sauveur, where she was baptized Gabrielle-Amélie with the holy rites of the Roman Catholic church.

I was schizophrenic from the start, said Amy.

Five

'I belong to a country that I have left.'

Jours gris

From the beginning, Eugénie was determined that her daughter should be fully aware of her French inheritance. The stories of Saint-Sauveur started early. Amy's first words were in French. At the age of five she went to Stockbridge School and there spoke Anglicized Scots in the classroom (broad dialect was strongly discouraged) and playground Scots outside, in the company of other children. She played Scottish street games, called a top a peerie, and skipped to the chant of 'One, two, three, a leerie . . .' Eugénie did not mind the street games, but she did object to the street language. It sounded so coarse. After hearing Amy rowing with another girl in the street below from her third-floor window, Eugénie reproved her.

'But she ca'ed me a Frog! I only tellt her she was a ba'-faced tatty-heid!' Amy had said a few other things as well, but those she would not repeat to her mother. 'And so she is. She's got a face like a ba'.'

'Ball,' said Eugénie, who had never imagined she would be trying to teach a daughter of hers to speak *English*. And they didn't even live in England! Her own command of the language still had its holes: she always forgot that it should be people, for instance, not peoples, her 'th's were difficult, and her accent caused smiles. Tolerant, even indulgent, smiles.

Men had told her that her voice was 'attractive'. Not George, of course.

Eugénie hated her daughter arguing and fighting in the street. George was no support to her in that; he said he was glad the lassie wasn't feart and could stand up for herself, the way he'd had to do.

'I want you to speak nicely, Amy,' said her mother. 'Say head, not heid!' That was one of the few Scots words Eugénie could understand. The rest sounded like double Dutch to her. Now she knew how he felt, said George, when she rattled on in French!

'Granny Balfour says heid,' said Amy. 'And ba'.'

Eugénie did not respond.

'I like French better than anything, though,' said Amy, knowing how to make her mother smile.

Amy longed to go to France. 'One of these days!' said her mother. But when Eugénie returned to Saint-Sauveur for a visit after an interval of nine years, she did not take Amy with her.

Amy begged to be allowed to go to Burgundy with her mother, but her father was adamant. She couldn't take time off her schooling, she had to 'stick in at her lessons' or she'd 'never get on in life'.

'It's only two weeks. I won't be able to *bear* it if you don't let me go! I'll die!'

'Don't talk rubbish!'

'Have you never wanted anything so badly you could've died for it?'

'I've said no, haven't I? And where do you think we'd get the money from?'

'All right, I know it doesn't grow on trees!'

'Don't be cheeky, madam!' Her father raised his hand, and Amy backed away. Not that he had ever struck her. When he hit her mother, Amy ran out of the house along the street to her Aunt Janet's, where no one ever raised their voice.

Amy and her mother had two places of refuge: the home of

my parents, James and Janet Balfour, and that of her mother's friend Liane. Her father did not know about Liane. Amy and Louise, Liane's eldest child, had been born on the same day. Liane was French, too, and married to a Scot, and she taught piano. She gave Amy a weekly lesson, and in return Eugénie would do some of her ironing. Liane had four children, and would have more; she was a Roman Catholic.

'You mustn't fret while I'm gone, now, Aimée,' said Eugénie. This would be their first separation; they had never been apart for a single night. 'The time will pass quickly.'

'For you, maybe. But not for me.'

'Don't pout, love. It spoils your pretty face.' Eugénie put her arms around her daughter and held her close. 'You know I love you, don't you?'

'If you did, you wouldn't leave me!'

'Now, don't be silly! You know I have to go and see *my* mother. You know I'll come back.'

George Balfour saw his wife off at the station. Amy did not go with them; from an early age, she hated standing on cold draughty station platforms waving goodbye. She went instead down to the Water of Leith, where she sat on the bank and fired stones at a rusted oil-drum bobbing about in the scummy water. It was quiet down there in the valley, away from the traffic, with the high green trees screening her; there was only the sound of the smack of the stones as they hit their target and the swoosh of the water as the drum swirled. As she fired she imagined that the drum was her father. 'Take that!' she muttered. 'And *that*!'

She heard feet slithering down the bank behind her and turned to see Danny McGrath, who lived in the flat below hers. His curly hair stood out around his head like a bush.

'You're no a bad shot fer a lassie.'

'What do you mean, fer a lassie? Are you wanting yer heid in yer haunds to play wi'?'

'Hey, hang on! No need to lose your rag.'

'I could beat you any day!'

'You're on!'

Amy jumped up. Swiftly they gathered stones and piled them into small cairns at their feet. They stood higher up the bank to fire, to get better aim. Amy went first. Her eyes narrowed, her lips protruded in a characteristic pout of concentration, then her arm came up and over in a wide arc and her stone went crash! right into the side of the drum, sending it into a frightful tizzy.

'The de'il seems to be in you the day!' said Danny, squaring up to take his turn.

Amy won the contest. And she was a whole year younger than Danny McGrath!

'You pitch like a laddie,' he said, and went sloping off, with his hands in his pockets.

For a few minutes Amy enjoyed her triumph, then she thought again of the train steaming south, snaking round long bends, sounding its mournful hooter, leaving a long plume of smoke trailing behind it. She trudged back along the path to the bridge at Stockbridge.

Granny Balfour was coming past, pushing the old pram she kept for transporting her washing to and from the steamie. She stopped when she saw Amy and put on the foot-brake.

'Where have you been?'

'Down by.'

'You shouldne go down by the river on yer ain. A bad man might get ye. Ye're no greetin', are ye?'

Amy had not realized that her face was wet. She wiped it with the back of her arm. She knew her grandmother thought she was 'tied to her mother's apron strings'; she had overheard her saying so to Aunt Nan. Aunt Nan had said, 'She's only a bit lassie yet.' Some said that Aunt Nan was still tied to *her* mother's apron strings. And she was forty!

Granny Balfour had on her thick hairnet and underneath her coat, which gaped open, her big wrap-around apron sprigged with blue and black flowers on a grey ground. She was seldom to be seen without the apron or the net: only on special occasions – christenings, funerals, visits to the panto at the King's Theatre and the like. For these celebrations she had her hair set at the hairdresser's in Raeburn Place, where Bunty MacFarlane's sister Jessie worked. Then Amy would find the sight of her grandmother's hair odd: like steel wool set in marcel waves. Amy preferred her netted and aproned.

'C'mon, hen, ye can chum me to the steamie. It'll dae ye guid to learn to work the mangle and fold sheets the richt way. Ah ken you've got some fancy notions in that wee heid of yours – put there by your mammy, no doot! – but ye micht still need to dae washin' when you grow up. Whit woman doesne?'

'I thought you were at the steamie yesterday.'

'This is your Aunt Janet's washing. She's no feeling so well the day.' She was pregnant, Amy knew; her mother had told her. Her grandmother thought that matters of that nature should not be spoken of in front of children; when Jinty Smith along the street, who was unmarried, had had a baby, Granny Balfour had given Amy some guff about her finding it under a gooseberry bush. As if there were any gooseberry bushes in Stockbridge!

Granny Balfour fished in her apron pocket and brought out a poke of sweets, black-and-white-striped balls, half of them stuck to the paper. 'Put one of them in yer gob and that'll cheer you up!' Amy did as she was told; she felt in need of some sweetness. The hard round ball, spiced with peppermint, bulged agreeably in her cheek.

'Bonjour, Aimée!'

Amy whipped round to see Louise, Liane's daughter. She was swinging her pink dancing pumps by their tapes. She went to ballet lessons on a Saturday morning. Amy's mother had asked her father if Amy might learn to dance – she yearned to dance – but he'd given a predictable answer.

'Bonjour, Louise,' muttered Amy, well aware that Granny Balfour's eyes and ears were on alert.

'Et ta mére? Elle est allée en France, n'est-ce pas?'

'Oui.'

'Veux-tu jouer avec moi cet après-midi?'

'Pas aujourd'hui.'

'Au 'voir, Aimée!'

'Au 'voir.'

Louise sped off.

'Who in the name was yon?'

'A girl.'

'I could see that! A Frog? What was she on about?'

'Nothing.'

'Do ye ken her?'

Amy shrugged. 'I just sort of see her about.'

Amy understood, without her mother having to tell her, why they kept quiet about their friendship with Liane and her family: it saved rows, being cross-questioned, as Amy had just been. So she learnt early on the art of concealment, of withholding pieces of information that she did not wish others to possess, thereby avoiding having to descend into the outright telling of falsehoods.

Granny pressed no further. She put out her foot and released the pram brake. Amy rested one hand on the handle. They waited for a tram to swing past, then they crossed the road into Hamilton Place.

As they drew near St Cuthbert's bakery, they saw that Aunt Nan was standing on the step talking to Jessie MacFarlane. Jessie's coat made a splash of red against the grey stone. Her sister Bunty had married and gone to live in Fife, and so they saw less of her now. Jessie too had been married, to a fisherman at Newhaven, and widowed. The fisherman had fallen into the dock when drunk; at least, that was how the story went in the street. Jessie was still only twenty-four. 'The Merry Widow', Granny called her.

'Look at the two o' them! Bletherin' their heids aff! I've tellt Nan her tongue'll fall aff yin o' these days.'

Jessie was smoking a cigarette; she held it perkily, at shoulder level. Amy saw that Aunt Nan was smoking too, but she was holding her cigarette behind her back; little feathers of smoke were curling round the edges of her white overall.

98

Granny Balfour thought that women who smoked in the street were common.

'Hello there, Mrs Balfour!' Jessie was quick with a greeting. She spun around on her high heels, her earrings birling. 'How're you doin' the day?'

'I'm takin' Amy tae the steamie. She's missin' her mammy.'

'What a shame! Thick as thieves, the pair of you, aren't you, you and your mammy?'

'I'll take you to the pictures, hen,' said Aunt Nan. She loved going to the cinema. They had a picture house – the Grand – in their own street and then there was the Savoy just down past the bridge and the Ritz over in Rodney Street, not far away. Aunt Nan spent nearly all her pocket money in these palaces of pleasure. She sat through most programmes twice. 'There might be a Roy Rogers on.' She particularly liked Roy Rogers; she'd sit right in the front row if he was in the film and talk to him. 'Ride 'em, cowboy!' she'd say. 'Give Trigger a pat for me, Roy.' 'Would you fancy going to the pictures tonight?' she asked Amy.

Amy nodded. She liked going to the pictures, but she didn't like it when Aunt Nan talked to the screen. People would snigger and glare at them and hiss 'Shush!', and worse.

'I'll come along for you after, then.'

'I don't know aboot the two of youse,' said Granny Balfour, shunting the pram forward, 'but Amy and I have got work tae dae.'

The steamie was full of steam. It didn't get its name for nothing, Granny would say. The steam snatched them into its damp embrace as soon as they opened the door and stepped inside, laying droplets of moisture on their faces and hair. No wonder Granny wore a net. The women's faces were brick-red and their hair clung in wet snakes to their heads. They were calling to each other across the deep-sided tubs. 'The boxes', Granny called them. They were wood on the outside, stone on the inside. Amy found it all strangely comforting, even though she'd hated the place when she'd come in before with her mother. But today she liked the way the women joked with one another and she liked the slap of the sheets and the whirr of the mangles as their big rollers turned. She felt half-hypnotized by the sounds and the steamy heat.

Granny Balfour was putting her waterproof apron on top of the other one and rolling her sleeves up her stout forearms. Then she ran hot water into a box and threw in a fistful of gritty soap powder.

'Git the sheets in then, hen, and dinne staund there lookin' glaikit! If ye keep yersel' busy yer mammy'll be hame in nae time, ye'll see.'

Amy was thinking about love when her mother came home; she had been to the pictures with Aunt Nan the evening before. They'd gone to the pictures five times in the two weeks that her mother was away. And nearly all the films that they'd seen had been about people – men and women – falling in love. She'd asked Aunt Nan if she'd ever been in love and her aunt had gone all coy and hinted that she might have been. 'What happened?' asked Amy. 'Why didn't you marry him? Would Granny not let you?' 'I love Roy,' said Aunt Nan. 'But that's not *real*,' said Amy. Aunt Nan looked huffed.

Eugénie brought back for Amy two books by the French children's writer the Comtesse de Ségur, *Les Malheures de Sophie* and *Les Petites Filles modèles*. Eugénie had read them when she was a child. Amy wrote her full name on the flyleaves: Gabrielle-Amélie Bussac Balfour.

For herself, Eugénie had bought Colette's novel *La Chatte*.

'I could read that, too, Maman, if it's about a cat. I like cats.'

'No, it's not suitable for you yet, love.'

'But why not?'

'It's a book for grown-ups. It's not so much about the cat as the man who owns it.'

'What does he do, this man?'

'He marries.'

'Is that all?'

'No, of course not. It's complicated.'

100

'Is he in love with his wife?'

'Their marriage is not what is called a love-match. It was arranged by their families – it is something that used to happen more.'

'But why is the book called *La Chatte*?'

'He is very attached to his cat, you see. And the cat does not like his new wife.'

'Does the cat win?'

'I suppose one would say that it does.'

'Maman, was yours a love-match, with Father?'

'Of course.' Eugénie's colour was high.

'Did you ever fall in love – before you married Father, I mean?' Her mother was looking away, towards the window where the light was failing. 'Did you, Maman?' asked Amy again.

'Well, yes . . . I did, once.'

They heard the key in the front-door lock. Eugénie got up, smoothing back her hair, which she now wore in a chignon, and went to meet her husband.

Three years later, Amy was allowed to go to France with her mother. On their way to Saint-Sauveur they were to spend a few days in Montmartre with the Lebruns.

'Can we go and see your friend Colette when we're in Paris?' asked Amy.

'Oh, I don't know . . .'

'Please, Maman!'

'It's a very long time since I've seen her. Must be eighteen years! She's probably forgotten all about me.'

'How could she forget? When she and Grand-mère were almost like twins. Write to her, Maman, *please*!'

Colette's answer came on blue paper. She was living now on the top floor of the Marignan building on the Champs-Elysées, with her third husband, Maurice Goudeket.

'Every time I see you, you're in a different place,' said Eugénie.

'I have moved thirteen times. Unlucky thirteen!' Colette did not sound troubled. 'How would you like to live on the eighth floor, Aimée?'

'I should love it. Especially if it looked over the Champs-Elysées.'

'Which floor do you live on in Edinburgh?'

'The third.'

'We do have a view,' said Eugénie. 'Of the Fife hills.'

'But it's nothing like this,' said Amy, irritated that her mother should even compare the two.

'Let me take you up on to my roof terrace and show you the view from there.'

Colette led the way up the ladder, which she said made her think of a ship's ladder. She liked it when it swayed in the wind. She had a cat on one shoulder and the other hand grasped a bulldog by the scruff of its neck. Amy, following behind, saw that Colette's feet moved surely and the calves of her legs looked muscled and strong, even though she was getting to be quite an old lady. She was sixty-four, the same age as Amy's French grandmother. Her mother had brought back a photograph of Grand-mère Bussac from her last trip, and she had looked grey and elderly then. She'd had a hard life, her mother said. Hadn't Granny Balfour's life been hard? Amy had asked. 'Yes, but perhaps not in the same way. She's always been in control.' That was the thing to aim for, said Amy's mother: to be in control of one's life. Not that that was easy, she had added, and closed the conversation before Amy could ask any more questions.

'Look at the clouds, Aimée!' Colette's ringed hand swept upward and silver bangles slid down her arm. 'See how the horizon shimmers! Look at Sacré-Coeur – wouldn't you think it was made of sugar candy? And there's the Opéra. I feel as if I have the whole of Paris at my feet when I come up here. I come in all seasons. Even on wild winter days. I like to watch the storm-clouds gathering and the rain advancing on the city like a curtain. Tell me, Aimée, how do you like Paris?'

Amy thought it wonderful, but felt too overwhelmed to say so. Looking at Colette, who was smiling broadly, her wiry hair lifted by the breeze, the cat sitting on her shoulder sniffing her neck, she realized that she did not need to. Colette understood the whirl of sensations going on inside her. Their eyes met; it was a moment of contact for Amy that was to stay with her for ever. She said she felt as if she had received an electric shock.

She went to the balcony rail and looked down into the avenue of the Champs-Elysées. 'The finest thoroughfare in the world', her mother called it. The street buzzed with traffic, the wide pavements swarmed with pedestrians. The pavement cafés too were busy; the customers lounged in their chairs, their faces turned towards the street so that they might watch the passers-by. They looked as if they had nowhere to go, nothing to do other than sit and stare and drink café crème and eat tartelette de fraises and smoke long, pungent-smelling cigarettes. They looked as if they might well sit until the sun went down. It would be good to have cafés like that on Princes Street, Amy had suggested to her mother as they'd walked down the avenue, but her mother had said that the wind was too cold in Edinburgh. You'd be blown to bits in no time. Besides, it was not a Scottish sort of thing. The Scots preferred to hug themselves inside their own houses. They didn't like exposing themselves to the stares of passers-by.

Colette came to stand alongside Amy. She leant both arms on the rail and the cat arched and curled its claws deeply but gently into the shoulder of its mistress's jacket. 'There's always something to see. Processions, military parades, funerals, traffic jams! I have a lot to amuse me.'

'When I grow up I shall come and live here on the top floor and I'll spend all day up on the terraces looking down into the Champs-Elysées!'

'And why not, Aimée? One must have dreams. But come, let us go back downstairs and I shall make you some hot chocolate.'

'Mother said you would give us hot chocolate.'

Colette's laugh was whipped away by the breeze.

The telephone was ringing as they came back into the

apartment. While Colette talked to someone called Marguerite (who appeared to be an actress, judging from the conversation), Amy let her eyes feast on the sitting room. Everything delighted her: the profusion of flowers, the bowls of fruit, the books, the crystal-glass paperweights, the lamps. She especially liked a mauve cyrstal lamp etched with lilac flowers. Some day she would have such a lamp. And she would fill her room with flowers like these flowers: curly-headed dahlias, velvet-petalled roses, glowing geraniums. She got up to look more closely at the paperweights; she did not think that Colette would mind or consider her nosy.

'Look, Maman, there's a paperweight almost like yours!'

The phone rang again, and the caller this time was called Nathalie. Colette must have millions of friends, thought Amy; they probably called from morning till night and had long, interesting, literary conversations.

'Ring me later, Nathalie,' said Colette. 'I have visitors.'

Amy smiled, pleased that Colette would put them before her friend Nathalie.

Pauline, the maid, brought in hot chocolate and Colette served it in blue-and-white cups. Amy sipped hers slowly, wanting to make it last for ever. She had never tasted anything so delicious. They had chocolate at home every morning, she and her mother, even though her father thought they would be better off drinking tea, like him, but it never tasted quite like this. Perhaps the milk was different. Or the cocoa powder.

'You speak French very well, Aimée,' said Colette.

'With a Scottish accent!' Eugénie smiled.

'There's Burgundy in it, too. Oh yes, I can hear it! You sound like a true Burgundian girl.'

Amy blushed. 'Maman and I always speak French when we're together. When Father isn't listening.'

'He doesn't like you to speak French?'

'It seems to make him angry, doesn't it, Maman?'

Eugénie shrugged. 'Men are sometimes like that.'

'That is true. But not all, thankfully. My Maurice is not, I am happy to say. I could never stay long with a man who did not like me to speak my mother tongue. With whom I could not *speak* in my mother tongue.'

Amy saw her mother look suddenly sad, bereft almost. They were closely attuned to one another's moods. She said quickly to Colette, 'Maman has all your books.'

'Not every single one, Aimée. Colette has published so many. I have just been reading *La Naissance du jour*.'

'Ah.'

'I liked the opening – you know, where you quote your mother's letter saying that she can't come and visit you because her rose cactus is about to bloom? And if she doesn't see it this time she may never see it again.'

'Shall I let you into a secret? I actually reversed what she said.'

Eugénie looked nonplussed.

'Oh yes, novelists are often guilty of turning their material around! That's how it becomes fiction. My mother wrote that not *even* the rare blooming of her cactus would keep her from visiting her daughter.'

'She must hve loved you very much,' said Amy.

'Yes, I think she did. I still miss her.' For a moment Colette looked sombre, then she brightened and lifted the jug, asking if they would like more chocolate. She replenished their cups and produced a plate of chocolate éclairs. 'Do you like éclairs, Aimée?'

'Oh, yes!'

'I do, too.' Colette bit into one with relish, then licked a sliver of cream from her top lip. 'I have an excellent appetite. What about you, Aimée? You don't look as if you eat enough – you have those telltale little salt-cellars in your neck. Not that they are not attractive. Now mine have long since vanished, alas. I love food. I like meat and crabs and apples and chocolate éclairs – am I not disgusting? – and ripe bananas and freshly ground coffee and mangoes. You might even say I'm a bit of a glutton!' She patted her stomach. 'It shows, eh? Do you like sugared almonds, child? You *must* like sugared almonds!'

'I've never tried them.' They were Aunt Nan's favourite sweet. Aunt Nan bought herself a poke of sugared almonds every Saturday afternoon as a treat, on her way home from the bakery, and ate them in the Grand Picture House on Saturday nights. Amy had always thought of them as old maid's sweets, along with peppermint pan drops, which old men and women sucked in church to stop them coughing.

'Try one now.' Colette held out a dish. 'Look at their soft sweet-pea colours; that is why I like them so much.'

Amy looked up, startled. Aunt Nan called them her sweet-pea sweeties. Maybe Aunt Nan wasn't as daft as some people liked to make out.

'Feel how smoothly they lie on the tongue,' said Colette.

From then on Amy shared with her Aunt Nan a preference for sugared almonds over all other forms of confection.

'You have such a lot of new things to look forward to, Aimée,' said Colette. 'How old are you?'

'Twelve.'

'Ah. On the brink.'

On the brink, thought Amy, liking the idea, even though she was not sure exactly what it was that she was on the brink of. Real life, she supposed. She felt suddenly older, on the way to being grown up, sitting here in this room high above Paris, drinking hot chocolate, three women together, talking.

'You have a good thick braid there,' said Colette, putting out her hand. 'Turn around and let me see it! You must be able to sit on it! Can you release it and let me see your hair? Would you, for me?'

Amy, blushing a little, fumbled to undo the blue satin ribbon at the end of the plait, then her fingers scrabbled through the three intertwined strands, running rapidly up to the nape of her neck. With a flick of her head she shook out her hair.

'What a glorious colour! Like a beech tree in autumn, with the sun lighting it. You are blessed to have such beautiful hair.'

'She wants to have it cut,' said Eugénie. 'All her friends are having their hair cut.'

'Don't!' said Colette. 'Not yet.' She glanced from mother to daughter. 'You seem close, you two?'

Eugénie nodded. 'We're good friends.'

'Where is your daughter?' asked Amy.

'Wherever she wants to be – a not unreasonable thing at her age. She is twenty-four now, my Colette. She spends most of her time on the Jouvenel estate in the Corrèze. She comes to Paris only occasionally. She comes and sees me when she wants to. She'll arrive unexpectedly and we'll talk for hours and then she'll go away and I won't see her for months.'

'*Months!* I should hate not to see Maman for months. I couldn't bear it.'

'Bel-Gazou married, didn't she?' said Eugénie.

'That lasted only two months. She divorced him, for physical disgust. An unimpeachable reason, would you not agree?'

Eugénie did not have time to comment before the door opened and a man put his head round.

'Maurice, come and meet some old friends!' Colette smiled warmly at him. 'Eugénie and Aimée, this is my best friend!'

Amy could not help feeling a little disappointed at the appearance of Colette's husband. He was quite dapper in appearance, but otherwise she thought him fairly ordinary: he was neither tall nor particularly handsome, and he had a largish mouth and ears that stuck out. She had expected him to look more *romantic*, more like a Chéri. He was sixteen years younger than Colette. He did seem to be nice, however, and he had very good manners; he gave them each a little bow when he shook hands and said 'Enchanté!', and he took the hand his wife was holding out to him and spoke to her in a kindly, affectionate way, which Amy had seldom heard her own father do to her mother. Her father seemed forever to be complaining, hectoring. Something was not right. The kitchen was untidy; there was a stain on the tablecloth; they had banked the fire too high, or not high enough; the dinner was late. She had started to notice it more in the last year and when she had commented on it her mother had said that his complaining was a bit like a nervous tic: on coming home, on opening the door, he seemed to be overcome by a compulsion to criticize. She had seen him standing in the doorway, looking round, looking for areas in which to attack her. Why does he want to attack you? Amy had asked. Her mother had shrugged. Her father hated it when her mother shrugged. 'You French!' he would say. 'Why can't you just *answer*?'

Her mother was gathering up her bag and gloves from the floor beside her chair. She was anxious that they should not overstay their welcome.

'Let me give you my new book,' said Colette. Goudeket fetched a copy from a shelf and put it into his wife's hands, along with a pen. 'It's called *Bella-vista*.' Colette inscribed it on the flyleaf: 'A Eugénie et Aimée, amies de Bourgogne et d'Ecosse, affectueusement, Colette.'

She embraced them both, told them never to visit Paris without coming to see her.

Going down in the lift Amy asked her mother, 'What does Monsieur Goudeket do?'

'I am not sure. Odile said she thought he was a dealer in pearls at one time. He's half-French and half-Dutch. Half-Jewish, too. He used to write a little himself, it seems.'

'But he's not famous, like Colette?'

'Oh no.'

'I wonder if he minds.'

'He doesn't seem to.'

'Maman, what does physical disgust mean?'

Eugénie blushed. 'It's difficult to explain. It's when a woman doesn't like to have a man near her.'

'But if Colette's daughter didn't like her husband why did she marry him?'

'Sometimes a woman doesn't find out until afterwards.'

On the Métro, Amy opened *Bella-vista*. 'C'est folie de croire que les périodes vides d'amour sonts les "blancs" d'une existence de femme,' she read. She contemplated the sentence. 'It is mad to think that the periods in a woman's life which are empty of love are blanks.' She was glad of that, otherwise her mother's life would be one long blank. Excepting, of course, that *she* loved her. But Amy knew that Colette meant *romantic* love. Men and women. As they sped through the tunnels underneath Paris, Amy thought about Colette's daughter, who lived by herself on a big estate in the Corrèze. Odile said the house was like a castle.

'Maman, Colette doesn't seem to mind if she doesn't see her daughter.'

'Her life is very crowded, of course, what with her writing and her friends. She travels, too. They go all over the place – to Belgium, Italy, Tunisia. They sailed in the *Normandie* on its maiden voyage to New York. Odile saw their picture in the newspaper. But she must miss her daughter sometimes. You'd think so, anyway. Her daughter was brought up differently – differently from you, that is. She had a nanny, and after that went to boarding school. It is what people in their milieu do. You've always been at home with me; I wouldn't have had it any other way. I'd never want to be separated from you.'

That was what made it so difficult for Amy to understand when her mother left her just over a year later.

They were on a train from Paris to Auxerre, Amy and Eugénie, on their way to Saint-Sauveur, having been seen off at the Gare de Lyon by Yvonne and Odile. They were alone together in the compartment. They had just finished a lunch of crusty bread and a ripe Camembert and peaches and were brushing the crumbs off their laps, when the door opened. Eugénie had been talking about Odile, saying what a pity it was that her husband had died so young, that she'd never had children, and had had to live so many years alone. It was as well she'd had Yvonne and Giles to turn to. Now there was a good marriage! They had always been so considerate – Eugénie stopped in mid-sentence. A man stood framed in the doorway. Amy felt conscious of him being framed; it was as if the moment was frozen. Yellow light seemed to encircle his head. He had dark, greying hair and dark, thickly lashed eyes. A handsome man, much more handsome than Maurice Goudeket. He might have been a Chéri when he was younger. He was wearing a pale jacket and a deep-blue shirt with a lighter-blue tie. He stood there staring at Amy's mother. She stared back at him.

'Claude,' she said, rising to her feet. 'Claude Laroche.'

Like a sleepwalker, she moved out into the corridor. The door closed behind her. Amy stayed in her seat, motionless, paralysed by a nameless fear, the last of the breadcrumbs sticking to her lap. When she got out at Auxerre, they trickled down her legs, into her white ankle socks. That night, taking off her socks in her grandmother's flat above the bakery, feeling the crumbs disintegrate between her fingers, the fear repossessed her.

They stood to one side of the compartment door, the man and her mother, so that she could not see them, though she could hear their voices murmuring, rising and falling, mingling with the rumble of the train wheels. The train swayed and rocked. She swayed and rocked like a stocking-doll.

After some time her mother came back. Amy could not say how long she had been in the corridor. Ten minutes. Or a lifetime? Eugénie said nothing. She sat down. She stared at the dusty velour back of the seat opposite. From time to time her top lip twitched and she seemed about to break into a smile, then, with a sideways glance, to think better of it.

Amy's mother did not speak the name of Claude Laroche again, not in her daughter's hearing. And Amy could not bring herself to ask, 'Who was that man? That man on the train? The one you called Claude Laroche?'

Amy both loved and hated Saint-Sauveur. The village and its surrounding countryside had featured much in her day-dreams: she had wanted desperately to come here, to see her grandmother and the Saracen tower and the ruined château and the garden behind the Colette house; to walk the streets, and take the paths through the woods. But something had shifted imperceptibly in her life, between stepping into the train at the Gare de Lyon and stepping out at the station in Auxerre. A remembrance came to her of a day at home when, riding her bicycle, the chain kept falling off. She had dismounted and, kneeling on the hard pavement, getting her hands covered with sticky black oil, carefully eased the chain back on to the ratchets until, finally, she had been able to spin the pedals freely between her hands. Then she had remounted and ridden off, but a few turns of the pedals later her foot lurched sickeningly down and there was the chain hanging loose again! She put it back three times, then in frustration flung the bicycle aside. Later her Uncle James had told her that it was the back wheel that needed adjusting.

She did not know what it was that needed adjusting now; she had only this sense of dislocation and an awareness that something which had once been taut was now slack. Walking in the woods one afternoon outside Saint-Sauveur, conscious that her mother's thoughts were not with her, Amy tried to take her hand and was reproved, gently and with a little laugh but firmly.

'You're too big a girl to take my hand now, Aimée!'

Later, looking back, Amy's most vivid memories of that holiday were of the times when her mother had gone off on her own to meet Florence or Sylvie, old school friends, or Anne-Marie, with whom she had nursed at the Front. Her mother would talk too much and too rapidly before going out. 'You remember me talking about Anne-Marie, don't you, Maman? We were at Cambrai together. She met George — your father, Aimée — she's from Sens, married now, to a man, an engineer, from Nantes, they have four children. They are living in La Rochelle, they have come to visit Anne-Marie's sister in Auxerre.' Berthe Bussac seemed not to notice the difference in her daughter. She said, 'Anne-Marie? I don't remember. You knew so many girls.' And on one occasion Eugénie simply disappeared. She went to the pharmacy, she had a headache . . . She did not come back for hours. Amy paced the streets. Two women standing at the intersection of the rue de l'Hospice and the rue des Gros Bonnets thought the girl looked a little demented with all that red hair streaming out behind her. Surely not another Juliette Colette? But then

Eugénie Bussac had mingled her blood with that of a foreigner, and who knew what strange concoction could result from that? Amy passed her Uncle Robert in the square with his son Alphonse and did not even see them.

Eugénie came back as dusk was shrouding the street. She said, 'I felt like some air. I went for a walk . . .'

After that visit to France Amy felt as if a shadow had appeared at the edge of her eye. Whichever way she turned her head, whatever she looked at, it was there.

On their return to Edinburgh, Eugénie paid regular visits to the General Post Office up in Waterloo Place, to the Poste Restante counter. She would then go into Princes Street Gardens to read her letter if the weather was fine, and Crawford's Tea rooms on North Bridge if it was not. Amy knew because she followed her. She told no one.

Amy went to the hairdressing salon where Jessie worked.

'I want my hair cut,' she said. 'Short.'

'Does your mammy know?'

Amy held out her hand. 'I've got the money.'

'I wouldne like to touch it without your mammy – '

'I want it *cut*! It's *my* hair.'

Amy swept some black hairs off the red mock-leather chair and sat herself down, facing the mirror. 'I'm ready,' she said, and folded her arms over the upper part of her chest.

Jessie covered her with a voluminous grey cloak and tied the tapes at the back.

'Are you sure now?' She held the scissors suspended.

'Sure,' said Amy fiercely.

'All right, keep your – !' Jessie stopped, realizing that what she had been about to say would be inappropriate, given the circumstances.

Afterwards, Jessie was uneasy about what she'd done. There sat the girl, glowering at her shorn head in the mirror, with a sea of dark-red tresses washing around the legs of her chair.

Jessie told my mother that she hadn't realized before just how strong-willed Amy was.

She asked her if she'd like to keep her hair. Amy said that she never ever wanted to see it again.

When she had gone out Jessie gathered it up in a bag, in case Eugénie should come asking for it. But Eugénie never even mentioned it to her.

Years later, Jessie brought out the hair; we looked at it, faded and lifeless then. Dead hair, Jessie called it. Next day, she threw it out in the bucket.

It was a full day before Amy's mother noticed the transformation that had taken place to her daughter's head, and it was her husband who drew her attention to it.

'I'm surprised you let the lassie cut her hair,' he said. 'Now that it's gone, she'll never get it back.'

The following year, 1938, Berthe became seriously ill. She had not been well for some months – a kidney complaint – but now her condition was deteriorating. Eugénie's brother Robert wrote to say that his sister should come, his wife could not cope, she had her own elderly father to look after. Eugénie prepared to go, leaving Amy with her father and Granny Balfour. It was early summer.

'Please let me come with you!'

'How could I?'

'*Please*, Maman! Don't leave me!' Amy clung to her mother.

'You can't take time off school. You know your father would never allow it.'

Berthe lingered, dying eventually in late August. Eugénie did not return to Scotland until the beginning of November. She wrote, saying that she had her mother's affairs to sort out. Granny Balfour snorted. What affairs could *her* mother have had? She hadn't even owned her house, had she?

When Eugénie did come back, there was a big row in the kitchen between her and George. Amy's mother emerged afterwards with the usual half-shut eye and next day her father said that he was sorry. Amy heard them behind the closed door of their room.

'You can say sorry once too often, George.'

'You'll forgive me, Jeanie, won't you?'

There was no reply.

Eugénie resumed her visits to the GPO. She hugged her secret to herself, did not confide in anyone. She stayed away from our house, fearing perhaps that my mother might plead for George. My mother often would speak up for him; she said he was his own worst enemy – not that that excused him. But she thought he loved Eugénie, in his own way. When he struck his wife, it was out of frustration; my mother did not condone it, but she understood.

Eugénie took to walking in the King's Park and on Arthur's Seat in stormy weather as well as fair. She was seen standing on the top of Salisbury Crags while the rain pelted down and others ran for cover. She began to look like a wild woman, with her muddied shoes and long hair tangled by the wind. On wet days she came in sodden. Placing her coat lengthwise over the rails of the pulley, she winched it up to the ceiling, where it hung like a spreadeagled scarecrow and dripped navy-blue water at irregular intervals on to their heads. She'd kick off her shoes and sit as close to the range as she could get, her hair hanging down over her shoulders like rats' tails. Her serge skirt steamed, giving off a wet-woollen, fusty smell. Her stockinged feet were stained.

The sight of her on those occasions inflamed George Balfour even more. She was a disgrace to him, to the name of his family. They were a laughing stock in the street. On coming home from work, he ranted about unwashed dishes, picked them up and threw them. Shards of broken china speared the carpet, tea spattered the ceiling, milk ran down the walls. His wife watched impassively. It was Amy who, trembling, jagging her fingers on the broken china, cleared up the mess.

In March, Claude Laroche arrived in town. Amy knew that he had without seeing him: her mother became transformed, looked years younger. She washed and brushed her hair. She smiled. She laughed. She stuck yellow daffodils in a blue-and-white jug. She pushed the kitchen window up high to let in the spring air.

George Balfour came upon his wife and Laroche behind the ruined chapel of St Margaret in the King's Park. Now he wore a bruise like a badge on his cheek. He had a broken knuckle too, on his right hand, which he had to take to the Infirmary to get set and plastered. For several weeks he carried a clenched white fist. The Frenchman left Edinburgh, taking Eugénie with him. She was not even allowed to come back to the house to collect her clothes.

From some points of view it might have been seen as romantic, this elopement, but not from Amy's. She saw her mother once more, at the school gate. It was lunchtime. The playground was milling with pupils, many of them knew the story of Amy's mother and her fancy Frog. They formed a sniggering cluster a few yards from the gate. 'French kisses!' 'French knickers!' 'Hoor! Hoor! Hoor!'

Amy and her mother put their backs to them. Eugénie had come to say goodbye and to tell Amy that she would send for her. She did not say how the sending would be done, nor how Amy's father would be induced to let her go. 'As soon as we have an apartment. I promise! I'll write to you at the Poste Restante in Waterloo Place. We're going to live in Paris. Won't that be nice? You like Paris, don't you?' Eugénie looked distraught, and happy. She embraced Amy, holding her close. 'Courage, mon enfant! Je ne t'oublierai pas.' 'I won't forget you.'

It was 1939, and Hitler was gathering strength in Europe.

Six

It must be said that when a young girl puts
her hand into a hairy paw, gives her
mouth to gluttonous and impatient lips,
and gazes serenely at the huge shadow of
an unknown man on the wall, it is because
of the powerful promptings of sexual
curiosity.

Mes Apprentissages

'C/o Laroche, 10 Boulevard de Magenta, Paris 10.'

Care of Laroche! She didn't trust *him* to take care of her mother. He had taken her away. The address at the top of the letter ran in front of Amy's eyes. 'Excuse me!' A man was glowering at her from under beetle-brows; she was standing between him and the counter. She had ripped the envelope open the moment the post-office clerk put it into her hand. She moved to the side, clutching the letter, and wiped her eyes with the sleeve of her navy-blue school Burberry. The man had turned his head and was staring at her. She turned and fled from the post office.

She went into Princes Street Gardens, where she sought out a quiet spot down in the hollow under the overhang of the dark castle rock.

'Everything happened so fast,' her mother had written, 'that I scarcely had time to catch my breath. I hated having to leave you like that, with just a few rushed words. The sight of your poor frightened white face stayed with me in the train all the way to London. But don't be frightened, ma petite. It will all come right in the end, you'll see. You'll come and make your home here with us in Paris. We'll move to a different flat, with more room, room for you. At the moment we are in Claude's flat – it's a bachelor flat, really. One bedroom, sitting room,

116

kitchenette. A bit gloomy, I have to confess, with its heavy furniture and dark walls. But it is handy for Claude's hospital.

'Let me tell you about Claude. You remember the man I met on the train from Paris to Auxerre, on our last visit to Burgundy together? That was Claude Laroche. He is a doctor, a specialist in renal diseases. I met him a very long time ago, long before you were born – in 1915, when I went to work in the hospital at Auxerre as a girl. He was a young intern there. We fell in love, we were happy for a time, then we had a misunderstanding. We were young. He married someone else on the rebound and I left Auxerre and went to the Front, where I met your father. The rest you know, more or less. Claude's marriage did not last; it broke up in 1920 and he went to Saint-Sauveur to look for me. But by then, of course, I was married to your father and living in Edinburgh.

'I'm sorry about your father, but I think you understand that I could not live with him any longer? Be kind to him if you can.

'Take care of yourself, my precious. I hope you are allowing your lovely hair to grow.

'Je t'embrasse – Maman.'

Amy read the letter aloud to my mother, translating as she went. 'But she doesn't say *when* I've to come.'

'You've got to be patient, dear.'

Amy snorted.

'You've got to give her time. You can't expect her to arrange everything straight away.'

'She's only got to send my fare.'

'She mightn't have the money.'

'She could get it from *him*.' Amy did not say his name if she could avoid it. 'I'll earn it myself. I'll wash stairs – anything!'

'They'll need to find another flat first. There's only the one bedroom.'

'I could sleep in the sitting room. On the settee. Or the floor. I wouldn't mind the floor.'

'He might not like that. I mean, not many men would, a girl

117

sleeping on the floor. And then you don't have a passport either, do you? You were on your mother's passport. You'd need a parent's signature to get a new one.'

'You could sign the form for me, couldn't you, Aunt Janet?'

'Me?'

'You've got the same surname.'

'You're asking me to forge – ?'

'It'd only be the teeniest lie. After all, you're like a second mother to me. Maman always said if I was in trouble and she wasn't there I should go to you. *Please*, Aunt Janet!'

My mother was saved by the arrival of Granny Balfour and myself. Granny had taken me to the steamie to give my mother a chance to get on with her ironing in peace. I was fond of the steamie at the age of four, so I was later told. The women made a fuss of me, let me put the soap powder in and trample the blankets, and they stuffed dolly mixtures and liquorice allsorts into my mouth, just as they had with Amy when she was that age.

Amy began to prepare for going to Paris. She got a Saturday job in the shoe department at St Cuthbert's and each week put aside the money without spending a penny, forsaking even the pleasures of a poke of sugared almonds or a visit to the Grand. She sorted out her clothes, putting in one drawer those she would take and in another those she would leave. She kept railway and cross-Channel ferry timetables under the lining of her desk drawer; she could recite the timings off by heart, knew which train connected with which ferry. She gathered Colette's books together and hid them in the kist under the winter blankets – her father was making bonfires in the back green of everything French. The neighbours complained that the smoke was fouling their washing but he paid no attention. His face had a tight, withdrawn look as he went about his burning. His eyes sparked. No one wanted to push him too far; it seemed possible that he might burst into flames himself.

When the coast was clear, Amy dug up the books from the

bottom of the kist and carried them, along with her mother's other memorabilia, to my mother's house for safekeeping. It was thus that they came into my mother's hands, and later into mine.

George Balfour forbade his daughter to utter a single word of French in the house. 'I can talk to myself, can't I?' she said. 'You can't stop me doing that. You don't own my thoughts.' They confronted one another. Both turned away. Amy went to Liane's, where she was able to speak freely and openly, and in our house she talked French to me. She formed an even deeper attachment for me, took me everywhere with her, cuddled me and rocked me and read aloud to me from *Les Malheures de Sophie*. My mother said it worried her a little at times, Amy was so intense, but she would have found it difficult to prise me from her arms.

Amy made daily pilgrimages to the Poste Restante, although Eugénie's letters came only once weekly. 'You never know,' she'd say. 'There *might* be one today.' She could not bear the thought that a letter of her mother's might lie all night in the cold, deserted post office. My mother thought that perhaps Eugénie didn't write more often because she wasn't sure what to write about; she would know that Amy was awaiting one piece of news and that alone.

Eugénie wrote about Paris, how beautiful it was in springtime. The café tables were out, the trees in blossom. She walked a lot around Paris while Claude was at his hospital. He worked long hours. She came home from her walks with aching feet. Those boulevards were hard! Oh, not that she was complaining about that. 'When you come we'll walk for miles and miles. We'll walk by the Seine and you can browse at the bouquinistes and we'll visit the Louvre and the Jeu de Paume – all the things we weren't able to do before. And we'll sit at a boulevard café – perhaps even on the Champs-Elysées! – and drink a café crème and watch the people go by.'

Eugénie wrote about Aunt Yvonne and Uncle Giles.

'He is not so well, he suffers a lot from ulcers. Aunt Yvonne is still pretty fit, as is Odile. They like to go out and about and have little treats, the two of them, to a café or the cinema. Both send their love.'

Eugénie wrote about Colette.

'I went to visit Colette today, at her home in the Palais-Royal. It is a first-floor apartment, a nice quiet situation. From her windows she can look down into the gardens of the Palais. When we took a stroll in the gardens I noticed she was walking a little unevenly. She fears she has the beginnings of arthritis. Monsieur Goudeket was with us, attentive as usual, anxious that she should not strain herself. She is anxious about him, should it come to war. He is half-Jewish, if you remember. We are all anxious. They say terrible things are happening in Germany and Czechoslovakia . . .'

Eugénie wrote to my mother. She wrote in English.

'In every letter Aimée asks when can she come. I would love to have her with me. But there is a problem. Claude is not anxious to have Aimée join us. He says it would be all right for her to come to Paris and live elsewhere. But where? There is no room at the Lebruns', and Odile lives in a single room. You see, Claude wants to have me on my own, for himself. You can understand that, can't you? He feels we've wasted all those years. He doesn't want to have to share me. He has no children of his own. We go out most evenings, when he is free. We go to restaurants, cafés, the cinema, the theatre. He is used to such a life. He is quite possessive. But, Janet, I don't really mind that! I am happy in a way that I have not been before. Except about Aimée. Do you blame me, dear friend, for taking this chance of happiness?'

I don't know what my mother replied – I have Eugénie's letters to her, but not hers to Eugénie.

One night Amy, wakening and getting up to go to the lavatory, was arrested by a sound coming from her father's room. It was a loud, strangled sort of sound. She stopped in the chilly passage, her feel cooling quickly on the linoleum. Perhaps her father was dreaming. He couldn't be *crying*, surely? She had never seen or heard him cry, couldn't imagine it, didn't want

120

to imagine it. The noise went on. Her toes were beginning to curl under; gooseflesh was forming on her upper arms. She was shivering. She did not seem to be able to move either forward or back. Should she go in to him?

She did not go. She scurried back to her warm bed, where she curled up in the foetal position, suffering the pressure of a full bladder rather than venture out into the passage again. On her 1965 visit to Edinburgh, she told me about this incident and how it had haunted her.

'We fail most of our friends and family at some point, to a greater or lesser degree. We can never give them everything they need.'

At the beginning of July Amy, by now fourteen, left school. She left at the insistence of her father; he said it would be a waste of time and money for her to stay on, when she could be out earning. The headmaster expressed dismay. Amy was one of his brightest pupils, excelling in English — and languages, of course — but history, geography and maths also. He even spoke of university. Scotland had always had its lad o'pairts; there was such a thing as a lass o'pairts, too, Mr Balfour should be aware of that. But Amy's father believed that women married and had no need of careers, in spite of his cajoling talk to her in her younger years about working hard at her lessons in order to get on. He had had no reason to think otherwise. Anyway, what was the point of a woman training to be a teacher, when she would be obliged to give it up when she married? Few if any of our neighbours — male or female — had what could be called careers; they had jobs. In the Co-op, on the trams, at the rubber factory, in a brewery. Mrs Craddock at No. 5 was a seamstress and Mr Flynn at No. 65 taught the violin and Jessie MacFarlane's father sold insurance. But no one considered these occupations to be careers. Careers were thought of in terms of advancement, moving out to the Victorian suburbs or even further to the land of bungalows, sending your children to fee-paying schools and dressing them in fancy blazers, getting a salary cheque at the end of the month instead of a weekly wage in your hand. (Nowadays the street has changed: it houses a school of dance and drama, an astrology centre, restaurants that serve French meals and bars where jazz can be heard on a Saturday afternoon, as well as shops selling many and various second-hand objects; and in the flats above, amongst the weekly wage-earners who have not all been dislodged, you might find a merchant banker in the early stages of his career or a university lecturer or an aromatherapist. Granny Balfour would have viewed most of these developments with grave suspicion.)

Amy had a notion to be an actress. She loved the theatre, and in her last year at school had starred in a school play, at the end of which the members of the audience, led by Danny McGrath, had clapped their hands boisterously and stamped their feet, and given Amy her first taste of applause. It made her feel good, gave her a glow inside. 'I think I was blooded then,' she said. She had enjoyed the actual performing, too. 'It was a relief to get out of being Amy Balfour for a while.'

It did not matter much to Amy what she did now that she had left school, since she was expecting to set out for Paris any day. In fact it suited her to be working full-time, and earning more money. And she would never have been able to persuade her father – or grandmother – to allow her to go on the stage. Granny Balfour had a low opinion of actresses. 'No better than they should be!' Though she would admit to enjoying the pantomime once a year at the King's Theatre, and Harry Gordon in the 'Half-Past Eight Show' in the summer.

George Balfour helped his daughter procure a job as a clerkess in St Cuthbert's head office in Fountainbridge, where he himself worked. They went up in the tram together in the mornings, sitting side by side, seldom speaking, their shoulders touching, holding their lunch 'pieces', which Amy had made up earlier. Her grandmother had told her she would have to be the woman of the house now. When Amy and her father were at work, Granny Balfour came in and washed the floor and scrubbed the bunker with bleach. She took their sheets to the steamie. 'Whaur wud a mon be withoot his mither?' she demanded.

Amy found her job mindless and boring, typing out invoices for tubs of lard and sides of bacon, and she hated the grey, narrow-minded people she had to work amongst. She heard their whispers. Scratch, scratch, scratch. They sounded like mice scrabbling in sawdust. Her father was pitied, her mother regarded as a fallen woman. She bided her time.

'Paris, 25 August 1939.

'Ma petite,
'It seems that war is certain to come now. Everyone thinks it is unavoidable, that there can be no last-minute efforts to pull us back from the brink at this stage. Claude has received his call-up papers, he will be in the medical corps. I can't believe we have to go through all this again. I have such a feeling of *déjà vu*. There is a chill in my heart. At least you are further away; you should not be touched there . . .'

On the first of September, the British government ordered complete mobilization. The newspapers were full of advice on how to cope with an air raid. 'Gerry isne goin' to drive me doon to any shelter below ground like a moose,' said Granny Balfour. 'Or to staund in a narrow passage wi nae windaes either! I'll stay in my ain hoose, thank you very much!' And she did, throughout all alerts, carrying on with her floor-washing and ironing, thumping her big heavy flat-iron down on the board with extra vigour.

On the second of September, the world held its breath.

The next day, Sunday the third, Amy came to see my mother.

'Do you think I'll still be able to get to France?' she asked anxiously.

'I doubt it, dear. Not with a war on.'

*

Men in the street were being called up. George Balfour was not amongst them; his wounds from the previous war precluded his passing a medical. The muscles and ligaments of his injured leg were in poor shape. He was allowed to join the Home Guard. Aunt Nan wanted to be an air-raid warden and get a tin hat and a torch but she had to make do with rolling bandages and knitting socks for airmen at the ARP post, alongside my mother. Aunt Nan brought along left-overs from the bakery at night to go with the wardens' tea: vanilla slices, flies' cemeteries, snowballs, angel cakes, and jam and custard tarts. St Cuthbert's had to do its bit for the war effort too, she said. My father was recalled to active service in the Royal Navy and sent to Skegness on the east coast of England.

'I dinne ken whit the world is comin' tae,' said Granny Balfour.

'Paris, 7 September.

'Ma chère Aimée,

'Claude has gone and I don't know where he has been posted. And I am alone in this dark flat. Paris has changed, as if an evil fairy has waved a wand. At night it is a strange city, like something from another world – not that I go out much now, not in the evening. I put out my lights and pull back the black-out and stare down into the boulevard. I see blue lights glimmering in the darkness; the streetlights have been swaddled in blue wrappings. Car lights are blue. People carry blue torches. There is hardly anyone on the streets after nine o'clock except for police patrols in their capes and helmets, on foot and on bicycles. They stab the passers-by with their torches. They allow the women to move on; they question all men, ask them for their papers. Métro services have been cut and hardly any buses are running. Sirens go even in the daytime. At night we go down to the shelters. We have been issued with gas masks – some of the women are making fancy covers for them. My neighbour said she was not going to carry that awful-looking putty-coloured object through the streets of Paris! I have made myself a tartan cover! I think of Scotland – and you – when I carry it. Even the street-walkers have their masks slung over their shoulders. I walked yesterday up to Montmartre to see Aunt Yvonne and Uncle Giles. Soldiers were putting sandbags in front of churches. Can you imagine if they were to bomb Notre-Dame or Sacré-Coeur? Some of the Métro stations had been roped off. Uncle Giles told me that they were packing up the Louvre. I passed a sign on a shop which said, "One son killed in 1914, one son wounded, third liable for call-up on Day Ten." The Monoprix stores have signs up: "French management – French staff – French capital." Let us pray that it will remain so . . .'

We were issued with gas masks, too, and barrage balloons flew like elephants above the city. Children tagged with luggage labels were herded out into the countryside, but I was not among them. I spent the war in St Stephen Street, with the rest of the family. Amy sat with her ear pressed up against the wireless. In the early days the French appeared to be advancing into Germany; there was a big push towards Saarbrücken. 'You see,' said Amy, 'We're going to win!' A headline in the *Edinburgh Evening News* asked: WILL IT LAST THREE YEARS? 'Three years!' she scoffed. 'Do they never listen to the wireless?' The French were tightening their grip on Saarbrücken, the RAF was blasting the Kiel canal. The Luftwaffe came over to have a go at Rosyth Dockyard and the Forth Bridge but didn't get the chance to do much damage. They came in daylight, over the North Sea, just like that, flaunting their Nazi signs. 'Cheeky buggers!' said Granny Balfour. 'At least our boys sent them awa' wi' a flea in their lugs!' I picked up a piece of shell and was told never, ever, to pick up anything in the street again, not while there was a war on. Granny smacked my hand and made me cry. 'That way, she'll mind!' A picture appeared in the paper of a German bomber spread-eagled in the Lammermuir Hills. Dead Germans lay in coffins in a church in Portobello.

'Paris, 20 October.

'Ma chère Aimée,

   'After the first few weeks, people have started to come out
again – it takes a lot to confine Parisians to their houses for
long! The women still look quite smart. Some of the restaurants which closed are opening up again, though menus
are limited of course and there are few waiters, only the
elderly. The young men have gone. So there are waitresses
now at the boulevard cafés. Yvonne and Odile and I had an
evening out. We went to the cinema. The queues were
enormous but everyone was in good humour about having to
wait. We saw James Cagney in *Angels With Dirty Faces*. While I
was watching the film I couldn't help wondering if you might
not be in the Grand watching it too.'

'Isn't it amazing?' Amy said to my mother. 'Aunt Nan and I
did see that picture, not at the Grand, but at the King's
Cinema! Just think, we might have been sitting watching it at
the very same time! It's quite possible. It's like telepathy, isn't
it?'

   My mother did not think it so surprising (though she did
not say so), since Amy, like most other girls of her age during
the war, went frequently to the pictures. When I was a little
older I was allowed to go on Saturday afternoons, or sometimes Friday nights. It was handy having our own picture
house right in the middle of the street. One of us would run
along and keep a place in the queue. Huge queues snaked
along the street, giving Granny Balfour cause to complain.
They stood on folks' doorsteps and dropped their fag-ends and
sweet- and cigarette-wrappings where they stood, even outside her stair door. She'd take her stiff broom and sweep the
litter up the pavement, through the waiting legs, without as
much as an 'Excuse me!' and deposit it on the steps of the
Grand. 'Tak' yer muck!' she'd say to the uniformed commis-
sionaire, who knew better than to argue. At sixty she was still

a well-built woman with powerful shoulders and hefty forearms.

Amy and I would look the other way while she was on the warpath and pretend she had nothing to do with us. We waited uncomplainingly for the queue to shuffle up, even Amy, who normally couldn't bear to wait for anything. We were prepared to stamp our feet on the cold pavement for hours if necessary. Then there'd be a little rush of excitement when we actually got inside and pushed our money under the glass grill and asked for two back-stalls. The organ would be playing and the people coming out would have faces flushed from the heat. We'd settle into the plush seats, Amy would say, 'Here goes nothing, kiddo!' and we'd let the American dream wash over us, giving us nights to remember and romance on the range; we were happily sucked into its world of turquoise swimming pools, sumptuous food (off the ration), beautiful women in slinky satin gowns and handsome, Bryl-creemed men.

Amy came out humming, walking in a slightly different way, swinging her hips a little. She asked whom she reminded me of. I tried Deanna Durbin. 'Rita Hayworth, you tumshie!'

My mother liked to go to the pictures, too, and so, of course, did Aunt Nan. Granny Balfour was scornful of picture-house pleasures. She thought they put foolish notions into folks' heads.

In November, Eugénie wrote to say that Claude had been taken prisoner at Saarbrücken. He'd been tending men right up in the front line. She was distraught. Amy's face was impassive while she read. She made no comment.

Shortly afterwards came another letter: Uncle Giles had died and Eugénie was going to stay with Aunt Yvonne. She would be glad to leave the gloomy emptiness of the apartment on the boulevard de Magenta.

Then, in June, came the fall of Paris. We felt the dull thud of it in the kitchen of our house. Amy white-faced, trembling.

127

My mother trying to comfort her. Holding her in her arms, smoothing her hair, which had grown long again, down to her shoulders. Telling her the Allies would soon push the Germans out. Telling her that her mother would be all right, that the Germans wouldn't be interested in her. Telling her that she would have to be brave.

Amy was sixteen when she went out on her first date. Danny McGrath took her to the pictures – not the Grand, that would have been too close to home. It would have laid them open to ribald remarks, whistles from Danny's friends and the penetrating scrutiny of Granny Balfour's open stare. He took her to the Gaiety at Leith. They came along the street together when I was out on the pavement playing hopscotch with a friend. They had to wait until I'd finished my turn before they could pass by. Danny had done his best to flatten his hair. It shone like a butter-ball; you could see the grease standing out on the strands. (I knew that Amy didn't like greasy heads, in spite of Cary Grant and co. She had very definite likes and dislikes where boys were concerned. They had to have clean fingernails as well. I sneaked a quick look at Danny's and thought they'd pass muster.) He had on his best grey flannels and a checked sports jacket that I remembered seeing his older brother wearing before he went off to the war.

The next day, I heard Amy discussing the evening with her friend Louise. The three of us were sitting on a bench in Inverleith Park. They were huddled together at one end, I was at the other.

'Did he try anything?'

'I didn't give him the chance! He held my hand.'

'You let him?'

'Better that than letting it you know what!' Amy eyed me. 'But after a while it got sort of sticky and clammy.'

'Yuck!'

That was what I was thinking.

In the next couple of years Amy went out with a succession of boys. Usually twice. Once to the pictures and once for a walk. They bored her, apart from the fact that she couldn't stand them pawing her; she'd rather stay at home and read a good book or go for a walk on the Pentland Hills, so she told Louise, who had started to go steady with a boy who attended her church, a nice lad whom she was subsequently to marry.

Amy had given up coming to St Stephen's Church of Scotland with the rest of us. She went sporadically with Liane's family to the Catholic church, where she lit candles for her mother. Amy reckoned that if any God would watch over her mother it would be the Catholic God. But since the fall of Paris to the brutal, jack-booted German armies, she had come to doubt if any god existed at all. The worst part for her was the lack of information, the absence of letters, being out of touch. It was as if a steel door had come down between her and her mother. She would alternate between spells of despair and rage, which would end in torrents of tears. And then she would pick herself up, for she was not one to lie down under adversity.

Her father and grandmother were much put out by her going openly to an RC church – she made no effort to conceal it now – but there wasn't much they could do about it, apart from a bit of ranting and raving. Granny Balfour had enough wit in her to know that a slap on the wrist was not going to deter her elder granddaughter from doing anything she wanted to do.

The only boy Amy went out with more than twice was Danny McGrath. He kept coming back. And she'd relent. As long as he promised not to Brylcreem his head! He laughed at that and looked sheepish. Afterwards, he always went about with his unruly curls standing out round his head like a halo. His hair made him look almost two inches taller, which brought him up level with Amy. Everyone said he was a nice lad. It was well known in the street that he carried a candle for Amy. And she was fond of him, though that was not exactly what he wanted. He took her dancing at the Silver Slipper Ballroom on the other side of town the night before his call-up and they had a good time. A happy time, said Amy. She was glad of that.

The day we heard he'd been killed in the desert I found her sitting slumped on the bank down by the Water of Leith, firing stones at an old tin can.

In 1943, when Amy and Louise were eighteen, they joined the Land Army – rather than the ordinary one – and were sent to work on a farm in East Lothian. Howking tatties would do them no harm, said Granny Balfour; might put a bit brawn into them. By this time she knew all about Liane's family, and, surprisingly, liked and approved of Louise. She thought she was a nice steady girl with her head screwed on, unlike some she could mention! The girls stayed on the farm during the week and came home at weekends.

One Saturday afternoon, Amy and I had to take a message along to our grandmother. Jessie, in the days of her widowhood and before marrying my father, lived in the flat below Granny Balfour's. As we were coming back down the stairs, Jessie's door opened, and she beckoned us in. It was Amy she wanted but I went as well.

Jessie was keeping up her reputation as a merry widow. She'd failed the medical to get into the WAAF, much to her disgust, owing to a heart murmur, which does not appear to have hampered her progress through life. Jessie had fancied the idea of being in the Forces, giving support to the boys in blue. She'd have liked even more to join the US Air Force. She was daft about everything American: the pictures, chewing gum, silk stockings, GIs. When the soldiers hit town in their pork-pie hats, Jessie was to be seen setting forth in her 'war paint'. 'You could scrape the stuff aff her face wi' a knife,' said Granny Balfour. 'Nan says they cry it "pancake" make-up. Mair the thickness o' a drop scone, if ye ask me!' Jessie went dancing at the Palais Ballroom in Lothian Road and the Palace at the foot of Leith Walk, in her ankle-strapped, white high heels. She demonstrated the jitterbug to Aunt Nan in her back kitchen. When she birled, you could see her knickers –

black lacy knickers, Aunt Nan reported – and the tops of her suspenders.

Jessie took Amy and me into the kitchen and shut the door. She seemed excited about something. She leant her back against the door, as if to stop it from being opened, and she spoke in a whisper after she'd shifted the wad of grey gum to the side of her mouth. I thought her lipstick looked like raspberry jam. Would any man want to kiss that? My friend Morag had seen her kissing a sailor under the arches in St Stephen Place. The kiss had lasted ten minutes, Morag said. We wondered how they'd managed to breathe. And how boring it must have been, going on all that time!

'I've a couple of fellas in,' said Jessie. 'Yanks. Airmen. I met them at the Palais last night. Asked them up for their tea. Nice guys they are, real nice. I think I've clicked with the older one. The other's about your age, Amy. Why don't you c'mon in and meet him? He's called Paul. Nice name, Paul, huh? Classy name.'

'Oh, no, Jessie, I don't think – '

'Ah, c'mon! You don't have enough fun in your life. A lassie like you should be goin' out more, havin' a good time while the goin's good. You only get one crack at life, you ken – this isne a rehearsal.' Jessie gave me a sideways glance. I knew what she was thinking: what do you want to spend all your time with a kid like *her* for?

I saw the resolve in Amy's face waver. It was true that she didn't go out much, not in the way that Jessie meant. Painting the town red. Tripping the light fantastic. Amy's idea of a night out was to go to the theatre and see plays like *Blithe Spirit* and *How Green was my Valley*, or even Shakespeare. Sometimes, for a special treat, she'd take me with her to the King's Theatre to see the Sadler's Wells Ballet and the D'Oyly Carte company playing Gilbert and Sullivan. We'd float down the hill afterwards, singing the music. Amy still talked of becoming an actress. Once the war was over. A lot of things would happen when the war was over, the main one being of course that she would go to Paris and join her mother and Claude Laroche. My mother said she couldn't see that happening.

'C'mon, Amy!' said Jessie again.

'Well, okay then, but just for half an hour. We want to go to the library before it shuts.'

'You and the library! You've aye got your head stuck in a book!' Jessie surveyed me. 'Maybe *you* could go to the library.'

'Ne va pas!' said Amy to me. 'Reste avec moi!'

'What are you saying to her? I wish the two of you wouldn't keep talking Frog to one another.' Jessie gave me another of her looks. 'Have you not got a wee friend you could be playing with? Where's your pal Morag?'

'I'm looking after her this afternoon,' said Amy.

'If that one needs looking after, my name's Rita Hayworth. I wish to God it was! *I hate men*,' sang Jessie, and shimmied her hips, and then Amy joined in, only she was better at it, and finally the two of them folded up in laughter. 'I dinne really hate men,' said Jessie, dabbing her eyes between the spikes of mascara. 'What about you, Amy? It might be better for us if we did! C'mon through, anyway, and meet the guys. Aye, you too, Little Miss Big Eyes. No show without Punch!'

She opened the door. We ducked our heads to avoid a flypaper barnacled with flies that was twirling merrily in the draught. Jessie never did take her flypapers down when she should. Housekeeping wasn't much in her line. She took us into the front room, where the two Yanks were sitting on the hard horsehair settee holding their squashed hats in their hands. They looked at if they couldn't make up their minds whether to go or stay. I thought they'd been about to go. If Jessie and Amy had spent another five minutes singing *I hate men* in the kitchen they might have skedaddled. And Amy's fate might have been different.

One of the airmen looked about twenty-one or -two, the other perhaps twenty-five. Jessie herself was thirty-five at the time, though I'm sure she hadn't thought twice about knocking off the extra ten years.

The men leapt to their feet as we came in.

'Awfy nice manners, haven't they?' said Jessie, sliding her hand through the arm of the older one, giving him a wink and a Deanna Durbin smile. He was on the short side with a craggy face (that's how *Woman's Own* would have described it at the time), and he looked a bit like Humphrey Bogart. Well, a bit, if you half closed your eyes. We were forced to say we thought so when Jessie quizzed us later. The other one was taller and more handsome and looked a bit like a young Robert Donat. Definitely quite a bit. He looked a real smoothie, too. I didn't like him from the start.

'Girls, I want you to meet Vance and Paul!' (Jessie was now trying to act like Veronica Lake – she had let her hair fall over one eye.)

The men shook hands with us.

'Pleased to meet you, mam,' they said to Amy.

To me they said, 'Hi, kid!' and Paul produced a stick of chewing gum from his pocket, reflex action from an American serviceman to a foreign child. He was to think that he could bribe me with a steady flow of the stuff during our association. 'Here you are, kid,' he'd say. 'Here's something for you.' To keep my mouth shut, was what he meant. I hated chewing gum, always had, always would. I put it in my pocket to give to Morag later.

'Let's sit down!' cried Jessie gaily. 'What about a wee drop port?'

She produced a half-full bottle and four of the six cut-glass sherry glasses my mother had given her for her wedding to Murdo Ward, the Newhaven fisherman. Usually their wedding photograph sat on the mantelpiece; today, it was not there. Jessie handed the glasses round and when she went by me she said, 'You're too young, kiddo!' and rewarded me with another of her 'Away home!' looks.

'Here's looking at you, buddy!' Jessie raised her glass to Vance. I noticed that she half-closed her eyes.

They drank. Vance produced a packet of Chesterfields and they all lit cigarettes except for Paul, who said he didn't smoke. I hadn't known that Amy smoked, apart from the odd Gauloise when she was younger, sitting beside me on a windy bench in Inverleith Park, her eyes skinned for approaching Balfours. I looked at her in surprise, realizing for the first time that there might be a number of things I didn't know about Amy.

'A clean-living guy, eh?' Jessie patted Paul on the knee.

'Do you have a shower every day?' I asked. We'd heard that Americans did.

'Of course he does,' said Jessie and flicked ash towards the McEwan's ashtray which she must have nicked from the pub. She was wearing false red nails about an inch long. When she'd plucked a cigarette from the soft packet the tip of one nail had bent back and I'd watched with interest to see if it would come off. But it had bounced back into shape again.

'I have a bath on a Saturday night,' I said. Most people in the street did.

'Speak for yourself!' I knew full well that Jessie didn't want me to speak at all. Before I had the chance to say anything else she started to tell us about Vance, how he worked as a garage mechanic in his father's business in peacetime, and hailed from Texas. She then gave us a chorus of *Deep in the Heart of Texas*, parking the cigarette in her mouth while she did the clapping bit, and swung her shoulders in time. She'd often burst into snatches of song; it just seemed to come over her. 'I'll get by as long as I have you'. Things like that. It wasn't unusual to hear Jessie singing when you passed her in the street. 'Paul's from Massachusetts', she said, when she'd removed the cigarette from her mouth and stopped choking on the smoke. She couldn't think of a suitable song for Paul's home state; she had enough trouble saying it. 'Quite a tongue-twister, isn't it?'

'Like the Leith polithe dithmitheth uth,' I said.

She ignored me. 'Where the hell is it anyway, Paul?'

'Kind of next to the ocean. The Atlantic ocean.'

'Do you live by the sea?' asked Amy.

'Not exactly. Sort of inland.'

'Near Boston?'

'See, she's a smart cookie, this one,' said Jessie. 'She's got brains coming out her ears!'

Amy was waiting for an answer.

'Yeah, kind of near Boston.'

'The Christian Science Mother Church is in Boston,' I said, trying to get back into the conversation. We had a neighbour, Mrs Craddock, who was a Christian Scientist, and it was her dream to go and see the Mother Church.

'Little Miss Know-all!' said Jessie with a laugh that was meant to tinkle but clanked.

'Y'all Christian Scientists?' asked Vance.

'*Course* we're not,' cried Jessie, who didn't even know what it meant. 'We go to St Stephen's Church of Scotland along on the corner.' And she gave Amy a look defying her to mention the Church of Rome.

'I haven't seen you at church for ages, Jessie,' I said.

'I've been busy.'

'Sometimes my mother goes to the Christian Science Church down Inverleith with Mrs Craddock. [It was something Granny Balfour was not aware of.] She wasn't feeling well, she gets this pain sometimes, so Mrs Craddock was helping her to know the truth.'

'What kind of truth?' asked Vance.

'That there is no sin, disease or death,' I rattled off. I was enjoying this more than I'd thought I would. 'That man is made in God's likeness. So if God can't be sick then man can't be sick. But God must look like an awful lot of people, mustn't he? I mean billions and trillions, if all the people in the world are made like him.'

'Who's for a bit more hooch?' Jessie got up and waved the bottle about and this time managed to give me a sharp kick on the ankle as she tottered past on her spiky heels. 'Ouch!' I went and glowered at her, but I didn't budge. Hadn't Amy asked me to stick with her?

Jessie gave up on me eventually and changed tactics. She started to tell Paul about the wonders of the Botanic Garden. Under cross-examination, he expressed an interest in plants.

135

'The flowers in the garden are awfy bonny. They've got everything under the sun there, from all over the place.'

'If they've got everything under the sun, they're bound to be from all over the place,' I said.

Again, Jessie ignored me. 'You should see them, Paul, seeing you're so fond of flowers.'

I could see that Paul was eyeing Amy, and he seemed to like what he saw. She was wearing a velour jacket in a soft pretty shade of green with a matching Alice band holding back her hair. And she was strangely quiet.

'I never knew you'd been to the Botanics, Jessie.' I assumed what I considered to be an air of innocence. It was well known that Jessie wouldn't walk two steps if she could hirple on to a tram. How could she, anyway, with heels the size she wore? Most of them were four-inchers. And as for knowing anything about flowers, she wouldn't have been able to tell a crocus from a cactus.

'Is it not time you were going home for your tea?'

'I'm going to Amy's for my tea tonight.'

Jessie, exasperated, came straight out then with her suggestion. Why didn't Amy – and *I* – take Paul for a walk in the Botanic Garden?

Thus began a number of expeditions in which I participated as the third wheel. I might not have liked Paul, but I wasn't going to abandon Amy. She came in now from the farm in the evenings whenever Paul was off duty. It seemed that no moment should be wasted. The boys were waiting to go to France. We climbed Arthur's Seat, strolled along the foreshore at Cramond, frequented the Fun Fair at Portobello and picture houses in different parts of town. I became acquainted with the Haymarket in Dalry Road, the Alhambra in Leith Walk, the Blue Halls at Lauriston. It was I who sought out fresh picture houses to go to, gleaning the information from the front page of the *Edinburgh Evening News*. 'Tonight it's to be the Dominion,' I'd announce. (They didn't care what it was.) My ambition was to visit every single picture house in Edinburgh; I liked collecting things. I kept a list, ticked each one off as we 'did' it. Sometimes Amy and Paul would go dancing with Jessie and Vance and then I was not invited, even when they were going to an afternoon tea dance at the Princes Ballroom. 'I'll just sit and watch,' I pleaded. 'No kids allowed,' said Jessie, glaring at me between those blackened eyelashes of hers that always reminded me of the bristles of a witch's broom. (I restrained myself from telling her, knowing there was a limit to how far I could go.) I'd chum the dancers as far as Princes Street, and there reluctantly leave them to their pleasures. Jessie wore silver shoes and carried a little silver filigree purse dangling from her wrist. She still has the purse, smelling faintly of face powder and stale Midnight in Paris, but not much else from those frolics. Except Vance's signet ring in a drawer somewhere. But she hasn't seen that in years. She was going to marry him – he asked her before he went to France – but she changed her mind after he'd gone.

On fine weekend afternoons my services would be required again and we'd be off, the three of us – Amy and Paul and I – down the coast on the bus. I was there not so much as a chaperone, more as an alibi and look-out. While they huddled together behind the whins and coils of barbed wire at Gullane, designed to keep invaders at bay, I sat up on a bank in the full force of the wind and scanned the skyline, like a scout, half-expecting to see Granny Balfour come rolling over the tops of the sand dunes in her wrap-around floral pinny. It might have livened things up a bit for me if she had; I got bored sitting there, with the grit blowing into my eyes and goose-pimples starting up on my arms. I'd go and walk along the beach for a change, keeping as close as I could to the sea's edge without getting my feet wet, and then I'd move a bit closer without bothering to take my shoes off. It was too cold for bare feet, anyway. When I came home my mother would say, 'How did you get your shoes so wet? Surely you and Amy weren't walking *in* the waves?'

'More like *on* them!' said my father, who was home on leave looking bronzed and fit. He laughed. 'Couple of drea-

137

mers, those two. The tide could be coming in and they wouldn't know it until it was up to their ankles.'

I was aware that a sea was washing round Amy's ankles and that she was getting in deeper and deeper. It would soon be up to her middle. I had a dream in which she stumbled and lost her footing in the cruel grey-green water and screamed for me and I went running down an endless, white, sunless beach, to arrive too late.

On the sands at Gullane Amy smiled dimpled, Shirley Temple smiles such as I'd never expected to see on Amy's face. She'd always hated Shirley Temple. That simpering marshmallow! Amy laughed and shrieked when Paul chased her, her feet floundering in the sand, her arms upraised to the sky as if appealing for help, the way she had in my dream. He always caught her – Amy who at school, in the playground, or in the street, could outrun any girl and almost any boy. And then Paul would tickle her and she'd collapse into soft giggles against him and he'd hold her and they'd forget all about me. The sun would be going down like a great big ball of orange-red fire over the land and the beach would be darkening to a deep gold and everyone but us would have gone home – the dogs with the sticks in their mouths and the children with their coloured balls and the elderly women in tweeds and brogues – and then Amy would look round and see me and say, 'Aw, honey, you look frozen!' Who could have blamed me for hating him?

'I guess I do kind of like him,' Amy told Louise as we walked along the path by the Water of Leith through to the Dean Village. They were walking close together; I was behind them. The sun was slanting down through the trees, lighting up their hair: Amy's red, Louise's black. 'He's – well, he's different. He's got a lot more go in him than most other boys I've been out with. And he doesn't talk about football! We have fun together.'

'Don't tell me you've fallen for him!'

'Well, what would be wrong with that? He's good-looking

and he kisses nicely . . .' Amy, with a quick look back at me, dropped her voice and switched to French, and from then on I caught only isolated, tantalizing words.

It was a warm afternoon, without wind. I sat on my dune feeling the heat of the sun on my face. The sea was calm, too. The waves came purling in and were sucked quietly back, and came rolling gently in again, and I could have almost fallen asleep. They were down in a dune a few yards away, hidden by whins. They were murmuring to each other, softly, softly, and the sound was like the rippling of the waves.

And then Amy screamed. It was the scream from my dream. Calling for me. A piercing scream, ending on a dying fall. I leapt to my feet and, slipping and sliding in the soft sand, lumbered across to their hollow. I looked down, and saw a tangle of white legs. He was on top of her. A fine spray of sand rose around them.

'What are you doing to her?' I yelled, and flung myself down the sandy slope. I caught hold of his hair and pulled. With a swift turn of his shoulder he repulsed me. I went flying backwards into the sand.

'I'm not doing anything to her, you silly little fool! She wanted it!'

I struggled up. I backed away from him. Then I fled through the sharp whins, skirting the barbed wire, grazing my knee, not noticing the jagged gash until later, when it began to turn septic and had to be bread-poulticed. I went down on to the beach, to the firmer, darker sand close to the water where my feet would find a surer touch and my legs could move faster. Amy caught me up at the far end by the rocks. Her hair was dishevelled, her clothes in disarray. She pinioned my arms, forced me to stand still, to look at her. My teeth were rattling in my head. I could feel grit in my mouth.

'Now, listen!'

'I don't want to listen.'

'You're too young to understand – '

'People always say that.'

'Maybe I shouldn't have done it, but he's going away.' She sounded feverish. 'It's wartime, you see. It's different. He's going to France, he might get killed.'

'I hope he does!'

'Don't say that!' I thought she was going to slap me. 'I love him.'

I said nothing then.

'And he loves me.'

'But he hurt you.'

She released me and turned to gaze out over the expanse of sea to the horizon. The wind had risen a little. White frothy waves were running over her bare feet; the tide was coming in. There was sand on the back of her hair. It clung to the strands, dulling the colour. I rubbed the red marks on my wrists. 'Maybe it wasn't exactly what I expected,' she said. She seemed to have forgotten me; she was speaking so quietly that I could scarcely make out what she said above the sighing of the sea. What had she expected? What had they been *doing*? 'He loves me. He says he's never met a girl like me before.' She looked back at me. 'Don't you believe him?'

I shrugged.

'We might get married.'

'*Married?*'

'People do when they . . . when they love one another.'

Was she really serious? Would she marry this man whom she hardly knew and go away and live in that place whose name I couldn't remember? I could only think of the Leith police.

'You can't go away! Not to *America*!'

'It wouldn't be yet. It wouldn't be until the war was over. You could come and visit us.'

'But your mother, what about her?'

'She didn't let me stop her when she went away with the man she loved, did she?'

I could think of no answer to that.

'I want you to promise not to tell anyone about this. Promise me!' She took hold of my arms again. 'Cross your heart!'

*

The row in George Balfour's kitchen was unlike the noisy stramashes that used to take place between him and his wife Eugénie. He was quiet and subdued, kept his voice down and made no attempt to strike his daughter.

Present were Amy and her father, Granny Balfour and my mother. Amy had asked my mother to come and stand beside her. I was banished to the stair, where I idled about watching the motes of dust dancing in the grey light, listening for sounds coming from the other side of the heavy brown door. The smell of damp stone tinged with ammonia filled my nostrils. The stair woman was washing the stairs. She'd already done the Balfours' landing and was working on the stair below. Hanging over the banister rail, I watched as the grey rag she clutched in her red hand made wide swirls over each step in turn. Slap, slap, went the cloth. She knelt on a mat of fawn sacking. Another piece was tied around her waist. She was a small woman with wispy fawn hair and thin shoulders.

Gradually she worked her way down to the bottom lobby, getting smaller and smaller the lower she went. I leant right over the banister until I was in danger of falling. I wondered what it would be like to fall. Blood was rushing into my head. I imagined my skull striking the concrete, the brains spilling out, spattering the newly washed floor. It was *I* who was there hanging over the banister rail, feet dangling, toes barely scraping the landing, inhaling the sour stench of ammonia and damp stone; and, at the same time, I seemed to be hovering above myself watching this young girl as she cantilevered further and further out into the abyss. Tempting fate, perhaps? Or merely toying with a notion of disaster? The bottom door banged, and I jerked upright, gasping for breath. The stair woman had finished and gone to tip her dirty water into the gutter. For a moment, on lifting my head, feeling the blood pound against my temples, I was not sure who or where I was. I leant against the clammy wall to let my heart subside.

They were taking a long time behind the closed door. They couldn't kill Amy, could they? At least my mother was there. She might not be all that strong physically, but they wouldn't dare harm Amy in front of her. The inside of my mouth was hot and dry. I sucked my lower lip into my mouth and bit down hard on the flesh until it hurt.

Amy brought Paul to visit us. He presented my mother with a pair of silk stockings that looked orange on her legs and me with the usual six-pack of Spearmint. My mother had used two weeks' meat ration to buy stewing steak for a pie and the butcher had thrown in a couple of kidneys. She'd spent most of the day making the pie and an apple charlotte to follow. I'd sat by the range and tried to concentrate on *Jo of the Chalet School*. I longed to go to the Chalet School in the Austrian Tyrol and share a dormitory with Jo. It would be a long way from St Stephen Street, Stockbridge, Edinburgh, Scotland.

Amy did most of the talking during the meal. She told us how Paul had been to New York and sailed round the Statue of Liberty, that he had three sisters and a dog that could do tricks, and he liked to go camping in the state of Maine. She spoke of Boston, Maine and New York as if she were personally familiar with them, or expected to be. She avoided my eye, even though I tried hard to make her catch it. He didn't have a lot to say for himself; he sat there smiling, looking dead chuffed with himself, the centre of attention. He reminded me of my friend Morag's cat when it sneaked the butter ration off the shelf and had a good tuck-in. It had cleaned its whiskers for hours afterwards.

I asked him if he had a swimming pool.

"Fraid not.'

'I thought *everybody* had swimming pools in America.'

My mother told me to pass the neaps. I avoided *her* eye.

He ate his steak-and-kidney pie and pronounced it swell. Amy beamed at him as if he had said something profound.

I asked him when he thought he'd be going to France.

'It could be real soon.'

I brightened at that. There was always the chance that a Gerry gun would get his plane.

They left soon after the meal was over. They had no need of

142

me to accompany them, now that the cat was out of the bag and leaping about washing its whiskers. They walked openly up the street arm in arm. I watched them from the window. He was kissing the side of her neck and making her giggle. It was the last time I saw him.

Amy came up to see what my mother had thought of him. She was full of fizz, like sherbet that's been shaken up with water in a bottle. She couldn't sit still; she got up and down off her chair, left her cup of tea half drunk, the scone on her plate untouched. She pulled back the curtain to peer down into the back green, asked if she could smoke, lit a cigarette, stubbed it out half-way down.

'He's nice, isn't he, Aunt Janet? You did like him, didn't you?'

'He seemed all right, Amy,' said my mother awkwardly. I knew she didn't like to hurt anyone's feelings. 'But to be honest – '

'Yes?' Amy looked at her sharply.

'I can't really see him as your husband.'

'Why not?'

'For a start, you're too young – '

'I'll soon be nineteen.'

'I don't think you're ready to settle down yet. I get the feeling that you don't really know what you want.'

'Oh, you do, do you? Well, *I* think I do know!'

My mother sighed. I am sure she had never anticipated being on the brink of a row with Amy.

'So that was for a start. Why else do you think I shouldn't marry him?' Amy's voice had a chink of ice in it; the fizz had fizzled out. I stayed in my corner, kept my head down.

'I don't think he'd be anywhere near good enough for you. Well, I mean you seem to have an awful lot more going on in your head than he does.' My mother was doing her best to be tactful but there was not a great deal more she could say, that Amy would listen to.

143

'I thought I could rely on you to stand up for me, Aunt Janet. I thought *you* would understand!'

After Amy had swept out, my mother said, 'He's good-looking, right enough, you can't deny that. But that's not enough to hold a marriage together.' I had the feeling that it was not looks she was talking about.

And Granny Balfour and Uncle George? What were they doing all this time? He was brooding in his kitchen, she was ranting in the steamie. No Yank was safe from her wrath. They earned three or four times what our lads did and came over here and snaffled the lasses from under their noses. And not even from under their noses! Behind their backs. For our lads were out there getting killed on the battlefields of France and North Africa. What was America doing that it took them so long to get into the war? Feart, the lot of them. The mangle rollers spun madly. And her George had had enough trouble in his life without having this to thole as well.

George, when he had finished brooding, went out to the US Air Force camp, where he had a few words in the ear of Amy's airman and his commanding officer. George warned the airman off. It hadn't taken much, he told my mother; he'd got the feeling that the lad had never had any intention of marrying Amy anyway.

Paul wrote Amy a brief note on a flimsy sheet of lined paper. I saw the sheet with its few scrawled, careless lines, saw her crumple it between her fingers and fling it against the wall, where it made no impact. He was too young, he wrote, he was going to war. He thought she might have got the wrong idea . . .

She didn't leave it there. She, too, went out to the camp, and hung about the gate for hours (along with a gaggle of other girls) until he came off duty. He came strolling out through the gates in the middle of a group of other airmen, talking and laughing. The laugh froze on his face like a mask when she saw Amy, then it dropped off. He took her arm, steered her aside. He didn't want a scene, you're darned right he didn't, not there right outside the camp with all his buddies looking on and listening in. He told Amy that her father had come out to see him and had told him to lay off. He didn't have to listen to *him*, she said, for she wouldn't. She could do as she pleased, and intended to; she was over sixteen, the age of consent in Scotland.

'Gee, Amy,' he said, 'I'm real sorry. We've had a swell time together, but – '

She blamed the Balfours. All of us. She said she didn't want to see any of us ever again.

'She's half Balfour herself,' commented my father, after she'd gone whirling out of our kitchen. 'She seems to forget that.'

'But she's not herself, James,' said my mother.

Who was she then? I wondered. I realized when I was a little older that it was one of the many facets of Amy: one that was capable of rounding on my mother, who was her best ally, and turning her back on those of us who loved her.

'She'll get over the Yank,' said my father. 'She'll simmer down and be back, before long, you'll see.'

But in that he was wrong. My mother was to be long dead before Amy returned to Edinburgh, and by then my father would be married to Jessie MacFarlane.

Seven

I ride at anchor under the blue lantern.

Le Fanal bleu

Amy, on her little dais, has brought us to the end of the war, in Paris. Colette is still in her apartment in the Palais-Royal, struggling to cope with her progressively incapacitating arthritis. The city is struggling, too, trying to put itself together again. Food remains rationed, queues are long, wine is often sold watered – 'baptized', as it is called – people are hard up and poorly dressed. But the city is free! Amy reminds us gaily, holding out her arms. And that is important. The American in the row in front of me is nodding vigorously. After the show he tells us he was in Paris as part of the liberating army that went in after de Gaulle had made his triumphant entry into the city; in a way, that's why he's here, this afternoon, in a small hall in Edinburgh. Since that time he's always had an interest in France. He remembers the smiling faces along the route, the cheering. He warmed to the city then.

'The lights are on again!' cries Amy gaily.

She was there herself, in those post-war years; and so was I, for a brief ten days, but that she does not yet know.

My mother, Jessie and I went to Paris in the summer of 1947. At that time we hadn't seen Amy for more than three years. After the dissolution of her relationship with the American airman she had asked to be transferred to the south of

146

England. She didn't tell even Louise she was going, she broke off with her and Liane also; she seemed to want to put the city of Edinburgh and all its occupants behind her. But she did send a postcard to Aunt Nan from somewhere in Kent. The postmark was smudged and we couldn't make it out properly.

'Working on a farm here now, still in the Land Army. Hope you are well. Love, Amy.'

'Doesn't give much away, does she?' said Jessie, turning the card over in case there should be a coded message on the other side. The picture gave nothing away either: poppies growing in a field. Amy must have forgotten that Aunt Nan didn't like fields. She felt nervous with too much open space around her, couldn't abide the windy exposure of the King's Park. The Botanic Garden was all right, she'd go for a walk there; it had trees and rhododendron bushes that were as high as she was. 'Don't know what Amy wanted to go away down there for,' said Jessie, passing the card back to Aunt Nan, who put it on her mantelpiece. Every time Granny Balfour saw it she trumpeted and said, 'Silly wee fool! We seem to mak' them by the mile in this family.'

We – my mother and I – knew of course why Amy had gone to Kent. She'd want to be positioned for take-off when the siren for the all-clear sounded and the war would be declared over. I pictured her standing poised on the white cliffs of Dover like a bluebird, ready to fly southward.

We thought of Amy when the Allies landed in Normandy on the sixth of June, 1944, and of Eugénie when they entered Paris on the twenty-fourth of August and the battle for the city was engaged. Two days later a victory parade went rolling through the boulevards; we saw it on the Pathé Pictorial News at the Grand.

'Amy'll be able to go to Paris now,' I said, but my mother thought not. 'She'll have to wait until the war is finally over. They won't be letting civilians travel to the continent.'

In the middle of October my mother received a letter from Eugénie, the first in four years.

'I wanted to let you know that I have come through the

147

German occupation. Claude remains a prisoner. But I have news of him from time to time. The last few years have been hard. We have had terrible shortages of food and fuel, at times went to bed starving. Sometimes my old aunt did not get up. If it was too cold inside, I would go out and walk. You cannot imagine how pleased we were to see the Allied armies!

'Many people stayed in the city throughout the war. Colette did. At the beginning she went to stay with her daughter in the Corrèze, but she said it was like a "green tomb"! There was no telephone, no mail. She hated being cut off, so they returned to Paris, she and her husband Maurice Goudeket. He was arrested by the Germans at the end of 1941, because of his Jewish blood. Colette was frantic. They released him after eight weeks. Odile says she heard a story that Colette had a link through to German High Command. The wife of someone important, who was a friend of an old friend. Who knows? There are many stories going around in Paris. They say there will be many scores settled.

'I visit Colette when I can. She has been good to me. She has happy memories of her days with my mother. Her arthritis is bad. She's having X-ray treatments, and sulphur and iodine injections. But nothing seems to make much difference. She is still writing in spite of the pain. She wrote several books during the war. Two I like very much, *Julie de Carneilhan* and *Gigi*. *Gigi* is amusing, not too serious. Good for dark days. And we've had plenty of those!'

It was Eugénie who let us know that Amy had arrived in Paris, in the late summer of 1945. A card came. 'Aimée is here,' it said, 'staying at present with Aunt Yvonne. Claude also is home, thank God.'

A letter followed two months later. 'Aimée is still in Montmartre with my aunt. She has taken a part-time job in a boulangerie to earn some money. She and Claude don't get on very well, I am sorry to say. Both are jealous! Understandably, I suppose. And I am caught in the middle. This seems to be something that often happens to mothers!

'It is taking time for Claude to readjust to normal life. After all, he was in prison camp for four years. He is terribly thin. I hardly recognized him when I met him at the station. But he is gaining strength little by little. I am trying to feed him up but it is not easy to get meat or eggs. Things are little better than they were during the Occupation . . .'

After that, letters arrived sporadically from Eugénie; none came from Amy. Then, in October 1946, we heard news that stunned us: Eugénie and Claude Laroche had been killed in a car crash on the road from Auxerre to Saint-Sauveur. He had been driving; they'd met a farm tractor head on, on a blind bend, and both had been dead when pulled from the wreckage. Eugénie was buried in the churchyard at Saint-Sauveur, in the Bussac family plot. The news was relayed first to George Balfour. He was still her legal husband; he had been notified as he was next-of-kin. Granny Balfour came along to break it to us.

'He looks like a man struck doon. When I think what yon Frechwoman did tae him!'

My mother left the room. I saw the tears spilling down her cheeks. The thought of Amy's pain stuck in my throat, and I could scarcely swallow.

We had fresh hopes then that Amy might contact us. She might need us again. We waited. Each morning I met the postman on the downstairs step.

'She's a stubborn bit lassie,' said Jessie.

'I wish I could write to her,' said my mother. But we had no address. How could we write c/o Madame Yvonne Lebrun, Montmartre?

The following year Jessie had a win on the football pools, a big one. She filled in the coupon every week, marking what took her fancy. The only football teams she knew anything at all about were Edinburgh's Hibs and Hearts and Glasgow's Rangers and Celtic. My father had a 'system' for doing the pools and on Thursday evenings no one dared speak in the kichen while he laboured at the papers in the hard-topped brown attaché case on his knee. He won smallish amounts, once even three hundred pounds (worth a fair bit then), but he never landed the moderately big money that Jessie did.

'A thousand quid,' he said gloomily, 'trust her!'

Jessie planned to have her flat redecorated from top to bottom, the kitchen modernized, the old black range removed, and a back boiler and fireplace with a tiled surround flecked in cream (spewed porridge, in my terminology) put in its place. She also bought a new gas cooker, a fur coat, five pairs of shoes, a lacy negligée that cost a bomb (her words) and a (real) ruby ring.

'The rest of the money we'll blow on a trip to Gay Paree! We'll go and look for Amy.'

She had another motive, too: a man, of course. What else? In the closing months of the war she'd met a Free French airman who was convalescing in Edinburgh from an appendicitis operation. Jessie used to go and visit the wounded in their convalescent home, take them tablet and shortbread which she said she'd made herself but had bought in Crawford's or McVittie's. I don't suppose they minded who had made it. Jessie said the way to a man's heart was through his stomach, but I could tell she didn't believe that.

The two women made an unlikely pair: my mother quiet, well-mannered; Jessie loud, brash. Jessie was good for a laugh, my mother would say. 'There's plenty life in her. It's good to have some life about the place.' The departure, first of Eugénie and then Amy, had left gaps in my mother's life.

Antoine had given Jessie his address and she'd written to him two or three times, or I had. She'd dictated to me a couple of matter-of-fact sentences (about the weather and her hairdressing business) which I'd translated into French and then I'd added one or two others for good measure. 'I have never known such ardour, Antoine, as I have known with you,' and 'I dream of your tender loving eyes nightly.' I thought I was being terribly smart and amusing. He had replied with a couple of postcards, one of Notre-Dame and the other of the Moulin

Rouge at night, but, as he himself said on the back of Notre-Dame, he wasn't much of a writer. 'Je n'écris bien.' At least he told the truth. When his missives arrived I was called upon to decipher them. My mother was not overly keen on me seeing them without prior censoring, but Antoine said little that could scandalize. He said little at all. 'Il fait chaud aujourd'hui.' I had thought that all Frenchmen were supposed to be good lovers.

Jessie stood in the middle of our kitchen floor holding her winnings in her hands and said, 'Let's go to Gay Paree! Let's go and find Amy and pay Antoine a visit!'

She hadn't had a card from him for some time but I didn't point that out; I didn't want to put her off the idea. I said quickly, 'Can I come too?'

'Sure thing, kiddo! As I always say, there's no show without our little Punch! Any road, you'll need to do the parlez-vousing.'

My mother stopped her scouring of the wood bunker. Water dripped from the scrubbing brush down her bare forearm into her rolled-up cuff. She was laughing and her cheeks were pink at the very idea of going to France. *Paris!* She'd heard so much about it from Eugènie and Amy but she'd never thought it was a possibility that she could go herself.

'Don't talk daft, Jessie! How could we come?'

'Easy enough. I'll pay the full shot for the both of you.'

'We couldn't let you.'

''Course you could. It's buckshee money!' Jessie threw it up in the air. The notes fluttered gently down to the floor, hovering for a moment in the draught before finally settling. I snatched one out of the air. I had never seen a ten-pound note before.

'I don't know what James would say.' My mother sobered and picked up a towel to dry her arm.

'I'll speak to him. You leave him to me!'

Jessie had a way of talking to men, telling them what was what and not taking no for an answer. You've got to stick up for yourself, she told me, nobody else is going to. Be bold, kid, be bold! I supposed it was because she was a widow that she was so much bolder than my mother. She had set up her own hairdressing business further down Stockbridge, on the main road. The salon was called 'Jessie Ann'; she'd had it done up in two tones of lilac paint and decorated the window with sprays of glassy artificial flowers and blown-up photographs of sleek-looking women who had just benefited from cold waves. My father admired her, thought she had a good business head. 'There are no fleas on Jessie MacFarlane! You could do worse than take up hairdressing,' he said to me. 'It's a handy thing for a woman. Maybe Jessie would take you on when you're fourteen.'

Jessie talked him into letting us go to Paris. (After my mother died, she became his lady friend; she strolled in Princes Street Gardens on his arm, had him up to her flat for his tea, gave him his favourite, tripe and onions, and he came home smelling of hair spray.) Our going to Paris would be no skin off his nose, he said, except that he would have to do for himself for ten days, though we knew full well that Granny Balfour would be in my mother's kitchen the minute she turned her back.

We seldom saw George now; he went to St Cuthbert's, did a day's work, stopped off at the pub on the way home for a carry-out of half a dozen bottles of McEwan's Export and shut himself up in his flat until the next morning. He'd even stopped going to the Lodge. The only person who crossed his threshold was his mother. She could be seen every evening at six o'clock, in fair weather or lashing wind and rain, bearing his dinner along the street on a tin tray. She continued to do so until the day she tripped on a cracked paving stone (obscured from her sight by the tray), tried to save George's mince-and-mashed-neap dinner and went sprawling sideways into the gutter, pulling a ligament in her right leg and breaking a hip. It was the beginning of the end for Granny Balfour. She was a heavy woman and never had full use of her legs again.

My father came to Waverley Station to see us off on the night train to London. He was wearing his best grey flannels and sports jacket and he whistled softly while he stood on the platform waiting to wave us goodbye. (Later, I wondered if it had suited him to get rid of us for ten days.) He put his hand into his trouser pocket, jingled the coins that lay there and brought up a half-crown piece.

'Hold out your hand.' He put the coin into my hot damp palm. I was sticky with excitement. 'Mind and sit with your back to the engine, now. You're not wanting any smuts in your eye.'

The guard blew his whistle, carriage doors banged, my father stepped back and raised his hand.

I couldn't believe it — I was actually going to set foot on French soil! And I was going to see Amy; I had already decided that. I had started to talk to her in my head, in French. My intensity nearly made me sick and I was quite unable to eat the sandwiches filled with pink spam and grey fish paste that the two women had made. They'd brought with them flasks of tea and milky Camp coffee, packets of oatcakes and digestive biscuits, tins of sardines and pilchards. Neither was sure about French food. Our provisions weighed as much as our clothes.

The Channel crossing was as smooth as milk. The sea glittered like satin under the sun's rays. I stood on deck, gripping the rail, as we glided towards the French coast.

Even the French train felt different.

'It *is* different, isn't it?' I said. I knelt on the seat for the entire journey with my face pressed against the grubby window. When we got out at the Gare du Nord, my legs were stiff and my knees red and marked from the scratchy seat-material.

'The last time I saw Paris,' hummed Jessie.

And Paris didn't disappoint me. Each little thing delighted me: the pungent smells of Gauloise cigarettes and strong coffee, the boulevard cafés with their striped awnings, the sound of French being spoken all around me, casually, the pavement kiosks, the flower-sellers, the names of the streets — rue de la Harpe, rue du Chat-Qui-Pêche. 'Can you imagine a street in *Edinburgh* called the street of the Fishing Cat?' I demanded. No wonder Amy had forsaken Edinburgh for Paris!

I liked, too, our Left Bank hotel bedrooms, hung with dark, dusty, red velvet drapes and crammed with top-heavy, mirrored mahogany furniture. Never mind the musty smell or the dust balls under the high double bed where I slept with my mother! Never mind that we emerged from its depths in the mornings with a couple of red bites apiece! We did not mention them to Jessie. She passed the nights on a lumpy truckle bed at the foot of ours. The room was cheap. It was in Paris!

Jessie couldn't get over the lavatory. A hole in the floor and a place for each foot. 'They're joking, aren't they?' she said, returning to the bedroom unrelieved, having groped her way back along the walls of the dark corridor (the light had gone off on its time-switch). She regarded the bidet; we had never seen one before, were uncertain as to its function. Perhaps it was meant to be a WC? In the bedroom? Jessie decided it was probably meant for men to pee in. She wanted me to complain to the woman on Reception about the holes in the floor.

'It's French, Jessie,' I said loftily. 'That's how the French go to the toilet. I expect Antoine's got one the very same. You'll need to practise, won't you, in case you need the toilet in his house?'

She was not amused. She gave me a look that was meant to indicate that I should not get above myself. But I already had: my feet were off the ground and I was flying high, totally intoxicated by the city and the fact that I could speak the language. I could and they couldn't. They were dependent on me, my mother and Jessie MacFarlane. There was to be no sending me home now, saying I was too young. I took charge of the map, sections of which I could recite by heart, led the way with confidence to Notre-Dame, the Eiffel Tower, the place de la Concorde, Sacré-Coeur. The places all appeared familiar to me. I had never heard of déjà vu then, but that was what it felt like.

We didn't mind that the city was still marked by war, that buildings were run down and in need of refurbishment, that food queues clogged the pavements. We didn't mind eating pommes frites out of a bag as we strolled along the boulevards in the evening and filling up with pilchards on digestive biscuits when we got back to the hotel.

Our first priority was to find Amy. Finding her was a foregone conclusion, as far as I was concerned. Well, we knew she was living in Montmartre, didn't we? It would simply be a matter of scouring the area until we tracked her down. And once having found her, I was confident that she would fall into our arms and all would be forgiven. Surely, if she were to see the three of us looming up in front of her in Paris, she wouldn't turn her back?

To begin with, we tried the telephone book. There were a lot of Lebruns. 'You canne phone all that number,' said Jessie. I dialled a Y. Lebrun and an M. Lebrun and both times got a man who answered shortly and was not prepared to waste his time. The clicks on the other end of the line made that plain.

We went up to Montmartre.

'Do you think Amy's aunt would live round here?' said my mother, as we passed doorways inviting us to enter and see sex shows. Her cheeks were pink. Sex was not a word that was ever said aloud in the family. Not even Jessie would have used it then. We passed two women leaning against a wall, one with orange-sherbet hair and black fishnet stockings, the other a peely-wally blonde with white stick-like legs.

'Hoors,' said Jessie. 'Imagine, even in the daytime!' There seemed to be a note of admiration in her voice.

Then I remembered that Amy had said something about her aunt living at the northern end of Montmartre.

I turned and faced north. There, above us, stood Sacré-Coeur, sparkling in the sunshine like a newly frosted vision.

'You dinne mean we've got to climb up all yon steps?'

'I told you it was built on a hill. It's called the Butte de Montmartre.'

'It looks mair like Ben Nevis to me.'

Jessie's feet were bulging over the tops of her high-heeled shoes by the time we made it to the summit. She kicked off the shoes and sank down on to the steps in front of the church. I scanned the faces of those who had already collapsed and of the women going in and out of the church. It was possible that Amy would come here to light a candle for her mother. She'd taken me to light candles in Edinburgh. 'Don't tell them!' she'd said, and I hadn't. Some secrets I could keep.

'This is murder,' said Jessie, drying off her face on her hanky.

It was midday and the sun shone mercilessly overhead. Paris was sweltering under a heat wave, and even the natives were complaining: the city was airless, intolerable, the grass was turning to straw, the leaves of the chestnut trees dehydrating, shrivelling, falling before their time. It didn't bother me, though; you could keep your east winds and grey skies and the cold clammy North Sea haar prowling up from the Forth to invade the streets.

Jessie put her handkerchief, streaked now with pancake make-up, over the top of her head.

'So what's the next move, madam?'

We were not actually at the northern end of Montmartre, I pointed out; to get there we would have to go down the hill at the back.

At least we were going down.

Gradually we lost most of the tourists and fund ourselves in streets where ordinary, everyday, not-very-well-off Parisians might live, in streets lined by rows of apartment blocks with the black wrought-iron balconies that had quickly come to seem familiar. The long lunch hour was in session; the pavements were virtually empty, the shops shut except for the boulangeries. I asked at a couple. Une écossaise aux cheveux roux?

'They do an awfy lot of shrugging, don't they?' commented Jessie.

We wandered about, hugging the shadier sides of the streets. I had imagined that Montmartre would be a little like Stockbridge, a fairly contained district that you could comb until you'd found what you were looking for, but it was turning out to be quite different: for a start it was much larger, and it sprawled in all directions like an inkblot, and then there was the whacking great Butte standing up in the middle of it.

I suggested that we make our way home via the boulevard de Magenta. How did I mean, 'via'? Jessie demanded. We could take the Métro, I replied. We couldn't just give up on Amy, could we, not like that, without trying any further? After all, we did have a number on Magenta, which at least was a starting point, and we *might* come across somebody who had known Claude Laroche and who *might* even know where Amy was now.

'It's a long shot.'

'Any shot is better than no shot.'

'You've always got an answer, haven't you!'

We studied the boulevard de Magenta on the map.

'It's a hell of a long street. The Frogs seem to go in for long streets.'

We elected − I elected − to get off at the Métro station Barbes Rochechouart instead of République, which brought us to the top of the boulevard. No. 10 turned out to be at the bottom, near the place de la République.

When we did eventually reach No. 10, I rang the concierge's bell. She emerged looking as if she had just wakened from a heavy sleep and I set about engaging her in conversation. She remembered Claude Laroche *and* Eugénie. Mais bien sûr! Une belle femme. C'était une vraie tragédie. So far, so good; I could follow at this level. Then she started to race on and I only caught half of what she said. I'd have got on better if Jessie hadn't kept butting in every two minutes to ask, 'What's she saying? She doesne half gabble!' But it did seem clear that the concierge had no idea where Amy was now. There were new tenants in the flat and they had nothing at all to do with Claude Laroche.

'We'll just have to keep our eyes peeled as we're going about,' said Jessie, as we tottered the last few yards to the Métro station at the place de la République, where we got caught up in the hectic mêlée of rush-hour Paris.

*

The next day we set our sights on Antoine. Or Tony, as Jessie referred to him. The rue de Courcelles – where he lived – was another long street over on the Right Bank. He lived at the other end from where we started.

Fortunately, though, the bottom door leading to Antoine's flat was open, and his name by the top bell. Jessie exuded a sigh of relief; she'd been afraid he might have moved away. She paused in the shelter of the doorway to renew her pancake make-up, which by now resembled baked earth fissured with rivulets of perspiration. She dashed Midnight in Paris behind her ears and under her arms. My mother decided not to come up, but Jessie needed me to do the talking; not that I had any intention of being left below. We entered a dark passage that smelled like the open-toed, open-topped iron pissoirs we passed on the boulevards. We fumbled our way up to the fifth floor. The sun sent a thin shaft through the skylight to illuminate the top landing. Jessie pulled Antoine's bell and hummed 'I'll be seeing you in all the old familiar places' while we waited.

'He might be at work,' I said.

Nothing seemed to be happening behind the scabby green door.

'We'll just have to hang about then, won't we, kiddo? I'm not going to have come all this way for nothing.'

Then we heard footsteps. Jessie licked her forefinger and smoothed the plucked line of her eyebrows. She re-settled her wrinkled satin skirt over her hips, squared her shoulders, pulled in her waist and stuck out her bosoms. The door was tugged open, as if it was inclined to stick. Jessie put out her hand and with a little laugh gave it a push.

She took a step back, jabbing my toe with her dagger-like heel. I suppressed my howl. Facing us was a young woman with hair scraped back from her temples and a skinny baby on her shoulder. Jessie dunted me in the rear unnecessarily sharply, I felt. I knew what to do.

'Antoine?' I enquired politely. 'Habite-il ici?'

The woman immediately looked suspicious. She was

Antoine's wife; it didn't take long for that to be established. 'Qui êtes-vous?' she demanded, her voice shrill, her eyes narrowing like cats' eyes in the dark.

'Personne,' I said and then, 'Bonjour,' and we retreated.

'Bugger!' said Jessie.

Jessie, though, was not one to sulk or spoil our holiday on account of a disappointment. Plenty more men in the sea, she was saying by late afternoon, and in the evening, after trawling around the boulevards, she hooked one and hauled him in. He was French. And a real nice guy, she said. A perfect gentleman. Scots guys had no manners, didn't know how to pay compliments, make you feel good, didn't even know how to hold a door open for you. Roland had glistening black hair and a bald patch on the back of his crown: that was all I ever saw of him. He took Jessie on forays around Paris, once darkness had fallen and brought a little respite to the overheated city. As I drifted into sleep I imagined them sitting on high stools in drinking joints and other dens of iniquity, rubbing shoulders with spivs and women in black fishnet stockings.

Every day, wherever we went, I kept up my watch for Amy. Each dark red head that went by turned my head.

And then, one afternoon, after we had been resting ourselves in the shade of the Luxembourg Garden, my mother and Jessie sleeping off their morning exertions, I reading *Claudine à Paris*, we saw her. All three of us did. We were coming out of the garden's gate; she was on the other side of the broad boulevard.

'Hell's bells!' exclaimed Jessie. 'There's Amy!'

'Come on!' I yelled, and went charging across the road without waiting for the lights to change, narrowly missing being flattened by a deux chevaux which brayed after me petulantly, its hooter blending into the overall Paris horn concerto. My mother and Jessie followed, once the lights had turned, half-running to keep up, breathless.

I crossed the wide mouth of the rue Gay-Lussac, found the opposite corner clogged with people and brasserie tables and chairs, barged into legs of all three, sending coffee slopping, raising exclamations of 'Merde!' I saw Amy's head turning right into the rue Soufflot. When I reached it myself, she was about to turn left into the rue Victor-Cousin. She was wearing a lime-green dress.

'Aimée!' I shouted at the top of my voice. 'Aimée Bal-four!'

She disappeared round the corner. I put on a spurt and was in time to see her turning right into the rue Cujas along the side of the Sorbonne. I caught up with her at the crossroads with the rue Saint-Jacques.

'Amy!' I had a stitch in my side, could say nothing more. I reached out and touched her shoulder.

She stopped and looked round: a stranger with dark-brown eyes and a thinnish mouth that was quite different from Amy's full-lipped one. I saw, also, that the colour of the dress was too sharp for Amy to have chosen.

The next time I sighted Amy I was certain that it really was her. I saw her in the rue Jacob. She glanced round briefly and there was something unmistakable about the lift of her chin. I thought she hadn't seen me. My mother and Jessie were in a shop doorway, peering in at the antiques. Amy turned into the narrow passage that went through to the rue de Seine. I didn't even wait for my mother and Jessie this time, I took off.

As I came into the rue de Seine, I saw Amy vanish into a doorway. I pounded along the pavement until I reached it.

It was an antiquarian bookshop. There were old scientific instruments in the window as well as books, and a big brass telescope. A half-curtain obscured the interior of the shop. I waited until I'd recovered my breath, then pushed open the door and entered.

It was quiet inside the shop. An ormolu clock ticked on the mantelpiece. A man in a cream linen jacket was sitting behind a desk with a leatherbound book open between his hands. I noticed his hands: they were elegant, and handled the book gently. And the fingernails were clean. They seemed almost to shine. I wasn't used to seeing men with pearly fingernals.

They were hands that Amy would like. The shop smelled of furniture polish and old, expensive books. They lined the walls; a double-sided case stood in the middle. The man was alone in the room. A door in the back wall was closed.

The man – the proprietor, presumably; he looked proprietorial – had looked up from his book and was regarding me quizzically. A man with dark hair broken by a thick band of white that rose in a widow's peak from his temple.

'Pardon,' I stammered, and backed out.

I must have been mistaken. Though I had felt sure . . . I wandered up the rest of the street looking in windows and doorways, then came back down, checking again. I peeped over the half-curtain of the antiquarian bookshop. The man was still reading. As I scanned the interior behind him, he looked up and met my eyes for the second time. I ducked down. I was sure, though, that Amy had not been in the room. It was as if the young woman I had seen had gone up in a puff of smoke.

When I returned to the rue Jacob I found my mother and Jessie on the brink of going berserk.

'Don't *ever* go off like that again!' said my mother.

'We thought you might have been kidnapped,' said Jessie. 'Sold into slavery. No such luck!'

They didn't believe I'd seen Amy.

'You're seeing her in your dreams,' said Jessie.

She was right about that. But I had seen Amy in the rue de Seine too.

'We are not going back *there* again!'

I had persuaded them to go once and Jessie had peered in at the door and seen only the man, who had seen her also.

'He'll be setting the polis on us. He'll think we're loitering with intent.'

There was only one other way to try to find Amy, I maintained, and that was through Colette. I had broached this idea before but my mother had not been receptive to the idea.

'Mind you, it would be nice if you could go and see her,' said Jessie, weighing in on my side, 'even leaving Amy out of it. You mightn't get the chance again, not if she's old.' I had told Jessie all about Colette; all that I knew, that was, from having read one or two of her books and from having listened to Amy, who had listened to her mother, who had listened to *her* mother. 'Why shouldn't you call and say hello?' said Jessie. 'After all, she's only a woman, like the rest of us.'

'Not quite,' said my mother, who could think of lots of reasons why one shouldn't call on a famous writer.

But Jessie had a way of making things seem possible. She didn't see why I shouldn't drop Colette a note and say I was in town, hoping to catch up with Amy. 'She doesn't have to answer if she doesn't want to. It's a free country, isn't it? And your Aunt Eugénie was an old friend, wasn't she?'

We overcame my mother's resistance. The next thing we had to do was to find out Colette's address. Jessie steered me into a bookshop, one selling new books. Chat up the assistant, she said, get her on to Colette, ask her if she knows where she lives.

It seemed that everybody in Paris knew where Colette lived. Mais naturellement! She was a kind of national figure. 'See!' said Jessie.

I wrote down the name of the street: rue de Beaujolais. 'It backs on to the gardens of the Palais-Royal,' said the assistant. She didn't know the number. 'Anyone will tell you.'

'Merci!' Jessie gave her a dazzling smile.

I bought a pad of blue notepaper (Amy had told me of Colette's liking for blue) and envelopes to match. I wrote the letter – in French, doing the best I could with the grammar – leaning on the mahogany dressing-table in the hotel bedroom. I could see the nib of my fountain pen moving over the blue paper in the spotted mirror.

'Now, just ask if she knows Amy's address,' said my mother. 'Don't be asking to visit her!'

'Tell her you think she's great,' urged Jessie.

'Don't tell her about Amy falling out with us!' said my mother.

'Butter her up a bit,' said Jessie. 'Give it all you've got!'

'Dear Colette,' I wrote, 'I am a big fan of yours. I think you are the best writer in France and the whole world. I am twelve years old, getting on for thirteen, and my Aunt Eugénie (by marriage) was the daughter of your old friend Berthe Bussac in Saint-Sauveur-en-Puisaye (Burgundy). I live in Edinburgh (Scotland) but I am in Paris on holiday with my mother and her friend Jessie MacFarlane, who is a widow. We have mislaid the address of my cousin Amy (daughter of Eugénie) and wonder if by any chance you might know it?'

I paused, bit the end of my pen, looked in the mirror, saw myself frowning, biting the pen, then made up my mind. 'I would love to come and see you. I realize that you must be very busy since you are so famous, so I will understand if you do not have time. But it would be lovely if you did.'

After three attempts – the first time I smudged it with my hand, the second I dropped a blob of ink right in the middle of the page – I decided that the letter would have to do. My hand was getting cramped and I was damp under the arms. On the envelope I wrote, 'Madame Colette, rue de Beaujolais, Paris, France,' leaving a space for the number in front of 'rue'. We then set out to deliver it.

We were very impressed by the Palais-Royal. 'She can't be short of a bob or two,' observed Jessie as we made our way through the stately gardens. Two children were playing with a large red ball, battling it about lethargically in the heat. A few people sat around in the shade on iron chairs, reading or dozing, but none looked like Colette. I had a definite picture of her in my head: I had gazed often at Amy's photographs of her, the ones that had come into my mother's possession. She'd be getting on now, of course, said my mother; she must be well into her seventies. I did notice one man sitting on a chair, holding a book between his long, thin hands, reminding me of that other man in the shop in the rue de Seine – he would not go away. The incident had stayed in my mind like a puzzle I could not fathom, yet felt I should be able to if only I had the vital missing clue. The face of the man on the chair also caught my attention. It was long and thin, in keeping with his hands, and sensitive-looking, with deep-set eyes and a slightly arched nose: a poet or a violinist's face, I decided. Grey hair receded from his high forehead. I'm pretty sure now that it was Jean Cocteau, who was a close friend and neighbour of Colette's. He lived in the rue de Montpensier, which, looking out from her window, was on the right-hand side of the gardens. I was too shy to approach such a man, whom I sensed must be someone distinguished. Instead we went through the little arcade (right under the windows of Colette's apartment, had we but known it) into the rue de Beaujolais and I asked a road-sweeper there. 'Numéro neuf,' he said, and pointed to the row of first-floor windows above my head. She might be looking down on us. The thought made me tremble.

Her reply came on blue paper also. 'I would be delighted to receive you and your mother . . .'

'Never mind,' said Jessie. 'I expect I'd be de trop.' She was picking up a few French phrases from Roland.

My mother and I went to visit Colette the day before we were to leave Paris.

I was nervous. I tugged irritably at my dress. 'It's awful, this dress,' I said to my mother; *I hated* it, I really hated it. I had never hated a dress so much. And I was sure that Colette would hate it, too. Mrs Craddock had made it for me on her creaking old foot-pedalled singer sewing-machine. The material was blue-and-white-checked gingham and around the skirt hem there was the ugliest crazy white rickrack you ever saw in your whole life and the sleeves were puffy and stupid-looking and, to finish the whole thing off, a broad band tied in a *bow* behind my back! It was *far* too young for me and far too tight. My budding breasts were stretching the cloth to the limit. I was torn between wanting the bodice to split, to prove to my mother that she shouldn't have let the hem down one more time and fearing that if it did rip we would have to turn back and I wouldn't meet Colette after all. And when I looked down I could see my feet clumping along in their Clark's school sandals and my knees bobbing out from under the hem of my dress. Everyone in Paris – well, perhaps not *everyone*, not the women we'd seen in the back streets around Montmartre, but the better-dressed, better-off ones – was wearing long, full, swirly skirts in the fashion called the New Look. Jessie had wanted to lend me one of her dresses and a pair of her high-heeled strapped shoes, but my mother would not hear of it.

I had another worry, too. I'd said I was a fan of Colette's, which I was, but I'd read only *Dialogues de bêtes* and the first two Claudines. What if she were to question me? 'What do you think of *Chéri*? Which do you prefer – *Le Blé en herbe* or *La Naissance du jour*? Please state your reasons. Which books have you *actually* read?'

Before we'd set out I'd fussed over the bow at the back of my waist, tying and retying it, until my mother had told me to leave it alone or it would end up looking like a dish-rag.

'It already does.' I gave it another twitch. 'The whole dress looks like a dish-rag.'

'We don't have to go, if that's how you feel.'

'We'll have to go now that we've said.'

I had marched out of the room before she could remove her white straw hat with the navy-blue ribbon and kick off the court shoes that were crucifying her feet. She was wearing her best going-to-church outfit: a navy rayon suit with a white, buttoned-to-the-neck blouse, and white gloves. Her face was brick-red, in spite of having been well powdered by Jessie, and her hair, newly permed before we left Edinburgh, clung damply to her temples in tight, round curls.

'I could murder that Jessie MacFarlane for putting the idea into your head,' she said, puffing, when she caught up with me.

'She didn't put it there,' I retorted and pressed on, carrying aloft like a spear the stiff bunch of blue gladioli I had purchased

165

earlier from a pavement flower-seller on the boulevard Saint-Michel.

'Madame is not so well today,' said the maid.

She stood stoutly in front us, blocking the way to Colette. I stared at her in horror. To have got this far to be told we could go no further!

'What's wrong?' my mother asked me anxiously.

Then we heard a voice calling from behind one of the closed doors. It was hers! A deep, rich voice. My spine tingled. 'Pauline! Have my guests arrived?'

Pauline admitted us. She opened a door and stood aside.

I paused on the edge of the room, which glowed and shimmered in front of my eyes. The walls were hung with dark-red silk wallpaper, the mantelpiece was marble. In front of the window, reclining on a divan bed with a writing table across her knees, was Colette. She lay motionless, her crooked hands resting on the table. She wore a blue satin kimono. Lace-edged pillows cushioned her back. A grey cat draped over her feet raised an eyelid and gave me an unfriendly look.

'Bonjour,' said Colette gravely, without any suggestion of a smile.

'Bonjour,' I replied in a small, quavering voice and wondered if my knees would be strong enough to carry me into the room. I advanced a little way.

Through the open window drifted the sound of children laughing and shouting in the gardens below. Colette liked the sound, even though she disapproved of the way the children trampled and despoiled the garden: she has recorded that, along with her many other likes. She liked to look down into the gardens and watch the children play and the lovers pass.

My eyes focused first on her face. I recognized it! Age might have blurred the contours, even shrunk it a little, but the chin was still pointed and that, combined with the broad forehead, served to give her face its triangular, fox-like look. Her eyes, black-rimmed with kohl, were sapphire-blue, like her gown, and brilliant. You could see that she'd been beautiful, *was* beautiful. Her hair was grizzled and grey and the curls arranged over her forehead were tinted mauve, but none of these changes mattered: I felt that I could peel away the layers and see, emerging from underneath, the girl with the long chestnut plait swinging in a hammock in the garden in Saint-Sauveur. The image was preserved amongst the photographs Eugénie had brought from France when she came to marry George Balfour. For a moment Colette's face, and the room, seemed to waver, like a negative in solution. I was with her in the garden behind the high wall of the rue des Vignes, a woman was stooping to lift fallen chestnuts, a boy was lying in the long grass, reading. I blinked, and the room in the rue de Beaujolais came back into focus.

Her eyes were holding mine. Her gaze was intense and quite sharp, even fierce, and not much friendlier than the cat's, but after a little while I could feel it softening, as if she had decided that she was going to accept me, perhaps even trust me.

I went up to the divan and proferred my bouquet. She took it solemnly, saying that it was très gentille of me to bring flowers. She gazed into the centre of the gladioli blooms and sighed. 'It's a marvellous thing, isn't it, a flower? When you stop to think about it? To look. A real marvel!'

I nodded. I was standing so still my head was swimming. The air in the room was warm and heavy in spite of the open window.

Colette passed the bouquet to Pauline, who went to find a vase. 'You know how much I love flowers?'

I nodded again. I was amazed at how many things I did know about this Frenchwoman.

'Sit down there, child . . . at the end of my couch – my raft! – where I can see you properly.' The cat streaked away at my approach. Colette said, 'Maurice, a chair for Madame Balfour.'

Maurice Goudeket, who had been standing in the shadows, came forward to shake hands with us and to pull up a chair for my mother. It had a tapestry back, embroidered by Colette herself, he told us proudly. In the days before her hands had become useless, she added. My mother perched awkwardly on the edge of the chair and twisted her gloves between her hands until they began to wilt. It was Jessie who had decided that she should wear gloves; she'd said it was the polite thing to do when calling, just as you should raise your pinkie in the air when you were holding a cup. 'Remember,' she'd said to us, 'remember to lift your pinkie if she gives you coffee!'

I glanced away from my mother. I felt ashamed that she did not know what to do and could not even speak to this famous writer, and at the same time I felt guilty that I had brought her into a situation where she was so ill at ease.

Colette allowed us to settle, gave us time to adjust, to take in her environment. I studied it covertly to begin with, then, when I saw that she did not mind, I looked more openly; in fact, greedily. Her room was like a treasure-trove. I noticed first a blue lamp set before a poppy-red curtain (much later I learnt that this lamp was her famous fanal bleu, made by fastening two sheets of blue paper together to form a lamp-shade), then her collection of glittering crystal glass paper-weights and her case of butterflies and a globe of the world and a barometer and a magnifying glass and a paper cutter and pens in a blue-green pot and –

'You see, I have everything I need to hand.'

I blushed, although she had not spoken reprovingly. I turned my attention to her books. Maupassant, Kipling, Cocteau, Gide, Zola, Balzac.

'Balzac! My mother has read Balzac!'

My mother, realizing that I was drawing attention to her, looked even more uncomfortable. One of her mangled gloves had slid from her knee down on to the carpet and now Monsieur Goudeket was stooping to retrieve it. He returned it to her with a little bow.

'She got him in our local library in Edinburgh, at Stockbridge,' I went on remorselessly. 'It's not a bad library, but it doesn't have many of your books in it.'

'I'm sorry to hear that! But Balzac – *he* has been my enchanted forest, my voyage of discovery. He knew it all! When you're older you must read him.'

'Oh, I shall!' I declared fervently. (After leaving Colette I dragged my poor long-suffering mother along to the bouquin-istes on the Seine, where I bought my first Balzac in a limp fawn cover. It was *Eugénie Grandet*. I chose it because of the name 'Eugénie'. To my twelve-year-old mind Amy's mother was a romantic heroine who had suffered and died for love.)

Pauline returned with a tray of blue-and-white china cups and saucers and a pot of hot chocolate.

'I knew you'd give us hot chocolate!'

'You did?'

'Yes!'

The echoes of recognition were coming fast and furiously. All the things that Amy had told me were true!

Pauline poured the chocolate and withdrew. We drank. Nectar of the gods, thought I, savouring both the taste in my mouth and the words in my head.

'You gave hot chocolate to my cousin Amy.'

'Ah yes, the lovely Aimée! Tell me, did you manage to find her?'

'No. As I told you in my letter, we've lost her address.'

'What a pity!'

'We were hoping that you might – '

'I'm afraid I can't help you, either. We've never had her address. Somewhere on the Left Bank!'

'Does she come often to see you?'

'We mightn't see her for a while – a month or two – then she'll drop in and brighten us up. She tells us what's happen-ing on the streets of Paris. She's a good mime, your cousin. She can play her concierge, the old man who lives in the apartment next door, the women in the boulangerie! She never tells us a great deal about her own life, does she, Maurice? There's a man in it, though; that much I can tell you.'

'With a white streak in his hair?'

'I wouldn't know about that. We've never seen him. She's very secretive about him. He may well be married. That's a fool's game if she's playing it! It was sad about her mother

169

Eugénie, wasn't it? So many old Saint-Sauveur friends have gone; I only have my memories now. Still, you are young, eh?' Colette's mood changed. 'What shall you do with your life? What would you like to do?'

'I'm going to be a writer,' I said, for the first time aloud. I had written my first book the summer before, a pseudo-Enid Blytonish adventure, but had already shaken off her influence and shifted my territory to the brooding, Brontë-haunted Yorkshire moors. After my visit to Colette I would write several Scottish versions of *Le Blé en herbe* – boy and girl on an East Lothian beach. The trouble was the wind blowing off the North Sea made it difficult to create a langorous, sensual atmosphere, and the remembrance of Amy and the US airman kept getting in the way.

'As a child,' said Colette, 'I didn't want to write at all. That's true! You look surprised. As long as I had books to read I saw no reason to write them. I only began to write after I was married for the first time.'

'Willy made you, didn't he? He locked you up in a room and wouldn't let you out until you'd written the right number of words.' Perhaps I shouldn't have said that? I glanced at Maurice Goudeket who, after all, was her present husband, and was relieved to see that he was smiling. I was thankful now that my mother did not understand French. She'd have been mortified, and furious with me. She considered it bad manners to refer to somebody's personal life unless you were invited to.

Colette laughed a deep-throated laugh, and my mother smiled and relaxed a little, thinking that everything was going all right. Which it was. I felt that Colette had become my friend, just as Amy had after she'd visited her with her mother in the penthouse apartment on the Champs-Elysées.

I asked Colette if she was still writing.

'Yes, I am, still. I don't know that I shall ever write The End. Until *I* end. There seems always something to be continued.'

At the talk of ending, her husband had got up to readjust

her cushions. She smiled into his face. He was her best friend: Amy had told me that.

I knew it was time to go. I felt very grown-up just in realizing that it was. Besides, my head was aching from having to sustain a conversation in French for so long and I'd reached that point when you start to nod, without always being sure that you have understood correctly exactly what has been said. I stood up and my mother followed suit.

'It was kind of you to take time from your holiday to come and see an old lady like me.'

'Thank you for letting me come. I shall never, *ever*, forget it!'

'You speak French very well. You roll your "r"s like a true Burgundian!'

'That's a Scottish thing, too, rolling your "r"s.'

'We have things in common, then.'

We laughed together, Colette and I.

She lifted a book from her table, and Goudeket, anticipating her need, took a pen from the blue-green pot on her table and put it into her hand. She wrote, with some difficulty, an inscription to me on the flyleaf: 'Pour que tu te souviens de ta visite au Palais-Royal, août 1947 — Colette.'

I was so overwhelmed that I could scarcely put out my hand to accept it. The book was *La Maison de Claudine*. I stood clutching it to my chest, gazing at her, fixing her image in my head. Then, hesitantly, I asked if I might take a photograph of her. Jessie had lent me her Box Brownie.

'Very well!' (Colette never minded having her photograph taken. In fact, she would often browse through old ones, admiring them; this was the performer in her, interested in her appearance. I was to find this in Amy, too, when we were reunited in the years to come.) Colette called for a mirror and frowned into it. She combed out her curls – 'I have such a monstrously high forehead!' – and refreshed the dark red lipstick on the thin line of her mouth. Her cheeks were already well rouged.

She posed, looking straight at me, straight into the camera.

171

Her dark, shadowed eyes stare out with intelligence and intensity from a silver frame on my mantelpiece.

In the evening, our last in Paris, we strolled at dusk through the gardens of the Palais-Royal, my mother and I, with my hand tucked into her arm. I had said I was sorry that I had put her through such an ordeal in the afternoon, I knew she had not enjoyed it and had found Colette, in spite of being sofa-bound, somewhat frightening. 'I think she could be a very demanding woman,' said my mother, who never demanded anything in her life; a virtue or a failing? I did not agree with her – at twelve going on thirteen I saw only what I wanted to see – but we did not argue. My mother had much preferred Monsieur Goudeket; she had thought him a real gentleman, with lovely manners. She was not one to hold a grudge, though, or nurse resentment, so she would put the discomfort of the afternoon behind her. She said I was 'an awful lassie', which she meant as an endearment, that I asked too many questions and my head was 'full of notions', which did not mean that she disapproved. She wanted me to lead a fuller life than she had.

We stopped at the northern end of the gardens to look up at the windows on the first floor. Colette's window was open, letting in the night air. Behind the glass, her blue lamp glimmered.

In the hall in the Dean Village, the lamp on the dais gave off a blue glow. Earlier Amy had covered the oyster-coloured shade with two sheets of blue paper fastened together. We, the audience, sat very still, awaiting the last moments of the writer's life.

It is the third of August, 1954; we are in Paris, in the apartment in the rue de Beaujolais. The weather has been very warm and the air is oppressively heavy, lying like a blanket over the city. Colette is finding it difficult to breathe. With her are her husband, her maid Pauline and her daughter.

A flock of swallows flies past the window. 'Regarde, Maurice! Regarde!' she says.

Her eyes are turned upward to watch the swallows pass. Her feeble hand goes up also, and then sinks down slowly, like a withered leaf settling on a soft bed of earth.

For a few seconds the silence in the room was complete. Then the Duchman cried 'Bravo!' and leapt to his feet, raising his hands high into the air to applaud. The other seven of us responded, getting to our feet without embarassment. After all, had we not shared a life together? Amy rose too, now, smiling and bowing her head in acknowlegement.

The audience clustered around her to offer their congratulations. The young man, Pascal, Amy's stage manager, stood to one side, leaning against the wall, his arms folded, smiling.

'You were just great!' said the American couple.

'Magnifique!' declared the Frenchwoman.

'We'll come again,' promised the bearded student in sandals.

'We'll tell everybody!' said the girl in the granny-print floral dress.

'I saw you perform in the Hague,' said the Dutchman. 'In the spring.'

'You did?'

They settled into a conversation. Amy had not yet emerged from her stage persona. She answered as if she were Colette. 'Yes, it was in '38 that I moved into the rue de Beaujolais.' I waited in the background. When Amy had lifted her head at the end of her performance, I had seen her eyes rest on my face with a look of enquiry. While she talked to the Dutchman, who seemed in no hurry to go, from time to time she glanced beyond him at me. Release came for her with the arrival of the janitor.

'Next lot's due in half an hour.'

'Sorry, won't be long! Pascal, we'd better start moving!' She spoke to him in French.

The Dutchman helped Pascal to carry the chaise-longue into a small side room. I followed with the lamp and the vase of flowers. We went back for the table and the pink velvet chair. Amy had retrieved the cash box from the back row where Pascal had left it.

'There!' she said brightly, though I could see that she was tired. 'It doesn't take long to strike set, does it? Especially when kind people like yourselves are good enough to give us a hand.'

The Dutchman was now asking if he might take her to tea. He already had a hand under her elbow. He wanted to talk to her about the possibility of giving a performance in Amsterdam; he had some connections, he might be able to give her an introduction. She glanced around for Pascal, who had gone in search of the janitor, and then uncertainly at me. She was in that limp post-performance state where she could easily be pulled in one direction or another.

'I would like very much to talk to you, too,' I said. 'It's personal.'

She nodded, and to the Dutchman said, 'That's sweet of you. But some other afternoon, perhaps?'

'Of course.' He retreated.

Amy cocked her head to one side. 'You're not – ?'

'Yes, I am!'

We embraced then, and our eyes were damp when we separated.

'I wondered, you know. I kept looking at you, but you were only a child when I left Edinburgh. It's more than twenty years, after all!'

Pascal returned and Amy said, 'This is my cousin! I told you I had family here, didn't I?'

He took my hand and said, 'Enchanté!'

I did not think he looked enchanted.

Now the janitor came in and began to drag chairs noisily about. Amy passed the cash box to Pascal, and we left.

I was surprised to find that it was still daylight, in the way that one is when emerging from a cinema in the afternoon. We stood blinking in the sunlight, looking up from the valley towards the roofs and spires of the city.

'How does Edinburgh strike you?' I asked.

'Beautiful. Bright. Lively. I've never seen it in such a mood.

You can hear people speaking *French* in the street, for goodness' sake! And Spanish and Italian!'

'It's Festival-time.' There had been no festival in Amy's day; it had not started until 1947.

'I never imagined I would come back!'

I did not ask why she had.

We walked up the steep slope of Bell's Brae towards the West End. I wondered if Pascal would join us for tea. But when we reached Princes Street Amy said, 'Why don't you go on back to the digs, Pascal, and I'll see you there later?'

He looked a little displeased, and for a moment I thought he might be about to become petulant, but he went without protest. We crossed the street to the Caledonian Hotel. I phoned home to say that I would not be back for some time, then we settled ourselves comfortably and ordered afternoon tea. When there is much to catch up on, starting is always slow.

Amy realized of course that some people would have gone – Granny Balfour, for example – and was sad to hear about my mother.

'And your father?'

'Still going strong, a bit bent at the knees, but otherwise doing all right. He married Jessie MacFarlane.'

'Jessie? Well, well! And you?'

I told her that I, too, was married, and had four children.

'Four! What a busy life you must lead!'

I did not like to ask if she had ever been married or had children. Nothing about her seemed to suggest it.

'We went to Paris one year,' I said. 'Jessie, my mother and I. It was in 1947. I thought I saw you in the rue de Seine.'

'The rue de Seine?' said Amy. 'It's possible.'

Eight

Rest assured, I am a pear that has been
ravaged by hail; you know that if it doesn't
rot then it becomes riper and sweeter-
tasting than the others, under its little
scars.

Lettres de la vagabonde

It was cold and wet the day Amy arrived in Paris in October 1945. The train from Calais had lumbered along with infuriating slowness, stopping at intervals for anything up to an hour; and there had been no heat in the compartments. There had been no light, either, once daylight had begun to fade. When Amy stepped down into the Gare du Nord, chilled to the core of her being, she was told the Métro trains had ceased to run. Most days they operated for only an hour. She stood shivering, waiting for a bus, and after forty minutes one came which was going to the place de la République. The queue surged forward. The bus was steamed up, packed with bodies. She did not get on.

In spite of the weight of her two suitcases, which contained all her worldly goods, she decided to walk. It was not so very far – it would have been only two stops on the Métro – but by the time she reached her destination her shoulders were aching, and she was soaking wet. Her hair was plastered to her head. She rang the bell marked 'Laroche', the door opened, and she went up.

Claude Laroche himself was waiting in the unlit doorway of his apartment. She saw his faceless silhouette as she rounded the corner of the stair. She had had a word on her lips ready to spill out; now it fell back into her tightening throat. Sitting

176

on the train, trying to read, trying to ignore the cold (a foretaste of the winter to come), she had not thought beyond this moment. She had lived through the scene often, but it was not developing as it had in her head.

'You must be Aimée,' said Claude. His voice was cool, as was the hand he proferred. 'Come in.'

He took one of her suitcases, and Amy saw his shoulder droop; in her letters her mother had said that he was still very weak. She made to take back the case but he shook his head and limped, lopsided, dragged down by the weight, through the dark tunnel of the hall into a room. Here there was a little brightness; not much. A lamp burned on either side of the empty fireplace.

'I'm sorry it's so cold. We can't get coal.'

'I know. Mother said.'

He was wearing a jacket over a heavy jersey and a scarf wound twice around his neck.

'What it will be like in winter, God only knows! Factories can't work full-time because of the electricity shortages, department stores have to shut two hours early. De Gaulle says it will take twenty-five years for France to recover itself. Some of us may not have that long!'

Amy was glancing around the shadowy room. 'Mother?' she asked nervously.

'She's gone up to Montmartre to visit your aunt – she was taken ill this morning.'

'It was one of the worst evenings of my life,' said Amy. 'He made me a cup of chicory-type coffee and I changed out of my wet clothes, but even then I couldn't stop shivering, and after a bit I started to sneeze! I went on sneezing.' She laughed and lit another Gauloise, blowing a stream of blue smoke out into the lounge of the Caledonian Hotel in Edinburgh. 'I always sneeze when I'm allergic.'

There was no question of Amy following her mother up to Montmartre. It was unlikely that buses would be running, it was still raining, and she was too exhausted to contemplate walking. And Aunt Yvonne was not on the telephone.

At ten o'clock, Eugénie's key was at last heard in the front-door lock, and a moment later she came into the room to embrace Amy, laughing and breathless, with tears escaping from her eyes. They clung to one another. For the first time since leaving Dover Amy felt some warmth creep back into her body. Over her mother's shoulder she saw the look on the face of Claude Laroche.

The two women had not seen one another for six and a half years. Eugénie had aged beyond her years; she was fifty now, but looked older. She was thin, and deep lines had gouged channels into the fine skin around her mouth and under her eyes, and her hair was almost white. It was the whiteness of her hair that shocked Amy most.

Eugénie turned to the man in the room. 'Chéri,' she said very softly, and went forward to kiss him. 'Comment ça va?' Her question was tender and anxious, and Amy saw that she loved Claude Laroche still, and he her. His arms had gone out to encircle her. His face softened. For a moment they forgot Amy, who moved to the window to look down on the wet boulevard. The lights were not bright in Paris any more, not in the way she remembered them, strung along the avenues and boulevards, glittering, full of promise; now they shone dimly, and some not at all. She stood with the tips of her fingers touching the cold glass and wondered if she should return to Kent. But to what? She had no connections in that part of the world and her friends in the Land Army had dispersed. She did not consider a return to Edinburgh.

Amy spent that first night in Paris on the hard horsehair settee in the sitting-room of Claude Laroche's flat. She slept little. She had a small hard pillow under her head and one blanket to cover her. Her mother apologized for not being able to make her more comfortable, but she had already had to take the blanket from their own bed. Don't worry, said Amy, she could wear her Land Army trousers and jersey and thick socks.

It was wonderful to see her again, said Eugénie, looking back from the doorway of the room.

Amy realized that would be the only night she would sleep there. During the long years of planning and dreaming, she had seen herself living with her mother again, en famille. Claude Laroche had remained a shadow at the edge of her vision; now he had come into sharp relief in the foreground of the picture. She faced reality: she saw that what might at least have been feasible when she was fourteen was not now that she was twenty. The next morning she moved her suitcases up to Montmartre, to her aunt's small apartment in the grey street scourged by winds sweeping down from the north. She should not expect to stay there indefinitely, her mother warned her. Aunt Yvonne's health was not good.

'She's changed as she's got older. People often do, alas! She's not the easy-going woman she once was – she's become finicky, doesn't like anything out of its place, complains non-stop. One can't blame her. The war years were hard on her. And now we have peace, but not much food in our stomachs or heat to stop us freezing to death!'

Amy had a little money saved, but she needed to find a job. It would not be easy; there were a lot of ex-Service people looking for work who would have priority over her. She was not even a French citizen, not then. She accepted a job in a boulangerie.

'A boulangerie, eh?' sad Aunt Yvonne. 'Must be in the family blood! The Bussacs were bakers, you know.' (She herself had been a Grenot before marriage, like Amy's grandmother Berthe, and *their* father had been a post-office clerk.) 'They won't be paying you much at the boulangerie. I thought a girl like you would be able to get something better. Your mother's always been telling us how smart you were. Top of your class, she said!'

'Lay off the girl!' said Odile, who still came most days to visit her brother's widow. She, although bothered with arthritis, had retained her interest in life and was affable. She would have invited Amy to stay with her but she had only one room,

179

further down towards Clignancourt. Amy often sought refuge there. They would huddle in front of a small paraffin heater and drink cheap red wine and eat the fresh bread and occasional croissant that Amy brought from the boulangerie. It was one of the advantages of working there: she could have all the bread she wanted.

There were other advantages. One, mainly: it was warm. She did not grudge crawling from bed into a cold room at half-past five in the morning, since she knew that she would be exchanging it shortly for a place of warmth, where she would be greeted by the reassuring aroma of baking bread and have a bowl of hot milky chicory placed in her hands. Her day started with breakfast and a chat with the baker's wife. She and Madame Maillot served the shop.

Amy enjoyed the customers, too; she came to know them by name and habit, could reach for their bread before they had time to ask. She learnt of the problems of their children, the ailments of their husbands, the births of their grand-children. They talked down the newly elected coalition government. Politicians, what did they know? Did you ever see them standing in hour-long queues, hoping to buy a piece of sausage or a sliver of cheese? Even the Communists. It was always the same: once they got into power, they forgot what it was like to be powerless. Amy found the life of the boulangerie comforting.

'And I was in need of comforting! I saw my mother only once a week, usually on one of my half-days off. I had two, one on Sunday, the other Monday. I seldom went to the apartment on the boulevard de Magenta. We would go for walks around the city, she and I, and then find a little café where we could have a cheap meal and sit for a couple of hours out of the wind. Sometimes we even went to the cinema. Claude had an army disability pension, but it was not a lot. They were hard up, too. He wasn't fit enough to go back to work that winter. It was as hard a winter as any in the war, they said.'

*

Amy left her Aunt Yvonne's and took a room close to the boulangerie. It was a squalid, dark little place, on the ground floor at the back, smelling of damp and mould and plagued by mice and cockroaches that had to be fought relentlessly, but it was hers. She could come back when she'd finished work and not have to meet the carping voice of her ageing aunt. To avoid that, she was prepared to accept the shared stinking toilet off the corridor and wash herself at the cold-water sink in her room. Once in a while she would have the luxury of a warm bath at the Laroche apartment, but they did not always have hot water and she felt guilty taking even two inches away from them. The evenings were difficult. She would eat her bread and whatever other small scraps of food she'd managed to buy and then burrow into her bed where she read (Sartre, Camus, Cocteau, Beauvoir, Colette) by the light of a torch until her eyes began to blink. She went every Sunday down to the Seine to see what she could afford at the bouquinistes which had started to appear again.

One Sunday, standing beside a bouquiniste stall trying to decide whether she could rise to the price of an almost new copy of a Sartre novel, she had an encounter that was to change the course of her life. A man came by and stopped at the stall. He, too, began to browse. He held his book between long, sensitive-looking hands. Amy could not help but notice his hands. He looked up and smiled at her. He asked her what she was reading. She showed him the cover.

'Ah, yes. *La Nausée.*'

'Would you recommend it?'

'It's probably not to my taste, but I find that a lot of people seem to be reading it at present, although it was published before the war. It may well reflect the mood of our post-war times. There is much nausea about. But don't let me put you off it!'

She had made to replace it on the stall. 'No, it's not that. It's a little too expensive for me, anyway.'

'In that case, let me − !'

'No, I couldn't possibly!'

But he was already paying for the book. He gave it to her with a little bow. 'Please! I'd like you to have it. It's not much.' He touched her fingers. 'You're cold!' It was January, and the wind off the river raw. 'Come, I'll buy you coffee!'

'So I let him pick me up for the price of a book that I didn't greatly like once I'd read it! Perhaps his opinion had influenced me before I even opened it. We went to a brasserie on Saint-Germain and drank lots of hot coffee, real coffee. They knew him there. Odile always said that people in the know could get what they wanted. At Christmas the shops had been full of goods that nobody – nobody we knew – could afford to buy. And then we had food: omelettes filled with cheese and ham, and a bottle of good red wine. He knew about wine. He was knowledgeable about many things. Food, painting, sculpture, architecture. I felt almost as if I were in a swoon. We talked and talked. He talked mostly, of course. I could have listened for hours. I drank in everything he told me. I was thirsty. And we talked about books. His taste ran to Proust rather than Sartre. He was an antiquarian bookseller.'

'In the rue de Seine?' I said.

'That's right,' said Amy.

By the end of the evening he had offered her a job. His assistant had left recently to get married. Amy would suit him ideally: she was interested in books, well read, and could type.

'And presentable,' he added with a smile. 'That's important, too! You have to be able to present yourself to my customers when I am out. I often buy from private homes, especially these days when so many old families are feeling the pinch.'

Amy looked down at her clothes, bought pre-war at St Cuthbert's drapery in Edinburgh. The white blouse was fraying at the cuffs, the black skirt beginning to look glassy at the seams and over the bottom. She expressed doubts about her presentability.

'Don't worry, I expect we can do something to remedy that. Clothes are merely details.'

It was arranged that she would come and see him the following afternoon, then he drove her back through the quiet late-Sunday evening streets to her room in Montmartre. Cocooned inside the warm, purring car, she said little; she felt as if she were in a dream and was reluctant, when they came to a stop and he switched off the engine, to open the door and face the cold blast of reality.

She lay awake for a long time thinking about him: he excited her. He was attractive, older – at least double her age – and cultured, and he belonged to a world that was warm and privileged. She said his name aloud in the little room. Olivier. Olivier Picard. She liked the sound and the taste of it.

She started work that week. Olivier took her to Printemps, the department store, and bought her two dresses, one a soft fir-green, the other a deep burgundy that went unexpectedly well with her hair. His long fingers moved deftly along the rails. Amy, liking his lack of hesitation, watched mesmerized. He bought her soft kid shoes and fine silk stockings. She changed in the little cubicle, emerged for assessment. His nod of approval flooded her with elation.

'I didn't know bookshop assistants got their clothes bought for them,' said Odile, 'like uniforms. I had to buy my own rubber aprons when I worked at *Le Matin*.'

'I have to fit in with his shop. It's a very, well, *refined* sort of place.'

'A bit different from a boulangerie, no doubt!'

'There's nothing wrong with me accepting them, Odile!'

'What else will he want from you, other than typing his letters?'

'That's all, I tell you! He's a very sensitive man, well read –'

'Reading books doesn't stop a man being like other men. And you're an attractive young girl.'

Amy blushed. 'He's not interested in me in that way.'

'It's your mind he's after, is that it?'

'He behaves impeccably,' said Amy, and indeed he had. She

183

shifted the conversation over to Aunt Yvonne, whom they had both been to see. Amy tried to visit her at least once a week, even though she found her trying. Remember that we must all grow old, had said Eugénie, who was not to do so herself. Aunt Yvonne's mind had started to wander; on that evening when Odile and Amy had called she had thought they had come to rob her.

'Old age isn't much fun,' said Odile. 'Forget what I said, Aimée. Have a good time while you can!'

Amy was having a good time. She loved the bookshop: she loved the peace and order, the slow tick of the grandfather clock in the corner, the sight, smell and feel of the books, and of Olivier Picard sitting serenely at his desk, unperturbed by rain lashing against the window, soaring inflation, impending strikes, or rumours of strife in the streets. He was in control of his world. When he smiled at her, her heart raced. When his hand brushed hers, she felt her cheek grow warm and she would have to turn her head aside. She liked her office, too, tucked away at the back: an inner sanctum. She was warm now all the time, even when she came back to her room in the evening. She returned as late as she could, going sometimes to a brasserie by herself for something to eat and a glass of wine, sitting by the window, a book between her elbows, reading, dreaming a little. She was only twenty years old.

Sometimes Olivier would take her for a meal after they'd closed the shop. 'You've worked hard,' he'd say. 'I think you deserve a reward.' She did not feel that she ever had to work hard; there was no rush, any movement within the shop was leisurely, and a raised voice was something that was seldom heard. The customers were male, mostly, keen collectors and other dealers, old rather than young. The occasional student who strayed in tended to find the prices beyond his reach.

Olivier came back jubilant late one afternoon: he had managed to buy a first edition of Verlaine's *Fêtes galantes* in excellent condition.

'Scarcely been opened, by the look of it. I'm going to keep

it. That's the trouble when you like good things yourself, you want to keep them!'

He was carrying also a bottle of champagne. 'I thought we might celebrate.'

It was seven: time to lock the door and pull down the blind. He turned the sign on the window to 'Fermé' and lowered the blind with care. Jagged movements pained him. His own were always smooth and unhurried. The evening traffic was rustling past in the street outside; Amy heard it as if it came from a distance.

They withdrew to the back room where he kept crystal glasses in a small corner cupboard. The moment of going ahead of him, into the secluded room, seemed almost to be ordained; Amy felt as if she had already lived through it. She took her time, as he had done with the blind. She cast her eyes downward, watched the gauzy mauve material of her dress swirl gently around her bare brown legs, saw her sandalled feet moving over the glowing red Turkey carpet, and his linen-clad legs following. The door clicked shut behind them. Now she looked up. He held the cold dark-green bottle against his chest, thumbs braced at either side of the bulging cork. She allowed his eyes to engage hers; she did not blink. The cork flew abruptly upward, and struck the ceiling. They laughed.

Amy bent to retrieve the cork. She cupped it in her hand; she would carry it home to her rancid little room that, after this evening, was to house her for only one more night. Olivier said it was unsuitable. He'd been horrified when she'd taken him to see it. He'd never seen such a miserable room in his life! He had a friend who owned a small two-room flat in the rue Visconti which he would rent for her. The rue Visconti would be very convenient, he said, since it was just around the corner from the rue de Seine.

They raised glasses to one another. The champagne sparkled, the crystal flashed in the light. Their eyes engaged once more, and they drank.

*

'He was a wonderful lover,' said Amy. 'Do you think we could have a drink now?'

We had finished our afternoon tea. I signalled to the waiter; Amy ordered a martini and I a gin and tonic. I was well aware that it was I who was going to have to pay; the money in her cash box would not allow her to drink in expensive hotels.

'Yes,' said Amy, 'he was everything that my American airman was not. Do you remember Paul?'

'Of course.'

'Well, you were only . . . what, nine, ten?'

'Nine.'

'But you were sharp for your age!' she laughed. 'Thank God, though, I didn't marry Paul and go to live in some hick town in the mid-west, or wherever it was he came from.'

'Massachusetts.' I had remembered more clearly than she had – or would admit to? I remembered Jessie trying to pronounce it and myself vying for attention, chanting, 'The Leith police dismisses us.'

'Olivier was kind and considerate,' Amy went on. 'And experienced. He knew how to make me happy. Oh yes, he certainly did! We made love on the chaise-longue in the back room, in my delightful little flat in the rue Visconti, in the country in summer, when he took me out in his car, in orchards, meadows, beside rivers . . .'

'Amy, how could he afford so much as an antiquarian bookseller? To run a car, rent a flat for you, buy you clothes? It can't have been that lucrative a business, surely, especially in post-war Paris?'

'He had a wealthy wife.'

Amy first met Solange Picard on a mild March day. Amy was sitting at Olivier's desk, on which she had placed a little vase of damp violets – he had gone to Neuilly for the afternoon to look over the contents of someone's library – when the door opened to admit a woman in her middle years. Her perfume came in advance of her. Amy knew at once who it was. The woman was tall and on the heavy side, with well-rounded hips and calves; she was wearing a cherry-red, figure-hugging suit with a silvery fur cape slung around her shoulders. Her full lips were cherry-red also, her cheeks ivory-white tinged with rouge on the high cheekbones. Gold hoops swung from her ear lobes. Bright stones sparkled on her red-tipped fingers. Her hair, parted in the middle and swept back into a chignon, looked so densely black and sleek it might almost have been oiled. There was something Spanish-looking about her, though her father had been an industrialist from the north and her mother the daughter of a vintner in Alsace-Lorraine. The other image that came into Amy's mind was that of Snow White's stepmother.

'Ah, you must be Olivier's new little assistant! What is your name again? He did tell me. Eulalie? Amélie?'

'Amélie Bussac,' said Amy stiffly.

'I thought you were supposed to be Scottish?'

'Half. My mother was from Burgundy.'

'Yes, I can hear it in your voice.'

Madame Picard dragged a chair over from the corner and sat down, facing Amy across the desk. Amy was concentrating on not trembling; she kept her hands out of sight. Her visitor tossed aside her cape and crossed her legs so that her skirt rode well up her thighs, showing the tops of her stockings and a hint of her suspenders. The sight of her both disturbed and reassured Amy; she could not imagne Olivier being content with such a wife.

'You were reading?'

'Yes.' Amy glanced down at the book. 'We were quiet – '

'Don't tell me what it is!' Madame Picard's laugh was in keeping with her appearance, large and overstated. 'Swann! I might have known! Myself, I prefer *not* to be by his side.'

'But he's a genius.'

'I don't doubt that. Give me Colette any day!'

Amy looked up, startled.

'I like a bit of red blood flowing, to feel the pulse beating strongly. Swann is too namby-pamby for me. All that fuss about madeleines! I'll take a chunk of fresh bread with a lump of ripe cheese. But I am well aware of Olivier's preferences.'

'Monsieur Picard' – Amy had almost said Olivier – 'likes Colette as well. He says her prose is rich and intricate, and that no one can match her when it comes to conveying the world of the physical senses.'

Madame Picard seemed amused. 'I am glad you are receiving literary instruction,' she said.

The visit threw Amy into confusion: it was almost enough to put her off Colette, though not quite. She could not decide whether Solange Picard had guessed about her relationship with her husband or not. She decided not, since she was inexperienced in such matters, and it suited her better to think that. She saw no reason why the woman should have guessed. It was the first time they had met, after all, and Madame Picard had not had the opportunity to observe her husband and Amy together. When she came in to the shop a week or so later she ignored Amy entirely, apart from a brief nod. She had been in the rue Jacob; she had seen a marvellous Louis-Quinze commode in an antiques shop and wanted Olivier to come and see it with her. He went.

Amy commented to Olivier that his wife looked Spanish.

'She's half-Jewish.'

'Oh.'

'We spent the war in Switzerland. We didn't leave Paris till the day before the Boche arrived. I had to drag Solange away. It takes a lot to intimidate her.' There was admiration in his voice, which Amy was quick to note; and of course she grudged it. 'She helped a number of Jews to leave Germany in the thirties, went in physically to help, ran quite a few risks. She still gives generous support to refugee organizations.'

It was easy to give if you had it to give, Amy was tempted to retort, but she knew it would sound churlish and childish, and not necessarily true. She said, 'Colette's husband, Maurice Goudeket, is half-Jewish,' and moved the converation on to easier ground, one on which she had some advantage over him: he had never met the writer or her husband.

1946 was a year of mixed emotions for Amy: she swung between happiness and sadness. Aunt Yvonne died in July, which was in many ways a relief since it seemed time for the old woman to go; Odile, Amy, Eugénie and Claude Laroche and a few neighbours gathered at Montmartre cemetary to see her laid to rest. Afterwards, the members of the family went for a meal at a local restaurant, and for the first time Amy and Claude Laroche were able to talk to one another civilly, without enmity; now that her life had found another centre Amy had tempered her demands on her mother and no longer expected to be her closest confidante. Eugénie knew about Olivier, though they had never met, and never would. She did not approve. She was afraid for her daughter. How could such a relationship end happily? But Amy had no thoughts in her head of ending. She was in love. Olivier could not let a day pass without making love to her. She felt powerful. When he opened the door in the mornings, she saw the desire in his eyes. He made her feel desirable. And beautiful.

From the time of Yvonne's death, Odile herself started to go downhill, little by little; she withdrew to her room, went out only for groceries, and after a while not even that, relying on the goodwill of neighbours. Amy, absorbed in her own life, did not notice much until it was too late. When Odile died early the following year, Amy realized with a sudden jolt that she had not seen her for two months.

But the biggest blow, coming before that, in the autumn of 1946, was the death of her own mother. The news of the accident was relayed first to Odile, who sent a young neighbour to the rue de Seine to tell Amy.

'Olivier was wonderful,' said Amy, lighting another cigarette. She had been chain-smoking. 'He was there with me when the girl arrived to break the news. He took charge straight away. He said he would drive me down to Saint-Sauveur,

189

there was no question of me going alone. He rang home – his wife was not in – and left a message saying that he would not be home that night. He was sorry to have to cancel their dinner engagement, but he had been called out of town urgently. Even in the midst of my grief I felt a little surge of joy that he had put me first, before *her*. Strange, isn't it?'

They spent the night in a hotel in Auxerre down on the quai overlooking the Yonne. They checked in as Monsieur and Madame Picard. He signed the register without appearing to give it a moment's thought. Amy was glad he had not assumed a false name. It seemed a sign that he was acknowledging her. Madame Picard. The sound of it was like a musical chord in her ear when the porter addressed her. 'This way, please, Madame Picard.' Madame *Amélie* Picard.

The night was peaceful; only the faint chiming of church clocks and the occasional swish of a passing vehicle broke the silence. A three-quarter moon shone in through the window, giving their room a silvery glow. Amy, leaning on the sill, let her eyes rest on the barges lying like dark lozenges on the pale water. She wished that she and Olivier could take off in a barge and glide down through the quiet waterways of France. She said so to him. 'It would be nice, wouldn't it?' He smiled. It was the first time they had spent a whole night together; when he came home with her to the rue Visconti he left usually just before midnight. She'd often teased him about that, asked if he was afraid he'd turn into a pumpkin if he stayed after the stroke of twelve.

Tonght she lay in his arms and he soothed her. Weep, he said; he didn't mind tears. Her father had found the tears of her mother difficult; he would leave the room. Amy talked about her family that night, about all of us.

Olivier came with her to Saint-Sauveur in the morning and stood by her side. He met what remained of the Bussac family: Uncle Robert, Eugénie's eldest and only remaining brother – the first-born child of Berthe Grenot and André Bussac – his wife Joséphine, and their unmarried slightly simple son

Alphonse who was a shoemaker. There seemed to be no Grenots left in the area, or none that any of the Bussacs had kept track of. Berthe's sisters Jeanne and Mathilde were dead, and their children grown up and gone goodness knows where! It was the way, nowadays; young people no longer stayed where they'd been born. Amy, walking with Olivier past the Grenot house in the rue des Gros Bonnets, saw a stranger standing in the doorway.

'Poor Eugénie!' lamented Aunt Joséphine. 'What a tragedy her life was! She didn't have much luck.'

Amy turned away. She had to think that her mother's spell of freedom on the mountain compensated for an early death.

Olivier said that he would stay with Amy for the funeral.

'Are you sure? What will you tell your wife?'

'Something. Don't worry.'

They stayed three more nights in Auxerre. She remembered them as happy nights, explosions of pleasure, after sorrowful days.

'We buried my poor mother in the churchyard at Saint-Sauveur in the Bussac plot, alongside her brothers Jean and Alain and her mother Berthe and father André. I thought she would have been pleased about that, except that Claude could not lie beside her. That was the thing that upset me most; I had never liked him, but I wanted them to be together. He was buried in his family plot in Auxerre. And so they both went back to their origins.'

Eugénie's death was a watershed for Amy, and changed even her relationship with Olivier; she came to rely on him more, and to want more of him. She had had him at her side in a time of crisis, had felt his comforting hand under her elbow, sustaining and guiding her, had seen the looks of approval on the faces of her relatives and the people of Saint-Sauveur. 'He is quite a gentleman, this man of yours,' said Aunt Joséphine. 'Very gallant. And very distinguished-looking with that quiff of white hair! [Amy called him Badger on account of that; he

191

called her his red fox.] Well off, too!' said Aunt Joséphine. 'No harm in him being a bit older than you, either. He'll have had time to sow his wild oats. My life hasn't been roses all the way, Aimée, I can tell you! You know what your Uncle Robert's like! Wandering eyes and hands. He'll go on sowing all his life. But your Monsieur Picard seems to think the world of you. Oh yes, anyone can see that. You can tell just by the way he looks at you. Protective-like. As if he wouldn't let anyone hurt you. I'd hold on to him, if I were you. There can't be many like him around.'

Amy had a friend, Camille, who lived across the landing from her. Camille worked as secretary to a junior minister in the government. She and Amy drank coffee in each other's rooms and discussed their lovers. Camille's was a journalist on *Le Figaro*, thirty and unmarried, so her affair was relatively uncomplicated. Except that he was reluctant to commit himself. 'He likes his liberty, as he calls it. Which of us is free? He is chained to his paper!' Camille was not so sure, anyway, that she fancied being tied down herself (she liked to have the odd little fling on the side) and couldn't understand Amy wanting marriage at her age. 'Time enough yet. A lot of wives have a pretty rough deal, after all. Think of your own Olivier's wife! How do you think she must feel, knowing he's got a mistress?'

'I don't think she knows.'

'You said she looks as if she wasn't born yesterday!'

From Amy's window they could see the chimneypots of the rue Jacob. Amy recalled Colette living there in her top-floor flat, looking out at the roofs in the rue Visconti, dreaming of Burgundy and home.

'Perhaps the thing is to live like Sartre and Simone.' Camille had been a student of Beauvoir's. 'Have as many lovers as you want, but remain faithful to each other in essence. Whatever *that* might mean – I suspect it's a movable feast. And it depends on who's moving the boundary lines. But I hear S and S tell one another all about their lovers and don't feel jealous – if you can believe it.'

192

Amy could not, nor did she feel that she could ever live that way; she wanted Olivier for herself. All right, so she was possessive and jealous; she was prepared to admit to both faults, if faults they were. 'It may just show that I'm passionate!' How could you not be jealous if someone you love makes love to someone else? She was monogamous by nature, she was in no doubt about that. Nature? queried Camille. Upbringing, more like. She maintained that Amy could not escape her Scottish Calvinist heritage. Amy said that was a stupid response, one that was glib and overworked. Anyway, emotions usually tended to get the upper hand of conditioning, especially when they peaked.

'Don't be a fool, now!' said Camille. 'You're not thinking of doing anything drastic, are you?'

Amy became obsessed with Olivier's wife; she began to follow her around in her free time. She was a woman Amy could not fathom, into whose heart she longed to see. Did she love her husband? What was her life, apart from buying clothes and antiques and going to soirées? The Picards lived in a luxurious apartment on the avenue Foch and mixed with the wealthy haute bourgeoisie.

'It doesn't seem the right milieu for Olivier,' said Amy. 'Most of them wouldn't know which way up to hold a book.'

'So there are contradictions in his life!' said Camille. 'As there are for the rest of us.'

One Monday – the shop closed Sundays and Mondays – when Olivier was out of town for the day, Amy rose early and went to the avenue Foch to take up a vigil. She knew Olivier would have gone; he had planned to leave for Orléans before eight. She had wanted to go with him, but he'd said that he had personal as well as bookshop business to attend to, and she would only be bored. She had known that she would not be – she could have gone to see the cathedral – but he had spoken with an air of finality, a tone of voice she recognized, which told her that he had taken his decision and did not want to discuss the subject any further. She'd felt a little

193

uneasy, had wondered if the personal business might concern a woman. He sometimes spoke with affection of an old friend in Orléans, known since youth, and referred to this person as 'she'. But she would be old, Amy reasoned, whilst she herself was young.

She had some time to wait before anything happened on the avenue Foch. First, the Picards' maid arrived, carrying a shopping bag with a baguette sticking out of the end, and shortly afterwards the curtains were drawn back on one side of the long window. Amy imagined Solange in a rose-coloured satin nightgown sitting up against a bank of lace-edged pillows, yawning, pushing back her long dark hair (though Amy found it difficult to picture her in disarray, without her chignon). Solange would be taking the breakfast tray, letting the maid settle it over her knees, asking what the weather was doing.

Amy's feet froze. She longed for a bowl of warm café au lait and a fresh flaky croissant that would melt on her tongue, topped by dark jam thick with currants.

Two hours later, Solange emerged, perfectly coiffed and made up, dressed in yet another expensive outfit – this time in egg-yolk yellow and black. She stopped on the pavement to appraise the sky and obviously decided to walk, in spite of the height of her heels.

Amy, who by then shifted her position from opposite the Picards' apartment to the corner of the rue Valéry, set off after her on leaden feet. Solange sauntered, her hips swinging from side to side; Amy longed to run, to get the blood pumping back into her feet. Solange strolled up to the top of the avenue, then cut across Victor Hugo, Kléber and Marceau to the Champs-Elysées. She looked like a woman with nothing particular to do, a casual boulevardier. She stopped to look in shop windows, she moved on. She did not once look back; if she had, she would have seen a woman in a fawn raincoat, hair obscured by a cinnamon-brown beret, wearing dark glasses. Amy's spying kit, Camille called it. ('Don't imagine I feel proud of this episode,' Amy said to me.) Halfway down the Champs-Elysées, Solange went into a café and settled herself in the glassed-in terrace, where she sat for a while drinking coffee and observing the crowds. Amy, stamping her feet behind a newsstand, began to regret her wasted day off. But when Solange rose Amy went too, drawn after her like an iron filing being dragged behind a magnet.

Solange turned right at the foot of the Champs into the avenue Montaigne. Amy began to feel now that she must have a target, some destination; she was walking more purposefully. She crossed the road and went into a brasserie on the corner of the rue Bayard. Amy saw through the glass a blurred shape – a man's – come forward to meet Solange. Their bodies merged, their heads bobbing from side to side in true French fashion as they exchanged double kisses, which could mean anything or nothing.

Amy had a further two hours of hanging around to contend with while they lunched. She walked past the window twice, saw their heads close together across the small table, talking, laughing. When she walked past the third time, she saw that the man had his hand on Solange's rounded, silken knee.

At half-past two, they appeared in the doorway of the brasserie. Solange took the man's arm casually and unself-consciously, and they turned into the rue Bayard. A few yards along they stopped to kiss, not the bobbing-about-type one as before. When they broke apart, Amy heard Solange's high curling laugh of anticipation.

They went to an apartment in the place François Premier, and there they remained for the rest of the afternoon.

'So, Aimée?' said Olivier. 'What am I supposed to do with this information?' He was cutting the pages of a new book (a rare object in the shop), and frowning with concentration.

'But don't you see – she's having an affair!'

'Yes, I do see.'

'But it changes everything, doesn't it?'

'Does it?'

'But if *she* has a lover, then – ' You can leave her, was that what Amy wanted to say? She did not finish the sentence.

She stared at Olivier. 'You knew about this man already, didn't you?'

He nodded imperceptibly.

'Does she know about me? *Does* she, Olivier?'

'Well, of course.' He laid down the knife. 'How else could I see so much of you? How could I have stayed with you in Auxerre for several nights? Now, don't get so excited, ma petite – '

'I am not your petite!' She ran from the shop without her coat or bag, round the corner to her flat, where she realized that she did not have her key. A neighbour let her into the building – it happened to be a rare occasion when the concierge had gone out – and she waited, shivering, on the landing until Camille returned home and took her into her flat and gave her hot coffee and cognac. Amy told her she was finished with Olivier.

'Un de perdu, dix de retrouvé!' said Camille.

'But I wasn't finished with him, of course,' said Amy. 'He came round later, and I couldn't resist him. He cared for me, I never really doubted that, but he wasn't going to rock the boat, be put out on his ear and have to pull himself up from the bootstraps or any such nonsense like that. Not at this stage in his life. They had an understanding, he and Solange. It was – wait for it! – "civilized"!'

I summoned the waiter, who came saying, 'Same again?' This was our third order.

'You've told me about her background,' I said, 'but nothing about his.'

'I never knew much; somehow I never needed to. He had some sort of connections in Orléans, apart from the old friend. For me he was Olivier Picard, a man complete in himself without any need to be defined by details of family background. He appeared uncluttered by the past. Unlike myself! Wherever I went I carried with me my twin poles of Edinburgh and Saint-Sauveur, swinging between them, unable ever quite to forget either.'

'How long did it last, your affair?'

'Four years.'

Amy came to terms with the situation, to accept that it would not change, although she admitted that a part of her, half-submerged, still hoped that it might; but by the time it did, it was too late.

Christmases were the worst times for her, and holidays, especially the long summer one. The shop was closed for the month of August and the Picards went to a villa near Cannes – the only exception being 1947, the year Jessie, my mother and I went to Paris. Solange had had a family complication that year, a niece's wedding or some such thing, and so they had closed for July instead. Otherwise I might never have seen Olivier Picard and caught that glimpse of Amy vanishing in the rue de Seine.

During Augusts thereafter, Amy wandered around Paris, trying not to appear forlorn; she had no desire to be an object of pity. Her pride ruled that out. Throughout her life she hated receiving sympathy. She was perfectly happy, she told Camille; she liked having time to herself. She frequented the bouquin-istes, was building up her collection of Colette in different editions. She walked in the Luxembourg Garden and in the Bois, lay under the trees, read, waited for September, and when it came breathed a sigh of relief, like most other Parisians, that life was returning to normal. One summer, she left the city with everybody else and went down to Burgundy, where she stayed with Uncle Robert and Aunt Joséphine, but that proved a disaster. Robert Bussac made a pass at her, and even after being warned off was unable to keep his hands to himself.

Christmases, though shorter, were worse than the summers; it was the deadly quiet that descended on the city which she found so oppressive. Now that all her Paris relatives had gone, she had no one to visit. She would eat a solitary chicken breast with a solitary bottle of wine and go out and walk by the Seine, where she would pass all the other solitary Christmas-

197

day people shambling along with heads down, unwilling to raise their eyes and admit their loneliness.

Four Christmases came and went.

The shop door opened one afternoon. Amy was immediately on guard when she saw Solange; her visits were seldom without a purpose. Olivier was away.

'I think it's time we had a talk, you and I.' Solange dragged up the chair from the corner and seated herself. She let her fur coat fall back off her shoulders. She crossed her legs.

Amy waited.

'Actually, I think it's time this whole thing came to an end. Now don't ask me what thing! That would be a waste of time and terribly boring. I'm talking about you and Olivier.'

'But why?' It was all that Amy could manage to stammer out.

'It's gone on too long, that's why. They don't usually last so long.'

'They?'

'His other girls, of course. Come, come! You don't imagine you're the first, do you? Or the last?'

'Why not the last?' demanded Amy, becoming bold.

'Don't tell me you foresee a permanent arrangement with Olivier? Living together? Why not? Are you going to ask again? I'll tell you why not: he has a good life with me. It would not be matched with you.'

'You're talking about material things.'

'Indeed. We have a comfortable home.'

'There are other places to live than the avenue Foch.'

'I'm sure. Fifth-floor flats out at Clignancourt, at the end of the line. Can you see Olivier living in such a place, coming in on the Métro every day to sell cravates over the counter in a department store?'

'He needn't sell cravates.'

'I own the lease of this shop.'

'You think you hold all the cards, don't you?'

'Most of them. And you're not so young any more that you

can imagine love in a garret with him. He would crumble to dust before your eyes. He would cease to be the man that you love.'

'I do love him,' cried Amy.

'I am aware of that. And that is why, more than anything else, it has got to stop.'

'They say money talks,' said Amy, 'but that's an understatement. Money screams and yells and grinds you into dust under its heel. Lack of it, anyway. It's the one thing that seems always to have been missing from my life. Due to misfortune or mismanagement?' She looked at her watch. 'Goodness, is that the time? We've been here for hours! Pascal will be wondering what's happened to me.'

I had forgotten Pascal.

Nine

I dress my wound, and nurse it in a
sheltered place.

Claudine en ménage

Amy came to Sunday lunch with the family. I asked if she
would like to bring Pascal, but she said no, not this time. He
could take in a few shows on the Festival Fringe. My husband
was abroad, on business, but everyone else was there – the
children, Aunt Nan, my father and Jessie. The children were
bemused by this strange woman, a new aunt they'd never
heard of. Auntie Amy. Amy preferred to have no prefix. My
daughter Vinca tried to climb up on to her lap at the table and
was firmly rejected. I saw straight away that Amy was not at
ease with small children, nor was she interested in them. She
was irritated by their claims for attention (as I often was
myself) and looked annoyed when one of them cut across our
conversation. She had been good with me as a child, had
shown great patience, but she was forty now, and in the last
twenty years would probably have had few dealings with the
world of the very young which, it must be admitted, can be
trying.

Vinca sought solace instead with Aunt Nan, who even in
old age was marvellous with small children. She'd become a
kind of Pied Piper figure in the district; one seldom saw her
without a number of children in her wake, and it was not just
for the dolly mixtures and penny chews in her pocket that
they followed her. She had time for them. She cuddled them

when they were miserable. She told stories plucked from the air. She'd put up her hand and snatch one. 'There,' she'd say, 'I've got one. Will we see what it is?' She'd squat on a step right there, wherever she happened to be, and the children would gather round; they'd lean against her, thumbs in mouths, wide-eyed. Her stories were not about once-upon-a-time, they were about now. Elves lived in the basements of St Stephen Street, kelpies played in the Water of Leith. She walked the children along the river-bank. They all saw the kelpies. 'We did so see them,' they told me, and I believed them.

Jessie thought I shouldn't let Aunt Nan take the children down by the river. 'They're only wee and she's half daft. She wouldn't notice if they were to go too near the edge.' But in spite of being an anxious mother, understanding only too well Sido standing in the doorway of her daughter's darkened room watching while she slept, I had faith in Aunt Nan and her protective instincts. She was whispering a story in Vinca's ear now.

'Well, Amy, it's good to see you again,' said Jessie, folding her arms under her pouter-pigeon bosom. Over the years she had changed shape; she'd plumped out and her neck seemed to have shortened but she still liked to 'get dolled up' and enjoy herself. Her hair, teased and lacquered in bouffant-style, looked like a marmalade-coloured bird's nest. It was seldom the same colour two weeks running. 'Though I must say we thought you'd gone for good. You never wrote.'

'I know, I should have . . .'

'So what's brought you back now?' It was my father who barged straight in to ask the question that I had myself been longing to ask.

'I met a man from Edinburgh at the Scots Kirk in Paris. He'd been to see my show. He said, "You should come to the Edinburgh Festival, you'd go down great!" So here I am!' Amy smiled. She was skilled in evasion.

'You're different,' said Jessie. 'Look who's talking! We're none of us getting any younger, eh, James?' She dunted my father in the side with her elbow. He was reaching out for the red wine, of which he would drink deeply and then, after lunch, subside into an armchair with the newspaper and snore. Jessie was fifteen years younger than he was and had plenty of energy in her yet. She continued to run her hair-dressing salon, working in it most days herself, though she didn't hesitate to take an afternoon off to go to Bingo. She went to dog-race meetings at Meadowbank with a neighbour (winning more than she lost) and frequented various cocktail bars with my father, when he would go with her, and some of her 'girl' friends when he would not. Sometimes, while Aunt Nan baby-sat, Jessie and I would pass an hour or two drinking gin and tonic in a hotel cocktail bar up town. She relaxed me. And I liked to hear tales from the salon and dog track.

'Aye, I wouldn't have known you, Amy,' said my father.

'She looks like Colette,' I told them.

Jessie twisted her neck to look at the silver-framed photograph on the mantelpiece. 'I suppose you could say there's a likeness. It's no a bad snap, considering it was my old Box Brownie that took it.'

Amy got up to examine the photograph, then she looked at me. 'Did *you* take that?'

'Yes, on our visit to Paris in 1947.'

'You went to see her?'

'We thought we might get news of you from her,' I said defensively. Did I need to be defensive? I sensed that Amy regarded Colette as her own personal territory.

She held the frame between her hands. 'It's good. You've caught the intensity of her gaze. I'm sorry I never thought to take one of her myself.'

There was a hint in that remark which I chose to ignore.

The children were restless; they'd had to wait while we had pre-lunch drinks. The boys were squabbling over a marble. I told them to stop. 'Not at the table, please! You know you shouldn't have marbles at the table. Now give it to me!' After a few seconds of direct confrontation the marble was surrendered; it was spun towards me across the table. It glanced off the soup tureen and hit me in the middle of the chest. I glared at the sender and put the offensive glass ball into my pocket.

I served the carrot-and-tomato soup, overruling an objection about its contents.

'It's got that taste in it.'

'Coriander. Just eat it up and don't crumble your bread in that disgusting fashion!'

'How can you *eat* soup? It's liquid. You can only drink it.'

'He reminds me of you,' observed Jessie. 'When you were his age. Always got a come-back.'

Aunt Nan was singing 'Heigh ho, away we go, riding on a donkey,' and jiggling Vinca up and down on her knee. I tried to restrain them, to suggest they wait until later, when we had finished eating – after all, we had scarcely begun – but Aunt Nan was away in a world of her own and did not even hear me. It had been a mistake to invite Amy to lunch; I should have made it dinner, without the children. But that wouldn't have pleased my father, who had grown fussy in his old age and didn't like to eat late; he claimed he got indigestion and couldn't sleep. He was the only one eating now, oblivious of all else going on around him; he liked his food. Aunt Nan's song ended with Vinca folding up into convulsions of laughter, which made her knees jerk and knock against the table-edge. We held on to our plates. Amy, who was not geared up to family life, did not. Her soup plate skidded and its contents shot into her lap. Tomato stains badly.

Wringing a cloth out at the kitchen sink, I made a face at myself in the window. Kids! Families! There was something – a great deal – to be said for the life of a single, independent woman. Amy had told me she was living in the rue de Grenelle in the seventh arrondissement – an ideal quartier, she said, très sympathique, with its brasseries, charcuteries and pâtisseries. There was a wonderful mouth-watering fromagerie close by which sold cheeses from the Breton coast, the slopes of the Pyrenees, the hill villages of the Auvergne. And every morning she breakfasted at her corner café, read the papers, wrote letters, took telephone calls and chatted with the patron and other interesting (childless) people who patronized the place.

Vinca and Aunt Nan had followed me out to the kitchen. Vinca was crying and Aunt Nan was rocking her, saying, 'It's all right, lamb, it's all right. You didn't mean to, did you?' The two younger boys appeared to have abandoned the table and were sliding up and down the hall on the carpet runner. Jessie and my father had remained in the dining room, trying to mop up soup and console Amy. I lent her – gave her – a new, emerald-green, velvet corduroy skirt I had bought only the day before.

After we'd eaten, Aunt Nan decided to take the children to the swings at Inverleith Park. She wound around her neck a green and white scarf that she'd found tied to the railings in St Stephen Street.

'Is that a Hibs scarf you've got on, Nan?' demanded my father, sitting up and taking notice. He was a lifelong Hearts supporter.

'Leave her alone, James!' said Jessie. 'What if it is?'

'I like green and white,' said Aunt Nan, stroking the scarf.

'Pape's colours,' snorted my father.

'Nothing changes,' said Amy, looking amused for the first time she'd arrived at the house.

With the scarf, Aunt Nan was wearing a none-too-clean pink blouse and a brown skirt she'd cobbled up from chenille curtains. It came down to her ankles. On her head she had a knitted tea-cosy that was pretending to be a strawberry.

'What a ticket she looks!' said Jessie, as Aunt Nan led her charges out.

'Mind the swings don't hit you on the head!' I called after them. 'Watch how you go down the shute!' I felt my warnings acted as some kind of charm, that if I failed to voice them disaster might strike.

'They're a handful, that bunch,' said Jessie as their voices dwindled into the distance. 'I must say I wouldne have had the patience for all yon myself. How's about you, Amy?'

Amy shook her head and took a gulp of wine. She was

twitchy; her hand shook as she lit a cigarette. I presumed she was still upset about the soup and the fate of her skirt, which was now soaking in a basin of cold water in the kichen. When one is used to the spills and disruptions of family fortune, it is easier to take these small upheavals with equanimity.

We drank our coffee in peace and Jessie and Amy smoked. It seemed almost eerily quiet in the room with the children gone. Part of my mind went with them, saw Vinca climbing on to a swing, Aunt Nan pushing, the hard tarmac below. Amy was telling Jessie something of her life in Paris. Jessie said she'd always wanted to go back, she had fond memories of the city. 'I met an awfy nice bloke.' She glanced over at my father, whose eyelids were going through that stage when they alternately droop and fly violently open before they finally give up the struggle. 'He was called Raymond.' Jessie said it French-style, and a little wistfully.

'Why don't you come over and visit me?' said Amy.

I slipped out to the kitchen to clear up and by the time I'd finished both my father and Jessie were asleep in armchairs on either side of the living-room fireplace. Amy and I went for a walk in the Botanic Garden.

'It can't have been easy for you,' I said, 'after you broke up with Olivier. I suppose you lost everything – the job, the flat . . .'

'And *him*. Don't forget him! That was the biggest loss of all. I seem to have a capacity for losing things. Whereas you appear to gather them round you.'

'Perhaps it's because I write; I hold on to the strings. Or try to.'

We seated ourselves on a bench in front of the sculpture garden, where we were able to regard the wide-angled view of Edinburgh. We let our eyes travel over the city's spires and rooftops and its castle battlements.

'I did consider coming back at that point,' said Amy, 'only fleetingly, though. I seemed to have thrown my lot in with Paris for better or worse.'

'You were back to square one, I suppose?'

'Except that I did have a little money this time. I let Solange buy me off. Don't look so priggish! What would you have done? I looked on it as redundancy money. But only *after* I'd begged him to come and live in a garret with me. I recognized the truth of what Solange had said, but it didn't stop me trying to hang on to him.'

'What *about* him?'

'He was distressed. Oh yes, he was! We'd been close to one another for four years, after all.'

Amy left Paris for a few weeks then and went travelling – she had to get out of the city. She visited the Roman arena at Arles, the Pope's palace at Avignon, Daudet's mill, the asylum where Van Gogh cut off his ear, saw superimposed on top of all these sights the image of a man's face with intelligent brown eyes and dark hair broken by a streak of white. She tried to let a man with blue eyes pick her up on a café terrace in Arles, went to the toilet, looked at herself in the cracked mirror, saw Olivier's face split from ear to ear, and slipped out the back way.

She returned to Paris.

'Don't go near the rue de Seine,' warned Camille, who was preparing to marry a banker and lead a provincial life in Rouen.

Amy could not face going to their wedding. Camille was to have four bridesmaids and the celebrations would last two days.

Amy wandered about Paris looking vaguely for a job. She rented a room in the thirteenth arrondissement near the place d'Italie. It was a cold, wet spring, with rain, sleet and wind persisting until May Day. And when the sun did break through it only increased her restlessness. She had money enough to last for a few months.

She heeded Camille's advice and gave the area around the rue de Seine a wide berth, the bouquinistes also. Once she saw Olivier in the distance coming towards her; shocked, she turned and ran the other way. When she rounded the corner she was sick in the gutter. She went to visit Colette, who told her that one died only of the first man and that resurrection was possible.

'I recovered!'

Maurice Goudeket, standing at the foot of her 'raft', smiled.

'But I suffered first,' said Colette.

Amy took a job as a receptionist at a small hotel near the Luxembourg Garden. The work was not arduous but the shifts were long; she worked twelve hours a day, six days a week. The hotel was run with minimum staff. When she fnished her shift or had a day off the patron took over the desk. His wife served the breakfasts in the cramped, dark dining room and helped the maid clean the rooms.

Amy's reception area was small, too, and poky, squashed into a corner of the gloomy entrance hall. She sat on a high stool behind a high brown desk and answered the telephone and handed over keys and gave out information on the tourist attractions of Paris. (She had got the job because she could speak English.) She felt like a robot, plugged in every morning, which then began to perform. *Emerging from the Métro, turn left for the Eiffel Tower* . . . It was a period in her life when it suited her to be a robot. In the evenings she went back to her room at the place d'Italie; the job did not come with accommodation. The patron was not prepared to sacrifice the income from a room.

Visitors came and went, arriving often in a taxi driven by a Hungarian called Janos, who spoke some English and whom the patron engaged to convey les américains et les anglais (which encompassed, of course, les écossais, les irlandais et les gallois) to and from the Gare du Nord. Janos was a man in his late thirties, small, brown-haired. ('Not noticeable in a crowd,' said Amy, 'not like Olivier.') At the end of the war, he had found himself near Leipzig and, following the partition of Germany, had moved westward with the great flux of refugees fleeing from the Soviet-controlled East. He missed his family in Hungary: elderly parents, brothers, sisters, aunts, uncles. Here, he was on his own. He had once been married, while still a student, but his wife had left him after a year and he was now divorced. He had been trained as a lawyer, but his qualifications were not recognized, of course, in France. These things Amy learned about him in idle moments of exchange over the top of the high brown desk while he waited for the next set of customers to emerge from the lift, lugging their suitcases behind them. The hotel did not run to a porter and the patron considered himself above such menial duties.

'So we are both refugees,' said Janos. 'DPs.'

'I belong here.' Amy bridled a little.

'But a part of you has been displaced and left behind, has it not? You know what I am talking about. The part in the centre of you that never quite settles.'

They spoke in English together, if only to keep the patronne guessing.

'Not that we had anything to hide,' said Amy. 'He was free. I was free. Technically, at least. I would not say emotionally. We started to go out together, to the cinema and for cheap meals, walks along the Seine and so forth. Then, one day, he asked me to marry him.'

'You said *yes*?'

'We weren't in love with each other or anything like that. We were both lonely. People marry for worse reasons; everybody knows that.'

'But it didn't last?'

'Getting on for four years. Temperamentally we were rather alike – inclined to flare up.' She grinned. 'So our relationship was pretty tempestuous, unlike mine with Olivier. Olivier was always able to calm me down. He balanced me out. I suppose my marriage to Janos might have survived if I hadn't been so stupid.'

They found a two-roomed apartment with a bathroom in the little rue de Commaille, off the rue du Bac, not far from the

Hôtel Matignon and other seats of power. They were lucky; a friend of Janos's knew the landlord, another Hungarian émigré, who allowed them to have it for a moderate rent. Their one-sided street overlooked a small square; from their windows they could enjoy the hawthorn and cherry trees in blossom and flowers in their season, and on sunny days Amy sat on the seats beside the elderly men and the young mothers chatting to one another and watching their children play. It had a very local feel to it, the little park. Amy loved the seventh arrondissement, on the left bank of the river but away from the more touristy streets of the sixth. This was the area in which she was to come to feel finally at home.

She set about making a home for herself and Janos out of their small flat. Olivier had given her a taste for good things. She spent hours rummaging in brocantes and at the flea market out at Clignancourt; she'd given up the hotel job because of the inconvenient hours. She bought for little money art nouveau and art deco lamps, oriental rugs, fine bone china and small, beautifully made pieces of furniture, which she renovated when she brought them home. She had an eye for a bargain, could spot something shining in a dusty, cluttered corner. Janos admired her flair, suggested she go into business, try buying and selling. But the idea did not appeal to her. She could buy only if she fell in love with an object, and then she wouldn't want to sell it. She flung herself into the creation of a home with the passion of someone conducting a love affair. She washed and dried the china lovingly, polished the silver frames of the art nouveau mirrors, cleaned the apartment windows until they sparkled, kept the fire burning brightly in the grate and cooked appetizing meals for the return of her husband, the breadwinner.

She even baked bread. It must be in her blood, she said. It made her feel peaceful: setting out the bowls on the table, sifting the flour, kneading the dough, and then there was the smell . . .

'Welcome to the Boulangerie Bussac!' she would say when Janos came in. 'The Paris branch!'

209

Janos smiled. He liked home-baked bread and appetizing food, a fire glowing at his feet and beautiful objects shining in its light; and Amy enjoyed his enjoyment. It was years since he'd felt so comfortable, he said. She understood.

When they could afford it, they'd go out, to the cinema or the theatre, which they both enjoyed. Sometimes customers would give Janos free tickets. He'd come in waving the ticket and say, 'Come on, get your coat on, we're going out!' That was the way Amy liked to live, impulsively. They were companionable, she and Janos. He liked to read and to listen to music also. In many ways it was a good life. They managed financially and could afford small treats. And they had a number of Hungarian friends whom they entertained. They would play music and eat Hungarian food (cooked by Janos) and the Hungarians reminisced about the good old days.

'All very cosy,' said Amy, with an attempt at sounding disparaging. It did not quite come off.

'Doesn't sound too bad.'

She shrugged, avoided my gaze. I couldn't expect her to give me a complete picture of her marriage, I knew that; she was making her own selections.

'You didn't go out to work, then?'

'I bought a second-hand typewriter and did typing at home – students' theses, the odd literary manuscript.'

'Wasn't it a rather lonely life working by yourself during the day?'

'What about you? You work at home.'

'But I have the children.'

'I had Paulette.'

Paulette was an American who lived in the flat below Amy. She was twenty-one years old and a student at the Sorbonne, supposed to be studying French language and literature, but her real interest lay in the theatre. She didn't often go to classes. 'No point, not with ten thousand other people there, half of them asleep.' She'd go to hear someone interesting, such as Sartre. She planned to go on the stage when she returned to the States – to New York, of course, not Milwaukee, which was where she hailed from. She'd had bit parts back home, mostly in amateur productions, and on one occasion had played the lead. She had portrayed the crippled Laura in *The Glass Menagerie*. She talked about Broadway and off-Broadway and off-that. She talked about Miller and O'Neill – he was the greatest in her book – and Tennessee Williams, as well as Anouilh and Asimov, Sartre, Gide and Cocteau. She spent most of her allowance, once she'd paid the rent, on theatre tickets. She took Amy with her to the Théâtre Marigny – they saw Cocteau's *Bacchus* there – and to Le Petit Marigny, the Renaud–Barrault workshop, and at another small theatre, the Théâtre de Babylone on the boulevard Raspail, they saw *En attendant Godot*, the Irishman Beckett's, which was hailed as one of the most stimulating pieces of theatre for years.

Paulette would come bouncing up the stairs, to disturb Amy as she sat slumped over her typewriter. Paulette's enthusiasm for the stage began to infect Amy and to bring back her own stirrings of desire to act. But, at twenty-six, she felt she'd missed the boat.

'Don't be ridiculous! There's more than one sailing. It's never too late.'

'But what would I do? Where would I begin?'

'Right here in Paris. Where else? The theatre's alive! This is a great era in the theatre. And you speak French, don't you?'

'Yes, but – '

'Look, you've got to have faith. You've got to have commitment. What you want to do is cultivate your mind and train your talents.'

Paulette decided to go to work on Amy. 'Look at your posture! Come on, straighten up, get rid of that hump. But don't arch the back of your neck! Your body's your instrument, never forget that! So is your voice. You've got to tune them, like a car engine. What do you think a car engine would be like if it wasn't tuned? It would stick, right? Splutter! Stall!' Paulette had picked up bits and pieces of theories here

211

and there, but Stanislavski and Strasberg were her main influences. She was into The Method.

They embarked on a programme of daily work-outs. They'd do deep breathing and then limber up with physical exercises: mobility was the key. 'Feet and ankles, fingers and wrists, every part's important. You've got to keep them mobile.' After that they had vocal exercises. The noises they made resembled those of a sick cat caterwauling, and brought the neighbour from across the landing to pound on the door. He was a retired policeman; he knew how to pound. So then they'd do something quieter, like ululating the Buddhist 'Ohm', letting it resonate in their heads until their ears sang. Or they'd exercise their lips with tongue-twisters. The Leith police dismisses us. 'Some things you can't escape,' said Amy.

Then they'd work on their emotions. 'Your husband has just told you he's leaving you for another woman. React!'

Paulette and Janos did not get on very well together. She thought him moody, which he was; he considered her brash, which she may have been. Amy accused him of prejudice and facile judgement. They often argued over Paulette. He'd come home after a heavy day at the wheel, having been snarled up in traffic, abused by customers, shortchanged by his boss, to find that his dinner wasn't ready. Paulette had been in and she and Amy had been 'tuning their instruments'. He had picked up some of Paulette's jargon and taunted Amy with it. 'That bitch!' He threw a pottery vase filled with violets at the wall; on another occasion a jug full of milk. Amy remembered with a shudder the violence of her father.

'I knew he did it out of frustration, but that's not a great deal of help when you're the target of the wrath. In his country he'd been a lawyer, someone held in respect. In Paris he was a nobody, frequently at the receiving end of abuse.' Amy turned up her collar. A lively breeze had sprung up in the Botanic Garden but we were loath to get up and lose our view of the city. 'Paulette was a good topic for us to argue over.'

'But she wasn't the reason your marriage failed?'

'Hell, no. In a way it was all a bit of a game, for me – The Method, and all that. I didn't really expect to take up an acting career, not then. But it was to stand me in good stead later. No, I was still centred in my home, for the one and only time of my life!'

'So what did bring your marriage to an end? Anything specific?'

'Oh yes! The return of Olivier into my life.'

At the end of 1953, when Amy's marriage was three years old, she bumped into Olivier in a local pâtisserie-cum-charcuterie. He was buying bread, an individual-sized quiche Lorraine and a tub of mushrooms à la grecque. Amy stared at him and his purchases. She had never known him to go food-shopping. And what was he doing in her area?

The shop was also a salon de thé and had four small tables at one side.

'Would you like some tea?' he asked.

They sat down.

'Pâtisserie?'

She shook her head.

A girl brought the tea. They stared at one another across the table.

'I'm living in the rue Vaneau,' he said.

'Which side?'

'The left.'

'Your back windows must look into the garden of the Matignon?'

'They do.'

They sipped their tea.

'Solange?' asked Amy.

Solange had fallen in love. Dramatically and absolutely, with a young poet. She wanted to dedicate her life to him. she had taken him into the avenue Foch and had bought Olivier his apartment in the rue Vaneau. She had also made the shop over into his name.

*

'She seems to be good at buying people off,' I commented.

'That was only fair – she couldn't have consigned him to the garret at Clignancourt.'

'Especially after having scuppered his love affair!'

'He asked me to have dinner with him the following evening. Just dinner, I told myself, that can't hurt; I wanted to catch up with what had been happening to him. What *was* happening to him. We went to a small discreet restaurant in a side street. You know the kind – ill-lit, with guttering candles and half-curtains in beige velour that conceal the interior from nosy passers-by, run by madame whose husband is the chef. I didn't go back with Olivier to his apartment that evening, though I wanted to, but I did the next time. I couldn't resist it, I was still in love with him – stupid fool that I was!'

Paulette provided cover for Amy's occasional meetings with Olivier, with some reluctance. Okay, she could see the attraction of Olivier, but if Janos were ever to find out he'd blow a fuse and probably blast Amy straight out of the window into the street. Was that what she wanted? 'You've got to ask yourself that, honey. You've got a lot to lose.' Of course it wasn't what she wanted, said Amy; Paulette was just being melodramatic. Janos needn't find out. She'd be careful. She didn't intend to throw over her marriage for Olivier. She still remembered that he had not done it for her. She met him in his apartment mostly, once or twice in the shop in the rue de Seine.

On one occasion, coming out of the bookshop, Janos's taxi swerved past her at the kerb. He saw her, braked, and backed up. He wound down the window and she was obliged to stoop to speak to him. He glanced past her at the bookshop.

'What are you doing up this end?'

'Looking for a book.'

He knew about Olivier; she had told him about her affair in those early days of chatting over the top of the high desk in the hotel near the Luxembourg Garden when there had been no reason not to tell him. She could not remember whether or not she had said where the bookshop was.

A car was honking; Janos's cab was holding up the traffic. 'All right, all right! See you later,' he said to Amy.

She would have to be more cautious from now on. She thought she could detect Janos's eyes watching her, when he thought she wasn't looking, and that he had been through her books and papers. She kept a journal but had written nothing about Olivier in it, or nothing that anyone else would be able to decipher. For a week or two she stayed away from Olivier, but when she heard his voice on the phone her legs trembled and her resolve weakened.

In the early spring he asked Amy to go away with him for a week. 'Just seven days, Aimée! So that we can have some uninterrupted time together. Arrange it – try to!' He'd rented a small villa in an orange grove near Antibes.

'You've got to decide what you're going to do,' said Paulette. 'You can't go on running two men. You're no Solange!'

'Help me,' pleaded Amy.

'Well, all right, but just this once more!'

Paulette was due to travel south to meet some American friends in Provence. She spoke to Janos. 'Amy needs a holiday,' she told him. Amy had recently had flu and been slow to pick up. Even Janos had been declaring himself worried about her. He agreed that Amy should go to Provence with Paulette.

'A winter cooped up in the apartment seems to have sapped her energy,' he said.

I couldn't really see what the problem was. Why hadn't Amy just left Janos – the marriage was obviously not working that well – and gone off with Olivier?

'It seems that you didn't love Janos, but you did love Olivier?'

'But I was married to Janos, and that meant something. There was a bond between us. We'd set up a life together, put effort into it. And most of the time everything was fine, in

215

spite of our spats. We were dependent on each other for many things. Walking out on something like that isn't easy. After all, it was the first proper home I'd had since I left Edinburgh.' Amy corrected herself. 'Before my mother left Edinburgh.'

I nodded.

'Anyway, I went away with Olivier. A week, I told myself, to steal out of time: that isn't much. You know how we can delude ourselves? I suppose we want to try to minimize the cost.

'The house near Antibes was beautiful. The site was spectacular, the furnishings exquisite, the weather perfect. We breakfasted on the verandah overlooking the blue, blue sea and the smell of thyme and lavender mingled with the perfume of the orange blossom! At night you could hear the cicadas, and the nights were good – '

'But?'

'Yes, there was a but.'

Amy had changed since the early days of her relationship with Olivier; she was now twenty-eight years old, had lived through difficult times and been married, but not to someone who expected to dominate her life and tell her what to think. Janos preferred her to have a mind of her own, in spite of the fact that he ranted against Paulette and the 'antics' they got up to. Whereas Olivier still thought of himself as her mentor and guide. He expected to take all the decisions. He was surprised when she challenged his actions or held opinions different from his own.

One evening, dining by candlelight, eating a daube provençale which she had spent the afternoon preparing while Olivier read Mallarmé, she remarked that the wine – a Beaune – was a little sharp.

'Don't be silly, Aimée,' he reproved her gently. 'After all, what do you – '

'Know about wine? I have taste buds, don't I? They may only be semi-educated but they are allowed to have a reaction.'

216

She spoke more sharply than she might otherwise have done if it had not been that they'd had a mild disagreement earlier, when he had cut her down over Simone de Beauvoir's *Le Deuxième Sexe*. He had said that she would do better to spend her time reading something worthwhile. 'What do you want to read a book like that for when there are so many great books waiting for you? She's full of hot wind, that woman!' 'I find her interesting.' 'And what of interest do you think she has to say?' 'That a woman's limitations are due to society. That they have been imposed upon her.' 'Simplistic!' 'She has more to say than that, much more! How can I condense a whole book into a sentence? Anyway, *I* think it's thoughtful and scholarly. She *is* a scholar of note. *And* of importance in the literary world.' 'On what do you base your judgement?' he had asked.

The relationship had begun to curdle. Like milk left in a warm room, said Amy: it goes off almost imperceptibly in the beginning, so that one cannot be sure it is turning, and then gradually the smell becomes stronger and there is no doubt left. I couldn't help wondering – though this naturally I did not voice – if there might not be some sort of perverse streak in Amy, so that when she could have what she wanted she no longer wanted it. But I thought *that* might be too simplistic.

Amy left early on the morning of the fourth day and travelled back to Paris by train. She arrived in the rue de Commaille to find Janos gone. He'd returned to Hungary. He had sometimes spoken about going home but usually in moments of despondency, after a tiresome day at work, and she had never taken him seriously. Go back and live under that regime? She never heard from him again. Two years later there was the uprising; she didn't even know if he had survived.

'So I lost my home and everything in it! The concierge told me he'd come back in a blue van *two hours* after I'd set off for Provence with Paulette and loaded it up with mirrors, lamps, rugs, record player, records – the lot! He'd obviously planned

217

it before I went. He'd left my personal possessions with the concierge along with a note. Looking back I realized how preoccupied he had been in those last few weeks. He said in the note that he'd known for some time that I'd been meeting Olivier and that I'd gone off with him. So I guess you could say I deserved it.' Amy's hand shook as she tried to light a cigarette in the wind. She kept her head turned away from me.

She hadn't been able to believe he'd gone until the concierge had opened up the flat and let her walk through the cold, empty rooms. On the walls there were marks where the pictures and mirrors had hung, and in the grate, dead ashes.

Amy stayed with Paulette for a short time, but she had to get away from the street and the proximity to the rue Vaneau.

'What happened to Olivier?' I asked.

'Solange's poet lasted only a year, then she and Olivier got back together again. I saw them earlier this year, sitting together on a terrace on the Champs-Elysées. His hair had gone completely white but hers was as jet-black as ever, and she crossed her legs with the same unselfconscious air of flamboyance. She was telling him a story; he was listening intently with his head inclined. Then they laughed together. He still has his shop in the rue de Seine but I make a point of never going past.'

Amy went back to life in a squalid room. 'I had no money to do anything else. That was the worst time of my life, so bad that I'll just skip over it if you don't mind.'

I did not question her then – there was so much to learn about her life – but the following year, when I was staying with her in Paris, I brought it up again. I had been thinking about it: this gap in her life which she was reluctant to fill in. It was late at night, we had been talking intimately, and had drunk many glasses of full-bodied red Burgundy.

'What happened, Amy?' I asked gently. 'After your marriage broke up? What happened to you?'

She gazed into her glass, then tilted it and drank. She reached again for the bottle. Her hand was unsteady.

For a while we sat in silence listening to the soft swish of rain falling in the courtyard, then with a sigh Amy got up and went to her bureau. She opened the drawer and took out a large notebook.

'My journal of the time!' she said, and tossed it into my lap, making me jump. 'Read it, for what it's worth, then burn it!'

I do not throw things away lightly, let alone burn them, especially when they concern the written word, so I took the journal back with me to Edinburgh, read it and put it away in a drawer.

Now, twenty-five years later, after Amy has disappeared, I bring it out and take another look at it.

'You know,' I say to Jessie, 'I never really understood why Amy was *so* devastated by the loss of Janos. When she lost Olivier the first time – with whom she was passionately in love – she didn't fly apart.'

'Things build up. You never know when they're going to get too much. It's like the hairline crack in the teacup. You go on drinking out of it and then one day it just comes apart in your hands!'

Jessie and I decide to read again the journal of Amy's breakdown, in search of a clue, any clue.

1 May 1954

May Day. Aren't you supposed to get up and see the sun rise? I did once, in Edinburgh, on Arthur's Seat, with my young cousin, many suns ago. The sun never rises here: from my bed I can see the courtyard wall. Stones. Grey stones.

I wake in the morning to a feeling of doom. That is my mood: backwards and forwards. Small things bemuse me. I turn small words around in my head for long stretches of time. Mood. Doom.

Here I lie in a seamy room on the outer edge of the

city. It is not all picturesque, this city, or touristique. Paris by Night tours do not come here. Turn left for the Eiffel Tower. Why not take a break from sightseeing and stroll through the cool shady Bois de Boulogne, so beloved of artists picnicking on the grass, talking about Art, and ladies walking small dogs? Why not indeed?

I see myself trapped in the outer seam of a vast, widely flung garment, amongst the other detritus – the fluff, the crumbs, the dead cells. I have sought it out deliberately, I daresay. Yes, I dare to say it. I admit that I wanted to get as far away from the city centre as possible, to go to the outer edge.

'It's no wonder she had a breakdown,' says Jessie. 'Lying in her bed, feeling sorry for herself.'

'You'd almost think she was punishing herself,' I say. 'But I suppose you can read into it whatever you want to read into it.'

May, still

I wake to grey light in the room. It's raining outside, out there in the world. I can hear the soft hiss of the rain as it falls between the buildings. Water is spouting from the broken gutter. After a while I get up, put on my dressing-gown and slippers, and grope my way along the dark landing to the lavatory. My hand skids on the greasy wall. Odours of cooking float up from the lower depths. The concierge is stewing grey fish-heads for her cats. She is grey, too, she speaks with a grey tongue, but it is not her fault. I suspect she was born to greyness. One of the cats – the ginger one with the crafty face and torn ear, victor of many courtyard battles – slinks past me, crouching low, his fur brushing against my bare ankles. The feel of his fur makes me shiver. I shiver easily. His belly trails on the torn grey linoleum. Everything is grey. Grey is the colour of my true love's hair . . .

I no longer have a true love. Or anyone to love.

I lean over the banister rail to watch the ginger cat go whisking down the stairs, bushy tail held high like a squirrel's. I remember the squirrels in the Botanic Garden in Edinburgh running up the trees, sitting on their haunches eating the nuts Aunt Nan and I had brought them. Only they were grey. Edinburgh seems light years away, like some country on the other side of a vast misty sea. I can't see even a trace of the shoreline.

Back in the room, I stand by the door. Time seems to have ceased. If I could move, it might move too. But there is nowhere to go: I am in a dead end. There is nowhere even to pace, except for a few feet of grey carpet.

Now this will not do! I can hear Paulette's voice in my ear. You've got to do something! Move! Walk to the window and turn, to the door and turn, back to the window. How many seconds have passed? Ten? Two? There is nothing to see at the window except a blank wall (grey). With rain falling. Falling . . . I do not need to record the colour of rain.

June
Can it be June? Does it matter?

I have such a feeling of emptiness. I'm hollow, like a gourd. Tap me and you'll hear the hollowness.

My hands are empty . . . I don't know what to do with my hands . . . except smoke. I am going up in smoke. Blue smoke. Hazy smoke. I wish I could . . . go up in smoke. It looks so effortless drifting its way up there towards the ceiling from the red-hot tip glowing between my two clenched fingers.

It is hot and airless in this room. The window is stuck. It can't be budged. I can't breathe . . .

Go out, for Christ sake! I hear Paulette's voice buzzing in my ear like a bluebottle. She is losing patience with me. And who would blame her?

221

'Aye, that's the trouble,' says Jessie. 'You lose patience with folk after a bit, if they willne help themselves. I'm with Paulette. I'd have told her to get the hell out of there, too!'

Paulette came yesterday. This is crazy living out here, she said. She's right: I can see the craziness of it. Look, she said, I know you've had a hard time and been through hell, but you can't let yourself go down the drain. The drains are blocked, I tell her. Can't you smell them?

Paulette doesn't live in the rue de Commaille any more; she's moved to a posher apartment on an île. Surrounded by water. But she's got a man called Luke to help keep her afloat. He's from New York, though she met him in Saint-Tropez. They fell in love: that's what she said. Head over. Amongst the thyme and lavender. He's a 'theatrical' lawyer. That means his clients are mainly theatre people. Lawyers like Luke are crazy about the theatre, says Paulette; they go to see every play, sit in at rehearsals, sometimes put up the backing money themselves. Directors manqués. We could all put manqué behind our names, couldn't we? Paulette didn't like me saying that. You've got to snap out of it, she said, and snapped her fingers, like that! There is no snap in my fingers. When Paulette goes back to New York she's going to live with Luke. He's got a wife over there but he's going to get rid of her. Paulette says she'll do all right, though, don't go wasting your sympathy on her; she'll get alimony.

I met Luke before I came to live out here on the outer edge. I like Luke. Yes, I really do. I like Luke a lot. In spite of his throwing off his wife like an old coat. He's been kind to me. He sent me fruit with Paulette yesterday. Oranges, bananas, peaches. Their bright colours look ludicrous in my grey room. They burn my eyes. I can't bring myself to skin them — my flesh creeps at the thought — let alone bite into them. Luke is very kind to Paulette, too, he buys her flowers. He *spoils* her, she says, and she laughs. They go to the theatre nearly every evening and afterwards he takes her out for dinner and then they go back in a cab to their posh flat on the Île Saint-Louis and they have a nightcap and he tells her he loves her. Meet me in Saint-Louis, Louis, I sang to her yesterday. But she didn't think I was funny.

'I mind seeing that at the Grand,' says Jessie. 'Judy Garland was great in it, wasn't she? Pity she had to end the way she did.'

Luke and Paulette took me to the theatre last night. They insisted. They came in a cab. Luke waited below with the engine running. Paulette dressed me up in her clothes. Now I'm like Paulette, I thought, I'll be all right. I'll pretend to be Paulette. But I had to come out halfway through the first act, right in the middle of a big scene. I started to cry, then I couldn't stop. I did try, I told Paulette I tried, God how I tried. So I had to leave. I had to say, Excusez-moi! Excusez-moi! Excusez-moi! and shuffle my way along the row, bumping into people's knees, knocking their programmes off their laps, trampling on their toes, and Luke and Paulette had to come behind me, saying, Pardon! Pardon! Pardon! The theatre-goers hissed as I went past. The noise swelled in my ears like the roar of a waterfall. I thought I was drowning. But I knew I was spoiling their fun. I began to cry again. The usherette glowered at me as she held the door open at arm's length to allow me to exit. A grown woman like me should know not to cry in public.

I tell Paulette and Luke they should give up on me. Paulette does not listen to me. She says she's not listening. She sticks her fingers in her ears.

Come and visit us, says Paulette on the telephone, which the concierge does not like me to use more than is absolutely necessary – that is, only if you think you're going to die or the building is about to go up in smoke. Come for brunch on Sunday, says Paulette. We always have a lazy day on Sundays, get up late, read the papers, eat eggs sunny-side up. The concierge is watching me through the slit of her door. I am standing in the hall with the receiver pressed hard up against my ear. Come on Sunday, says Paulette, speaking loud and clear, I'll send Luke for you, and puts down the phone.

The concierge's slit widens and she emerges. She says, What about the rent money? She is a rent-collector as well as a caretaker. I say: Tomorrow, I'll have it tomorrow. Guide's honour. I half-rise my hand. She says, DEMAIN ou DEHORS! She spells it out so that I will not misundertand. D-E-H-O-R-S. She makes a chopping movement with her hand. Comprenez? Demain est dimanche. Back in my room the refrain runs in my head; it runs and runs.

Luke comes for me. He comes in a shiny black car, which impresss the concierge. She has been about to open the grey maw of her mouth and say DEHORS! but now she gives me a squint-eyed look that says PLUS TARD! I get into the shiny car and Luke drives me through the streets, the Sunday streets, the quiet streets. He talks to me in a quiet voice. A soothing voice. He reminds me of Olivier. Luke is Paulette's guide and friend, an older man, a father-type figure and lover also. Everthing rolled into one. Useful, that.

Paulette serves brunch in their elegant black-and-white living room overlooking the river. She sits cross-legged on the thick white rug to eat, her plate balanced on her knees. She is wearing black velvet trousers and a white silk blouse. She has a black velvet ribbon in her hair. She tells funny stories, which make Luke laugh. She scolds me for not eating enough and I make another effort. Just try a few more spoonfuls of scrambled egg, there's a good girl. Someone else used to say that to me but I can't remember who. I'm getting too thin, Paulette says. I drink cup after cup of black coffee and smoke cigarette after cigarette.

After a while Luke excuses himself. He has work to do: he has to telephone New York. He makes deals. He goes into another room to make his deal. They have more than one room, more than two rooms. I am left with Paulette so that she can give me yet another pep-talk. I have just got to snap out of it. I have got to snap.

I ask Paulette if she can lend me money for the rent. I say I'll pay her back. She uncrosses her black velvet legs and gets up to fetch her purse. She stuffs notes into my hands, says I don't have to pay anything back.

Get a job, Paulette tells me. Work. Work's a great healer, the woman in the next room to mine tells me. She sells stockings in a department store and she's religious. Jesus hangs crucified against her freckled throat. She prays in church thrice daily. She confesses her sins. Now that appeals. I ask the woman what silk stockings have to do with the Holy Spirit and she tells me everything has to do with the Holy Spirit. Could be. She offers to pray for me and I say, okay, I don't mind if she prays. I remember praying in a church in Edinburgh where the candles flickered in front of the altar and the air was thick with the smell of incense. It was not St Stephen's parish Church of Scotland.

'You're telling me it wasn't!' says Jessie. 'You ken what Granny Balfour used to say about being an RC?'

'Amy was brought up Protestant, though.'

'Aye, well, that's as maybe! But I'm sure her mother was putting plenty other notions into her head.'

Paulette comes for me. She says, Get up, put on these clothes, comb your hair, we're going out to find a job. The job is for me, not her. She has Luke. I'm a student, she says impatiently.

As we come down the stairs the concierge opens her door. she doesn't speak. *She* knows and *I* know that I owe her two weeks' rent. So what is new? They say there is nothing new under the sun. When they made the atomic bomb, that was new, wasn't it?

Paulette takes me to a department store. She does the talking. The woman gives her a what's-the-matter-with-her-can't-she-talk? look. She gives me a look that says that I couldn't manage to sell a hot-water bottle to an Eskimo. She's not daft, that woman. She wouldn't be where she was if she were, would she? It seems she can get along just fine without my services. I believe her.

Paulette then takes me to a café. We drink coffee and consider my chances. Paulette considers them. She says I might have to be prepared to take anything. I am prepared for anything.

I get a job in a grubby suburban store selling cosmetics. I stand behind a battery of lipsticks, wearing red lips and green eyelids. The supervisor says I have to look soignée. To look cosmeticated – aren't we trying to sell products? She is image-conscious; she spends hours standing in front of the mirror, rearranging her cravat. She walks like she thinks she's Sophia Loren. Maybe she is, for all I know. I don't know much. The lipsticks have red tongues sticking up out of their shiny gilt cases. I smear the tongues on the insides of women's wrists to let them see how their lips will look. Gashed. I open up the powder boxes and try not to let the powder overpower me. The smell is nauseating. Are you all right? asks the supervisor. She says, Perhaps you had better go out into the street for a minute and get a breath of fresh air. I go and stand at the door and watch the traffic screeching past. Car bodies glint in the hot sun. Trucks backfire. Men shout. What a lot of noise there is out here in the street. I forget that I am supposed to be selling face powder and stand there until the supervisor comes to see if I have recovered. She is annoyed now. There are two customers waiting at the counter to buy lipsticks and face powder. I follow her back meekly.

I drop a powder compact. When I pick it up I see there is a zigzag line across the mirror. There is a zigzag crack across my face, too. I didn't mean to drop the compact. Please miss, I didn't. Honest, I didn't. My hands were slippery. The supervisor's red mouth is open in a round red O and she is screaming at me. Imbécile! Don't I know that it's unlucky to break a mirror? Seven years' bad luck, as far as I can recall. That's what Granny Balfour used to say. She used to say it with satisfaction. She liked the idea of someone being visited with seven years' bad luck. She was never so cack-handed herself as to break a mirror.

I am given a week's pay and released from cosmetics.

I have found another job. Waitressing. It's a cheap bistro. Only the cheap places will have me.

Bonjour! Comment ça va? Il fait beau aujourd'hui, n'est-ce pas? I have learned the lines. Be cheerful, says the patron, who has a face the length of Leith Walk. I carry the bleeding steaks to the tables. They like their meat saignant here. The blood spurts under their knives. I make some remark about the Blood of the Lamb and the woman looks at the man and the man looks at the woman and then he gets up and goes to complain to the patron. There's been a customer complaint, the patron says to me. You have been warned.

The next evening I am doing my best, I am not speaking except to say Bonjour! etc, but it is not so easy to keep the same control over my hands. Don't tell me! says Paulette the next day when I do tell her. Yes, I dropped two steaks. I admit to my guilt. They slid off their plates, I tell her. On to the floor? she asks. I shake my head. Don't tell me! she says.

'I know how she must have felt,' says Jessie. 'I dropped hair dye on a woman's frock once. It was her best frock, her only frock. It was pale blue. The dye was cried "autumn beech".'

August
I am walking along a street – some street, any street – when I see a billboard.

COLETTE EST MORTE!

That is what it says. I read it over and over and over again. I am trying to comprehend it.

'Yesterday, 3 August, at half-past eight in the evening, the writer Colette died at her home in the rue de Beaujolais overlooking the garden of the Palais-Royal. She was eighty-one years old . . .'

Do you want to buy that paper? The man who owns the shop has come out of his shop. I see that I have taken the newspaper off its stand and have squashed it between my hands. I fish in my pocket and find some coins.

Then I go to the Île Saint-Louis. I walk all the way, I have no more money in my pocket.

For heaven's sakes, says Paulette, you've actually come here on your *own*? What's gotten into you?

She was always so full of life, I say. She didn't waste any of her life. She never stopped looking. She didn't sit looking at the wall. Except maybe in the rue Jacob when she was Mrs Willy. But she pulled herself up, she moved on. I can't imagine her *dead*. With her eyes closed. For ever and ever, amen. She was born on the same day as my grandmother, Berthe Grenot, in Saint-Sauveur-en-Puisaye. I hadn't been to see her for months.

Who? asks Paulette. Your grandmother?

No, I say, Colette. I'd *forgotten* her! How could I forget her? And now it's too late! So often it's too late and you can't get back what's been taken away.

It's like the end of a chain, I say; the link has snapped.

Good, says Paulette, you're upset. You're reacting.

8 August 1954

Yesterday, Paulette and I attended the funeral of Colette in the Cour d'Honneur du Palais-Royal. She was the first Frenchwoman ever to be accorded the honour of a State funeral.

We went early, at half-past seven. Tout Paris was there. We queued in the rue de Montpensier (that's where Cocteau lives – we heard he was ill and wouldn't be able to come to the funeral). At a quarter past eight we were allowed into the court. Everyone was quiet as we filed slowly past the great catafalque draped with a silk tricolore. When I was passing, a little puff of wind arose and the flag billowed out. I felt she was saying goodbye to me! Leaning against her coffin was a black velvet pillow on which rested her cross of the Légion d'Honneur with its bright scarlet ribbon.

There were flowers banked all around the court, the colour blue predominating. Pale-blue and dark-blue gladioli. One wreath was from the French parliament, another from the city of Lyon, yet another from the King of Belgium's grandmother, with her name 'Elisabeth' on the card. The Association des Music-Halls et Cirques had sent a sheaf of lilies and her Compatriotes de Saint-Sauveur-en-Puisaye a big bouquet of dahlias looking as if they'd come in fresh from the country, the dew still on them. That was the wreath that moved me most.

Then we moved back into the gardens, behind the fenced-off area, to wait. The notables arrived: the writers, artists, musicians, politicians. The crowd murmured their names as they arrived. Roland Dorgelès from the Académie-Goncourt. Prince Pierre of Monaco. Marlene Dietrich.

'Dietrich,' breathed Paulette. 'Isn't she something?'

'Hey, Paulette, look over there!' I nudged her. I had seen a face in the crowd I thought I recognized. 'Isn't that Graham Greene?'

'Gee, I think you're right.'

(I was, for today there's an article by him in *Le Figaro littéraire*, written in the form of an open letter to Cardinal Felton, Archbishop of Paris. Colette's family and friends had asked for her to be given a burial service at the nearby Église Saint-Roch and he had turned it down. Just because she was twice divorced and une libre penseuse! Not that I think she'd have wanted a religious service particularly. Were two civil marriages so unpardonable? asks Greene. To non-Catholics it would seem that the church itself lacked charity.)

Colette's family, flanked by members of the Académie-Goncourt, took their places facing the catafalque: her daughter Colette de Jouvenel, husband Maurice Goudeket, and her old faithful servant Pauline.

The Minister for Education, Jean Berthoin, gave the address for the French government. He called her 'pagan, sensuous, Dionysiac'! I wanted to cheer.

After all the pomp and ceremony they took her quietly off to Père Lachaise to give her a private burial. The crowds dispersed. She belonged to Paris, they said. There will never be another like her.

Paulette and I went to a brasserie and ordered a bottle of red Burgundy, a basket of fresh bread and a hunk of ripe Camembert.

'She was certainly somebody,' mused Paulette, who had been impressed by the crowds and the presence of the famous. 'I was thinking, while we were standing there . . . You know you've always wanted to do something?'

'*Do* something?'

'Go on the stage. Act. Well, what about a one-woman show?'

'A one-woman show?'

'Don't keep repeating what I've just said, for Chrissake! The thing about a one-woman show is that you can get it under way on your own. You don't need a backer, a director – '

'You think I should *do* Colette?'

'Why not? Now quit that trembling! You're not going to start all that up again, you've just come out of that tunnel. Look, you've got the background, and you knew her. I'm serious. I really am!' Paulette raised her glass. 'Colette est morte – vive Colette!'

Ten

There came to me the strange sensation
that it was only when I was on the stage
that I could feel really alone and safe from
my fellow-creatures, protected by a barrier
of light.

La Vagabonde

'The first thing we're going do is cut your hair and then frizz it.'

Amy sat in a chair with a waterproof cape tied round her neck whilst Paulette, armed with a large pair of scissors, snipped and hummed and pulled her head back from time to time to admire her handiwork.

'Okay, stage two: the permanent,' said Paulette.

'Are you sure I need a perm? My hair's pretty wavy already.'

'I'm not talking waves, I'm talking frizz!'

'When Colette was young her hair was wavy rather than frizzy.'

'You've got to go in around the middle years, then you can move backwards and forwards. Don't forget you've got to be eighty at the end. Anyway, you ask people what their image of Colette is and they'll tell you she had frizzy hair. And we're in the business of image-making, right?'

'Are we? I don't know. I'm not sure about this whole business . . .'

The perming chemicals tickled their noses and brought tears to their eyes. Amy was not allowed to look during any of the stages. She was placed in front of the window where she could watch the bateaux-mouches going by. 'Just wave to the tourists!' said Paulette. When Amy's hair had dried, Paulette

232

took another glance at the photograph she had propped up on the shelf alongside her. 'Now we've got to arrange the bangs across your forehead, like so! It's lucky you've got a high forehead. We're getting there, I reckon. Okay, okay, I'll let you look now!' With a flourish she produced a mirror. 'Madame Colette! So what do you think?'

Amy made a face at herself. 'Not bad, I suppose, considering.'

'Considering what? The poor material I had to work on? Don't be so darned grudging! It's pretty good, if you ask me! A transformation is under way. Tomorrow I'm going to put chestnut dye on it, to tone down the red.'

'Tone it *down*?'

'Her hair wasn't red like yours, was it?'

'Now, look here, Paulette!' Amy sat up and threw off the waterproof cape. 'There is a limit!'

'You haven't reached it yet, honey! If you want to be an artist you've got to be prepared to make sacrifices. Think of Van Gogh! Just as well you're not going to play *him*. I'm not going to ask you to cut off your ear!'

Amy sank back into the chair.

'Now for the make-up.' Paulette closed in on Amy's face. 'Darkish shadows on the upper lid . . . kohl to ring your eyes . . . lots of lovely thick black mascara. Now, half lower your lids. Look sensuous. That's it! Beauty spot high up on the right cheek. Carmine red for the lips. Pity yours are so full. Can't you pinch them in a bit? You've got to *think* your way into Colette, *feel* your way, *will* your way . . . I'm doing the outer stuff, you've got to do the inner and bring the two together. Co-ordination is the name of the game.'

It seemed like a game to Amy: she was willing to let Paulette have her way. She felt bemused as she submitted to her hands; she had not felt so relaxed for a long time, mesmerized almost. Paulette appeared to be in her element, Amy commented. Perhaps she should take up directing? Paulette thought she might, but didn't get around to it before falling pregnant and returning with Luke to the States to get married and live happily ever after. Their marriage was one of the success stories, said Amy. Paulette didn't become an actress, either. She was not so good at subsuming her own personality, entering into the skins of other people; no matter which part she played she was forever Paulette, with bouncy movements and a perky voice.

She was back now to talking about inner resources and tuning up their instruments. Every morning Amy would leave her new room – she had gone back to Montmartre and was lodging with an elderly woman, a former neighbour of Aunt Yvonne's, in return for domestic help – and make for the Île Saint-Louis. She would find Paulette waiting impatiently in black leotard and leg-warmers beside a rigged-up barre, ready to begin the exercising of their bodies and their voices.

'Now we've got to dress you like she dressed.'

That was not so easy. Colette's lifetime had spanned eighty years. Paulette decided they would have to go for something neutral and adaptable: a black skirt, an embroidered blouse, a broad belt, a shawl to throw around the shoulders when they were beginning to hunch and the frame was shrinking.

'After all, you've got to go from youth to old age in a couple of hours.'

'A tall order,' murmured Amy, who had no real intention at that stage of appearing in public impersonating Colette.

'Now your voice. It must be deeper . . . huskier . . . sexier . . . You say she rolled her "r"s? Let them roll. Yes, that's better . . . Don't you feel yourself becoming different, becoming *her*?'

Gradually Amy found herself becoming absorbed into the life of Colette. She *felt* it happening. She said it was like being taken over. Yet she was aware at the same time that she was willing it: she set herself to look at the world through Colette's eyes. She walked in the Bois, with all her senses on alert, noticed patterns of light and shade, listened to the small sounds, the crackle of twigs, the soft sigh of branches in the wind, and then the birds' last full-throated chorus before falling silent for the night. She particularly enjoyed walking in the Bois during the hour 'entre le chien et le loup'; she liked the filmy greyness that stole in amongst the trees and blurred the edges of the paths. Colette had said that Paris was full of ghosts. 'Restless ghosts, illrecovered from blows received in the past.' Amy was conscious of the ghosts in those twilight hours.

She went to the Palais-Royal and sat in the gardens, watching the children play and the lovers pass. She thought of Maurice Goudeket, who could be sitting at his window looking down on her; he had remained in the apartment and would do so until he remarried. What would he think if he knew that she was impersonating his wife, trying to inhabit her mind and body? She had written a letter of condolence, but had not yet approached him or Colette de Jouvenel to ask permission to portray Colette and use her material. Time enough when you're almost ready to start performing, Luke said. Time enough, agreed Amy.

'I suppose what all this play-acting was doing was taking me out of myself and my depression. Though I still had my black moments.'

I did not say that it could be dangerous to be permanently 'out of oneself', though that was what I was thinking. By immersing herself in the life of Colette, Amy was able to escape the pains and inadequacies of her own life. But where did it leave *her*? Of course we each have our own methods of escape; we are not all 'in ourselves' all of the time. God forbid.

'Now we've got to work out a programme for you,' said Paulette, 'select which bits of her life you're going to do. You've got to go for the key episodes. So what do you say we start with her childhood in Saint-Sauveur?'

Step by step, working their way through Colette's life and work, they built up Amy's programme. Paulette did not know a great deal about Colette when they began but she had a strong dramatic instinct. She sat in a corner and watched critically. Too long . . . too boring . . . take that bit out . . . okay, we've got the idea, she hated the apartment in the rue

Jacob, no need to go on about it any more, we'll all end up yawning . . .

Then came the day when Paulette said they should let Luke see it.

'*Luke*? I don't know that I want *him* to see it.'

'You've got to start with somebody. You're not just going to play to me for the rest of your life, are you?'

Paulette arranged props in the living room: a velvet-covered chair, a small table draped with a lace cloth and a bowl of roses. Luke was brought in. He cracked jokes – 'Where's the candy, then?' 'How about a martini in the intermission?' – trying to put Amy at her ease. She was exceedingly nervous, and began hesitantly, stumbling over words. And at one point she stopped and looked at Paulette and said, 'This is hopeless! I'll never make it as an actress.'

'Sure you will! Get on with it! Remember, you're in Burgundy, it's 1885, you're twelve years old and queen of the earth! Forget us! We're not here!'

Amy got on, and slowly her nervousness decreased, as did her self-consciousness; her voice steadied, grew stronger, and she became absorbed in the part. She held on to the threads until in the end she lay on the 'raft' in front of the window looking over the Palais-Royal and finally let her eyelids sink down.

'Bravo!' Her audience rose to applaud.

'You were great,' said Luke.

'You're just being kind.'

He denied it. She had some faults to straighten out and she'd need to continue to work at it, he said, but she had the basis of a professional performance there.

'Professional?'

'You don't think we've been doing this just for laughs, do you?' demanded Paulette.

Amy went to see Maurice Goudeket. Paulette propelled her there and waited below, on one of the iron garden chairs, while Amy went up.

Pauline opened the door to Amy. She had stayed on to look after her mistress's widower. Goudeket looked startled when Amy was shown in (as if he'd seen a ghost?), though he recovered quickly and was his old gallant self. He shook hands and made her comfortable in a chair before returning to his own at the desk by the window.

He cocked his head. 'I didn't recognize you for a moment!'

'I know,' Amy said nervously, but did not explain, not yet.

He told her he was writing a memoir of Colette, mainly because he did not want her to be misunderstood. Amy commented feebly that it was probably difficult for anyone fully to understand another human being, while underneath she was pondering how to ask the man permission to bring his dead wife to life.

'Her behaviour often astonished and shocked people,' said Goudeket. 'But she had her own private code of conduct that governed her. So what if it didn't always coincide with current standards of morality? She hated hypocrisy. And hypocrites. She was not an angel, certainly. But who would want to live with one? She was a complex woman. Some thought her arrogant and self-satisfied, but that wasn't so. In private, she was really rather scornful of her fame. She didn't wholly believe in it.'

'Perhaps no one ever quite does?'

'Perhaps not.'

Goudeket talked then about Colette's death. They had known she was approaching the end for some weeks; she had grown daily more silent. She couldn't write; her hands hurt. She had lain for hours immobile, and after the third week in July had not got up at all. 'On the evening before her death she rallied a little and even took a sip of champagne. She looked at the case of butterflies beside her bed, then her eyes went to the window. She saw a flock of swallows passing and she said, "Regarde, Maurice, regarde!" Those were the last words that she spoke.' He paused, and Amy wondered how many times *he* had spoken them. She repeated them to herself in her head, for future use, and immediately felt guilty, as if she were trying to steal something. 'After that she went back into her own world, to that country she had lost. I believe that then she was in her garden in Saint-Sauveur.'

Goudeket gazed out of the window and Amy waited apprehensively, trying to brace herself to raise the purpose of her visit. When Goudeket looked back at her, he said, 'It was good of you to call, Aimée. I appreciate it, and I know she would have, too.' He rose from his chair.

Amy got up also. She thought of Paulette sitting on the iron chair below.

'Actually,' she said, 'there was something I was wanting to ask you.'

Amy's first performance in front of an audience (other than Paulette and Luke) took place in their sitting room on the Île Saint-Louis. The audience was all American. Some were friends of Luke's who happened to be passing through Paris; they were keen supporters of the arts back home. They attended first nights, private viewings, bought paintings, read all the latest novels hot off the press, entertained literary lions and when holidaying in Europe took in the Uffizi, the Louvre, the Prado, the Salzburg Festival, and even the Edinburgh International Festival.

'In spite of all that, they're okay,' said Paulette. 'No, I'm not kidding, they are!'

The others were a motley bunch, mostly jean- and sandal-clad, whom Amy suspected Paulette of scooping off the streets.

In spite of Paulette's reassurances, Amy found herself shivering as they waited in a back room listening to Luke greet the audience.

'The culture-vultures. That's what they are, aren't they?'

'They're not going to eat you.'

'No? I bet they've got sharp beaks.'

'But you're not dead, are you? You still seem to be kicking, as far as I can see. And vultures only attack corpses, unless they've changed their habits. Anyway, Luke is going to give them cocktails to soften them up.'

'Why are you doing all this for me?'

'Because we want to, stupid!'

'I was worried about getting my nervous hands back. Once they'd start to tremble I couldn't stop them. When we went into the room I wanted to die. All those faces staring at *me*. Waiting. Expecting to be entertained. What an expectation! I wanted to run. But I felt bolted to the floor. And my legs were full of lead. Then I looked over at Paulette and I saw her eye trained on me and I rose to the occasion. I felt myself rise. At one point, when I was well into my performance, I looked at the audience in their well-cut suits and off-the-shoulder dresses and the others in their jeans and sandals and I thought, okay, I see you there, but you are *there* and I am *here* and *I* am doing what *I* want to do, so right now *I* am calling the tune, and if you don't like the way I sing then that's too bad, but I can't alter it just to please you.'

'And you were a success?' I asked.

'Amazingly, yes!'

Amy might have been able to face an American audience but a French one would be quite a different matter.

'They'd tear me to shreds! "Who does she think she is, daring to portray *our* Colette!"'

'All artists risk – '

'Okay, okay! The Impressionists were jeered at and they laughed at Rembrandt, but I've got to stand there for two hours in *front* of them, performing. Exposing myself.'

'It's unlikely, though, that they'll throw orange peel at you. And if they do, then think of Colette at the Moulin Rouge! She survived, didn't she?'

Paulette scoured the Left Bank and came up with a studio near the rue de Seine for a moderate rent.

'*He* won't come. Stop fussing!'

They scrubbed the studio floor, brushed down the cobwebs and flung the windows open wide to rid the place of the smells of turpentine, mice and cats. They hired forty chairs. Hard ones, with backs unsuited to the human form. 'You'll just have to be riveting to take their minds off their bodies!' Paulette put up posters in bookshops round about (not Picard's, of course) and in the university area, and left fliers on café tables.

AIMEE BUSSAC AS COLETTE!

Twenty people came. About half the audience was French; the rest was made up of tourists from Britain, America and Holland. Amy began hesitantly, fluffing words, feeling fright gripping her, then she got herself under control and gradually won over the audience. Most of it, at any rate. She noticed that a couple of the Frenchwomen tapped their hands together only perfunctorily at the end and raised critical, plucked eyebrows at one another, and there was one man who did not even go through the motions of applause. He turned out to be a critic. He wrote a small piece in *Le Figaro*, saying there were moments when Aimée Bussac had brought Colette alive but she had not managed to get the full measure of the writer. Another review in a student paper cavilled a little at the way she moved, but was otherwise approving. 'A sensual, sensitive performance.'

Amy brooded over the poor review. 'I told you I wasn't good enough for a public performance.'

'That's only one crummy review! One man's opinion.'

'I saw those two women yawning.'

'Those two would yawn if Daniel was getting torn apart in the lion's den right under their noses.'

Luke said, 'How could you expect to get the *full* measure of Colette? You're only beginning. You've only given two performances. You'll grow, and the show will grow and develop. Your understanding of your character will deepen. Every performance that you give will be different. Isn't that the exciting thing about it? If art isn't exciting, forget it!'

The takings for the evening covered costs, just, with a few francs left over. Not enough for a meal with a bottle of wine; Luke had paid for their after-show dinner. Amy unpacked her old typewriter and set about finding typing work again. Paulette organized another studio performance. This time twenty-five people came and the profit was slightly larger. Next day, Amy was back at her typewriter. Thus was established a pattern of living which enabled her to survive financially. She moved, too, into a cheap, cold-water, ground-floor apartment on the rue de Grenelle, where she was to remain for the rest of her life in Paris.

'My life seemed finally to have got on some kind of even keel, and then the blow fell. Paulette and Luke were going back to New York. They were going to get married.'

A few drops of moisture had touched our faces. We got up from our seats in front of the sculpture garden. A swathe of rain was crossing in front of the castle and old town roofs, threatening to move our way. People on the path below were scurrying for shelter.

'Paulette was pregnant,' said Amy. 'I hadn't even realized.'

She saw them off at the Gare du Nord, waved until the train vanished to a dwindling point. Then, infected by the three glasses of champagne she had drunk in their apartment beforehand, she returned to the rue de Grenelle, to her corner café, where she telephoned a contact Paulette had given her. The director of a small theatre, no more than 'a hole in the wall', as he himself called it, said he would be delighted to have her perform there. She hung up the receiver and went to tell the café patron that she had made her first engagement. All by herself.

'Bravo!' he said, and put a glass of marc on the counter.

Later, returning home to her cold apartment a little drunk, switching on the light, seeing the empty space, the dishes lying on the draining board since morning, a film of dust on the round mahogany table, she became aware of the hole that Paulette's going had left. It seemed to yawn at her feet. Another step, and she would tumble into it. The room looked dismal; there was no other word for it. Except grey. She hadn't made a home of it, the way she had the apartment that she'd lived in with Janos. It hadn't seemed worthwhile, just for herself. Outside, it was raining. She could hear the soft hiss of the rain as it fell in the courtyard. Not that again! Oh God no! She put her head against the mantelpiece and wept. *Now, that won't do! You've got to be positive, do you hear? And what do you think you're worth?* Amy looked round. No, Paulette was not there, she was heading for the Statue of Liberty.

In the morning, Amy resolved to spend some time and a little money brightening up her environment, to look for coloured glass lampshades at the flea market, to make bright cushion covers, to buy posters for the walls; then she went to the café, where she telephoned her friend Camille in Rouen. They had not spoken together for a while. Amy told Camille about her Colette project.

'Good for you! Nothing much has been happening to me. I really envy you doing something like that. You're so adventurous, Aimée. A truly independent woman. I do admire you. Listen, why don't you come and do your show in Rouen? I'll fix something. Gérard has contacts, so many contacts you wouldn't believe. That's the trouble – I can't go anywhere without being seen by someone who might contact him.'

'Don't tell me you've become a Madame Bovary!'

'I don't ride around in closed cabs or leave messages in holes in the wall – I wish I could, think how romantic that would be! – but I do have the odd assignation. With the same man!' He was the local doctor. Wasn't that dangerous? asked Amy. Perhaps, Camille agreed. But it was also part of the attraction, Amy could see. 'Don't worry,' said Camille, 'I shan't end like Emma Bovary. She wasn't very intelligent.'

Camille had organized a good evening for Amy. The hall was full and the audience paid handsomely for the privilege of seeing 'Aimée Bussac, direct from her outstanding success in Paris, portraying the writer Colette, friend and schoolmate of her own grandmother in Saint-Sauveur-en-Puisaye.'

'I told them we were lucky to get you, you were in great demand. You've got to put a high price on yourself, Aimée.'

'You haven't been talking to my friend, Paulette, have you?'

'Paulette?'

'Forget it!'

'But it's true, what I say. If people think you're successful, they'll treat you as a success.'

The audience was dressed as if for a performance at the opera, furred and jewelled, and applauded warmly. Amy, glowing, was introduced to Camille and Gérard's friends and acquaintances, including the doctor, who was dark and bearded like someone out of a Chekhov play. His name was Charles. He inclined his head over Amy's hand and murmured, 'Enchanté!', but did not otherwise speak. She saw his eyes under their bushy black brows swivel frequently to where Camille stood laughing and accepting congratulations as if it were she herself who had been the performer. He appeared to be unaccompanied by a wife.

Camille gave a champagne supper for Amy after the performance.

'I haven't enjoyed myself so much for ages,' she said next morning, when she and Amy were breakfasting together, Gérard having gone off to do his banking. 'You must come again! Wouldn't it be an idea for you to start touring the provinces? Isn't that what Colette herself did when she became a music-hall artiste?'

Amy set off on a mini-tour to Auxerre, Dijon, Lyon and Saint-Etienne. 'In the footsteps of Colette', as she wrote on a postcard to Camille. *Les Envers du music-hall* kept her company; she read it in bed at nights in the cheap little rooms where she lodged, usually near the railway station, ready for a quick departure the following morning. And so the little ingénue with the peroxide hair and the grande cocotte with her black feathers and the under-manager with the fag hanging to his lower lip went with her, and Colette herself, the Colette of 1909, thirty-six years old.

Amy's first stop was Auxerre, a place of difficult memories for her, but she was resolved to confront them. Before her performance she walked along the towpath beside the Yonne and stopped in front of the hotel where she had stayed with Olivier. She looked up at the window of their room. Although she felt a twist of anguish over what once had been and was now gone, it was almost as if it had been another person who had gazed out at the barges lying motionless in the night.

The old theatre where Colette had played Claudine, the Salle de Comédie, had been demolished. There was now a new, brash-looking Théâtre Municipal, too large really for Amy's one-woman show but she would have to make do in it. She learned in the years to come to play in any kind of space, from barns to church halls to purpose-built theatres, behind proscenium arches, on apron stages, on no stage at all, with and without lighting, to audiences that ranged from two to two hundred.

In Auxerre she had about a hundred, a goodly number. There was much interest in Colette in the area, of course. It was the first time she had to play behind a proscenium arch, to try to draw her audience into the intimate atmosphere of a salon.

She was well received. Afterwards, two elderly women came backstage to speak to her and offer their congratulations. She had caught Colette miraculously well! Did she remember them, by any chance? They had lived in the rue de la Roche as children and known her grandmother. And their mothers had known Colette when she was a girl. 'The Colettes always had a high opinion of themselves, you know. They thought they were a cut above the other villagers.' Amy detected their resentment, passed down from one generation to another. Not that they weren't proud of Colette, they hastened to add.

Amy was removing her make-up in front of the mirror, when there came another tap on the door.

'Entrez!' she called, thinking it would be the concierge anxious to lock up.

A dark-haired young man – little more than a boy – entered. He introduced himself. 'Pascal Audry.' He had thought she was wonderful, had come round to tell her so. He hesitated by the doorway, blushed, studied his feet, then in a rush asked if he could take her to supper?

'I'm afraid not,' she said gently. 'I'm tired and tomorrow I have to go on to Dijon.'

He was there in the audience the following night, in the front row. She saw his dark eyes beamed on her like searchlights as soon as she entered. Here in Dijon she was playing in a small hall; she was on the same level as, and much closer to, her audience. She was aware of his eyes throughout the performance, found it difficult to look away from them, and was by the end somewhat annoyed at him. She felt he had broken her concentration. Going to the small boxroom that served as her dressing room, she told the concierge not to let anyone come round to speak to her. She slipped out of a side door and scuttled through the dark streets to her lodgings.

He was there in Lyon, also. He sent half a dozen dark-red roses with a note. Could he come and pay his respects? Tell him no! she told the concierge.

He was waiting for her in the street. 'Don't be annoyed,' he said, laying his hand on her arm.

'But I was,' said Amy, drinking her tea. We had sought shelter from the rain in the tearoom at the Botanic Garden. 'I'd had one or two like him pestering me before – oh, not as persistently as Pascal, going to the extent of following me around! – but the idea of Chéri seemed to inspire a certain kind of romantic young man. It was as if they thought I should actually be playing out Colette's life. They were confusing her life with mine. They were usually theatre-mad. Mostly they just wanted to talk to me, tell me how much they had admired my show, which was flattering and nice; one sent me a bunch of pink and purple dahlias. Another wrote me a letter on blue paper. "I know blue is your favourite colour," he wrote! But Pascal's pursuit of me was much more serious.'

*

Amy went for supper with him in Lyon. The night was cold and wet and she was feeling cold and lonely. After the exuberance of her reception, the let-down was always difficult. She thought, too, that it would be better if she tried to talk some sense into Pascal's head.

He ordered champagne. She hoped he would have enough money to pay for it, for she did not. She was touched by the way he was trying to act in an adult fashion to the waiters.

'I'm in love with you,' he said over the supper table.

'Now, that is silly! You're far too young.'

'I'm advanced for my years.'

She smiled. He had a faint line of dark fuzz on his upper lip. 'What age are you? Come on now, don't lie!'

'I wouldn't lie to you.'

Under lowered eyelids, he confessed to being sixteen.

'And I am thirty-two!'

He said that he did not mind. She said that she did.

He lived in Auxerre and his parents did not know where he had gone. She made him promise to return home the next morning. He said that he would, in return for her address in Paris.

Pascal wrote regularly for the next couple of years. She replied from time to time, only a few lines, usually on a postcard that she would send from some place where she was playing. She returned to Rouen, went on to Caen, down to Nantes, on to Bordeaux and then to Biarritz. On another tour she did the southern towns and cities of Toulon (Captain Colette's birthplace), Aix, Marseille, Arles, Nîmes. Each trip took a great deal of organizing.

'I wish I could help you,' wrote Pascal. 'I am good at making arrangements. And I would like to make my life in the theatre.' His father was an accountant and, as is often the way, wanted his son to come into the family firm.

'You must work at your studies,' Amy wrote back.

*

Maurice Goudeket came eventually to one of her performances in Paris. She had run into him a few days before, at Père Lachaise, on the twenty-eighth of January, the birthday of Colette and Berthe Grenot. Amy had brought blue hyacinths and laid them on the grave and was standing on the path looking at the headstone of pink-and-black Burgundian marble with its simple inscription 'ICI REPOSE COLETTE 1873–1954', when she became aware of someone coming up behind her. Turning, she saw that it was Goudeket, bearing his own floral tribute.

They talked. He had heard that she was having success with her show and asked when next she would be playing in Paris.

'On Saturday.'

He came, and was impressed. 'Uncanny,' he said. 'You've caught her well. There were only a few moments when I was not convinced.'

'Perhaps you would give me some advice on those?'

'I would be delighted.'

He invited her to have dinner with him. In the restaurant she noticed that they were attracting a few glances. People would look at them and frown and then look away. Surely that couldn't be . . . No, of course not. She *died. Didn't* she?

Goudeket told Amy that he was to remarry, a Madame Lelong, widow of the designer Lucian Lelong. She was wealthy, Amy gathered, though he did not say so. And much younger than he, by more than thirty years. He was to leave the rue de Beaujolais and go and live in the Lelong apartment on the Right Bank; and at the age of seventy-one he would father his first and only child, a son. Colette de Jouvenel was to move into her mother's old apartment.

'You seem happy,' said Amy.

'I was happy with Colette, too.'

'It may be that by nature you are a contented man?'

He smiled. He would like to think so. 'Though *she* called me "une flamme couverte"! People sometimes ask me if it was not difficult to live with a genius. It's usually Anglo-Saxons who

247

ask! No, I don't count you as one. You're a Burgundian, aren't you?'

In 1960, Amy went on a tour of the States arranged by Paulette. On arrival in New York she stayed several days with her and Luke in their apartment on the Upper East Side, saw that they were happy, met their two small children and did her show at Gotham Book Mart. After that, she set off alone, moving north first to Boston, then westward, playing in arts theatres, private homes and university French departments across the country. She sent postcards to Pascal from Philadelphia, Cleveland, Chicago, New Orleans, Albuquerque, San Francisco.

She returned to Paris exhausted but, for the first time, with money in her pocket. The universities had paid well. She went into her corner café to have a coffee and brandy and found Pascal sitting there, waiting for her. He had taken his baccalauréat, as he had promised her he would, and left home.

'So here I am.'

'But what about your military service?'

'They've turned me down.' He was slightly asthmatic.

He had rented a room down at the quai near the foot of the boulevard Saint-Michel and was working part-time in a bookshop.

'The rest of the time I can be your manager. And when you go on tour I'll give up my job to come with you.'

'So I gave in,' said Amy. 'I was tired and jet-lagged and I had just had three months of arriving alone in unknown places to unpack my cases and set up my props. To think that a decision that affects your life can sometimes hinge on how tired you are at a given moment!'

But she hadn't regretted her decision?

'Oh, no. Pascal is an excellent manager. He'll pursue a contact until he gets an answer! He has set up tours for me in Holland and Belgium and Germany, as well as various parts of France. And every now and then he'll find a new venue in Paris itself. Next year we're going to Sweden, and he's got lines out to Australia and New Zealand. I don't know what I should do without Pascal.'

'Here are your gloves . . . Your hat! On the floor, of course. Where else? I know all your little habits . . . Put your coat on, there's a nip in the air. Au revoir, mon Chéri, au revoir . . .'

I would have liked to turn round and look at Pascal – was he watching this scene with extra attention, would it be a blueprint for one that he himself would play out at some future date? Or was I trying to dramatize him too much? On either side of me sat Jessie and my father, as absorbed as everyone else. Beforehand, my father had made it plain that this was not 'his cup of tea', that he'd come only because it was Amy. It was her last performance of the 1965 Festival. Aunt Nan was baby-sitting for me. I had brought her one afternoon – she had so much wanted to see Amy on stage – but it had been something of a disaster. She'd kept making remarks. She couldn't get over the fact that there wasn't a proper stage (which was clearly a disappointment). Or curtains, either. 'Do they no' usually have curtains? Maybe somebody's took them. We'll need to ask Amy after.' She was used to the King's Theatre, all red plush and gold tassels. She fluttered her fingers at Amy, who was trying not to look in our direction, and she clapped when she should not have done, which was at regular intervals, almost every time Amy shifted from one scene to another. I had had to take her out.

On the dais, Léa has closed the door behind Chéri. She droops, and now she shows her age. What else did she expect from a liaison with a much younger man? She is resigned. She lifts the curtain so that she can look down from her window and watch him go. She sees him cross the courtyard. Then he stops.

'He's coming back!' she cries, and holds out her arms to us, so that we can rejoice with her. 'He's coming back!'

I heard a sigh of relief from Jessie. She doesn't like sad endings.

Chéri is looking up at the sky and at the chestnut trees in

flower. It is springtime. He takes a deep breath and fills his lungs with fresh air. Then he hastens on, invigorated. Free.

'Like a man escaping from a prison,' says Léa.

And Amy, alias Colette, alias Léa, lets the curtain drop back into place at the window.

There was a long pause and then Amy moved briskly, changing the mood for the next stage in Colette's life. Enter the Baron! Jessie inclined her head towards mine to murmur in my ear, 'I might have known!'

So now Colette is in love again, at least for a while . . . The marriage is not a bed of roses, but who wants roses? He has affairs, she is jealous. She gives birth to a daughter.

Watching this last episode, it struck me that Amy was not giving enough weight to it; she was skating over it as if it was only another incident in Colette's life. I made a mental note to discuss this with her; she had said she would always welcome hearing my reactions. (Within limits, I was aware; too critical a one would not be well received.) I didn't find time to talk to her about it before she left for Paris the following day but I did take it up in a letter. 'The birth of a child is a major event in a woman's life,' I wrote, 'even for someone like Colette who was obviously not very maternal. Strange that she was not more so, when she valued so much the bond with her own mother. Was it pure selfishness on her part?' Amy replied cryptically: 'It seems to me that the arrival of a daughter did not much affect the course of her life.'

The hall was full that afternoon; many in the audience had been before. I picked out the Dutchman and the flower-power couple. The show had been well reviewed during its three-week run. This was the first time that Amy had played every day in the week for such a long stretch. She'd thrived on it. And her performances had gone from strength to strength.

On stage now, Amy brought us to the final scene of Colette's life in the Palais-Royal. 'Regarde, Maurice, regarde!' Our eyes swept upward with hers to watch the flight of sparrows pass, then dropped when hers did. There was silence in the hall.

Amy rose and faced her audience, with head inclined. We

applauded enthusiastically. Jessie clapped with her hands raised to shoulder-height and was the last to stop.

'That was a grand show.' She leaned across me. 'Did you enjoy it, then, James?'

'Aye, it was no' bad.' My father was anxious to get outside and have a cigarette. He left us.

The usual cluster of people had gathered around Amy to compliment her. Her face was flushed and she was laughing. Pascal had moved up to stand where he could watch over her. She is in her prime, I thought: on a peak. That is why she has come back to Edinburgh at this point; she has felt confident enough to do so.

We were having a farewell party for her in my house afterwards. She invited the Dutchman, and the flower-power couple, and several others who were standing around.

'I want all my friends to come!' she cried gaily.

More than sixty people turned up. I never did find out who they all were and some, I suspected, did not know why they were there. Amy and Jessie did the cancan. Pascal sat on a stool in the kitchen, drinking red wine and looking gloomy. 'Why does she want all these people?' he asked, as he popped salted peanuts into his mouth. I felt that he should know the answer to that better than I.

I wanted to talk to Amy about her mother's books and the Baccarat paperweight. I thought that she should have them. I caught her as she was whisking into the kitchen to fetch more wine.

'Hang on to them,' she said. 'How could we get them back to Paris on the Magic Bus?'

In the morning, Jessie and I saw Amy and Pascal off at the bus station. We were all a little hungover, but Amy was feeling happy. I thought Pascal looked relieved to be departing: Edinburgh had taken too much of Amy away from him, relegated him to a part on the sidelines.

'I'll see you next year,' said Amy. 'I'll be back. By popular demand! And you must both come and visit me in Paris!'

I said I'd try. 'But you can see it wouldn't be easy for me to get away.'

'Aunt Nan can look after the kids.'

I was not so sure about that. Aunt Nan was marvellous with them, and it was all right to leave them with her for two or three hours, but a few days? Goodness knows what they'd get up to!

'You fuss too much,' said Amy, and climbed aboard the bus. Pascal was keeping their places. He got up so that she could slide into the window seat, where she cleared a circle on the glass to look out at us.

'Write!' I mouthed.

She nodded.

Jessie and I waved them off, then walked home down the hill. Jessie took my arm and leant on me. She still wore ridiculously high heels, even though she had trouble with her back and her knees were puffy.

'Are she and Pascal . . . well, you know?'

I thought it likely, could not say for certain. During several late-night chats I'd probed a little, but Amy had always missed the point. Deliberately, I felt. I thought she rather enjoyed creating a little mystery around her life, confusing fact with fiction; and so when she was ultimately to disappear, in one way I was not wholly surprised. I even wondered if she might not have staged the disappearance herself. But then, do we not all to some degree fashion our own ends?

Eleven

Some peaches, forgotten in a bowl, recalled
themselves to me by their sharp perfume; I
bit into one and it reawakened my hunger
and thirst for the round material world,
laden with savours.

La Naissance du jour

Amy came to the next Festival without Pascal. She had written
to tell me that he would not be accompanying her. 'He says
that I don't need him in Edinburgh, with all the family there
to help me.'

She lodged in Jessie's spare room. 'I would stay with you,'
she said to me, 'but the children . . .'

'Of course.'

'It's just that I need rest and quiet in between shows.'

She talked Jessie into doing the box office for her. But Jessie
didn't mind; she enjoyed sitting at a table selling tickets,
having a bit of a blether with the folk. She liked meeting all
kinds.

'I don't suppose you could spare the odd afternoon, could
you?' Amy asked me. I was earning enough money now to
employ a girl to help with the children. I was enjoying my two
or three hours of freedom to write in the afternoon, when I
could close the door of my study confidently behind me. 'On
the busier days?' Amy pressed. 'It's just that it's such a help to
know that someone is in charge of the props and the effects,
to put on the music and so forth. It means that I can
concentrate on my performance.'

Where was Pascal now? I asked. Still in Paris? Until then I
had spared asking her. She said that he had gone to the South

of France; a friend of his had rented a house and Pascal was going to set up engagements along the coast for Amy for the following spring. 'He's not lounging about doing nothing.' The implication seemed to be that I was.

'Who does she think I am?' I demanded of my husband when Amy had gone off to watch opera at the King's with an American woman who had come to her show in Paris.

'You tell me.'

I glared at him.

'Why don't you just calm down!'

'Oh, well,' I said, with a sigh. 'I suppose she needs all the help she can get.' Any discussion that I had about Amy always ended on the same note: that she was basically alone, in spite of Pascal, her life had not been easy, and she was perched most of the time on the edge of survival, whereas other people were, as I was, well cushioned, with homes of their own stuffed with possessions, husband and children. 'And she's a performer,' I would add. 'Her whole life is built on projecting herself. It's understandable that she's come to see her needs as being more important than anyone else's.'

Amy could be generous too, however, and when she had money she did not hesitate to spend it on presents: books and sweets for the children, flowers and bottles of wine for us. 'Full house this afternoon,' she'd cry gaily, holding up a bottle of wine in each hand. She loved to celebrate, to enjoy herself, to move on a whim. I could see that family life would not have suited her. Or had she made herself unsuited because she had no family? She would pick up starving young Fringe performers and bring them back with her for dinner; she ate most evenings at our house. 'You don't mind having Daniel, do you?' she'd ask sweetly, when he would be standing out in the porch, with a sheepish grin on his face, waiting to be admitted. 'He hasn't had a square meal since he arrived in Edinburgh. There are so many of you, you won't notice one more!' Jessie and my father would often be there, and usually Aunt Nan. We kept a seat for her at the table. It was the only way I could be sure she would have a square meal. She liked it when the evening developed into a party and Amy was persuaded to 'do' Juliette Greco or Edith Piaf. Aunt Nan and Jessie would join in, soon knew the words of Greco's *Mon Homme* off by heart. I'd hear Aunt Nan singing it along St Stephen Street, giving it the same intonation that Amy – and Greco – did. On those evenings of merriment the children stayed up until almost midnight. They behaved well, stayed quietly in the background, knowing that to step forward centre stage would be to hear the dreaded word 'Bed!'

The following spring, I went to stay with Amy in Paris. Jessie had hoped to come with me, but my father was ill and she felt she couldn't leave him. As she said, he was handless enough without her at the best of times.

Amy met me at the Gare du Nord. 'You've actually made it! I was half expecting to get a last-minute call to tell me someone had measles!'

I slept on the bed-settee in her sitting room. She had made it into an attractive room; she had covered the scabby chairs with swathes of coloured cloth, scattered bright cushions around, pinned theatre and art posters on the dirty-yellow walls, set lamps in strategic places. The lamps were especially good, glass-shaded, etched with flowers, of the twenties and thirties. There was a pretty pink-and-green one shaped like an inverted tulip. And a petalled pinkish-lilac one, reminding me of another I had seen in an apartment in the rue de Beaujolais.

The kitchenette of Amy's flat was tiny, no bigger than a cupboard, and windowless. There was no bathroom. We boiled water in kettles on the gas ring and washed ourselves in the sink. We cooked very little. Would I want to go to Paris and *cook*? When we couldn't afford to eat in restaurants we brought back crusty loaves, pâté, cheese, olives, tomatoes, fruit, pâtisserie, wine. For ten whole days I revelled in the simplified life of a single woman, free to get up in the morning and do what *I* wanted to do, eat breakfast in a café – of all places! – without kids spilling rice crispies on the floor and knocking over the milk bottle after I'd told them for the tenth time to be careful and not to wave their arms about. I could read the morning paper without a child wailing about lost gym shoes or no clean socks or insisting that they *had* to have twelve toilet-roll middles for a class project that very morning or else they couldn't go to school. Which would then remind me that someone had stuffed half a toilet roll down the lavatory. No one, needless to say, would own up. 'It wasn't me!' The eternal cry. 'It must be me, then,' their father would say, and four heads would nod. From my child-centred house in Edinburgh I had viewed Amy's apartment in the rue de Grenelle with envy.

Pascal kept a low profile during most of my visit, appearing from time to time, usually on a matter of business – or so he would say, stressing the word 'business' and looking pointedly in my direction. I would then retreat, go walking for an hour or two, happy to have time-out in Paris on my own. I was well aware that he regarded me as a visitor from enemy territory. He was polite enough, but cool, and adopted an air of boredom in my presence. He would lean languidly against the mantelpiece in his blue denim suit with his silver identity bracelet dangling from his wrist. At the time, denim suits were de rigueur on the boulevards Saint-Michel and Saint-Germain, as were the bracelets. He would study his nails. Amy admitted that he was possessive. 'Don't you mind?' I asked. She shrugged. 'It's part of his temperament. He's a very passionate young man. I accept him as he is.' I saw that this acceptance was mutual; he was never critical of her and let her moods wash over him, as she did his. They knew when to leave each other alone, when to offer consolation. Back in Edinburgh I had to admit to Jessie that they seemed at ease with one another.

When I had an opening I slipped in a question I hoped would come over as guileless. Did Amy see him often? 'When I'm not here, I mean?'

'Well, of course. Every day!'

'But he doesn't live here?'

'Oh, no! I need my own space; I've got used to it. And once

one does, one needs it. He has his own room round the corner. That is the best way to keep love fresh: each have a place of their own to retreat to.'

'It's not always practical, though, is it?'

'Not if you have children.'

Coming back to the flat by myself on one occasion, I heard Pascal's voice. He and Amy were in the sitting room. I waited in the narrow hallway, unsure whether to advance or retire. I had no wish to eavesdrop, nor did I want a rerun of the scene on the beach at Gullane of more than twenty years ago. 'I feel lost without you,' he was murmuring. 'I miss you, Aimée.' 'I miss you too, mon chéri.' 'I need you.' 'Come on, now, Pascal, you can't . . . She'll be back soon.' 'No, she won't, she'll be along at the bouquinistes again. She'll have forgotten the time.' So that was how he saw me, my head buried in books! 'It's only for ten days,' Amy was saying soothingly. 'That's a lifetime!' said Pascal. I took a step back on to a creaky board, then stopped again. The hall light went out on its timer. 'You're impossible, Pascal!' Amy's low, amused laugh suggested that she found what he was proposing to be perfectly possible. I groped for the door handle, knocked over Amy's umbrella, cursed softly and opened the door, letting in a shaft of light. I closed the door very quietly behind me, though I need not have bothered; I doubted if they would have heard even if I had slammed it.

I went to the corner café and read one of my newly purchased books.

'You are Colette's cousin?'

I blinked, and looked up. An elderly man at the next table was smiling at me. 'Aimée Bussac! Colette — that's what we call her in here. She really does look like her, doesn't she? You wouldn't know the difference, would you?'

'I think I would,' I said.

He tried to pick me up. He asked if he could join me and slid over on to a seat at my table before I could say yes or no. He was a bore and a nuisance and I was forced to retreat from there also. I went along and sat in the gardens in front of the Invalides until I thought it would be safe to return to Amy's.

There was neither sign nor sound of Pascal now. Amy was lying back on the settee with her arms behind her head. Juliette Greco was singing *Mon Homme* on the record-player.

'Where have you been?' asked Amy. 'I'd thought we might have gone to the theatre, but now we're too late.' She broke off to listen, holding up a hand to quieten me. 'Ma seule joie . . . mon bonheur . . . c'est mon homme!' She was smiling to herself. And I thought I could hear her purring.

'Rather an old-fashioned sentiment, isn't it?' I said coolly. It had been chilly in the Invalides garden; the sun had gone down before I left. What was more, I did not believe that Amy believed in the sentiment, that a part of her was play-acting. I thought that a measure of Pascal's attraction for her was that she was not required to make a total commitment to him.

'Who cares what fashion it is?' she said.

Another record that she played frequently was Piaf's *Je ne regrette rien*. She played it with some defiance, I felt, and at full throttle, so that it bounced off the walls, but whether it was for my benefit or her own I could not be sure. But of one thing I did feel certain: whilst singing this song herself she could not have laid her hand on her heart.

Pascal had forsaken bookselling in order to buy and sell antiques. He appeared to earn some sort of a living this way and it was an occupation he could put into cold storage while he went off touring with Amy. He had an eye for a good buy, said Amy; in the middle of a heap of rubbish he would pick out the jewel. 'She taught me,' he said, and she smiled at him.

We all three went out to Clignancourt to the Flea Market on the Sunday, one of the few outings we did undertake together, going on another occasion to hear jazz in a cellar along Saint-Germain. Pascal was partial to jazz and the boîtes; he often went alone in the late evenings, Amy said; when she was tired or wanted time on her own she would tell him to run along without her.

We spent a couple of hours rummaging around the antiques section of the Flea Market. I found a pretty, inexpensive paperweight and Pascal bought Amy another glass lampshade in an art nouveau design. Could he afford it? she asked, holding it up so that the light shimmered through the semi-opaque apple-green glass. She would love it, but was he sure? He said he'd made a good sale on a painting the day before.

'It's yours!' He kissed her over the top of the lamp and took a roll of well-used banknotes from his denim pocket. The painting sale must have been a good one. I couldn't help wondering if he might not be engaged in some shadier activity – trading in stolen goods or peddling pot, perhaps. Then I chastised myself. Why should I be so ready to think ill of Pascal? What did I have against him? That he was sixteen years younger than Amy? That was not a crime. And he did seem devoted to her. I set myself to be nicer to him.

We had a rollicking lunch in a restaurant packed with Parisians enjoying their Sunday out; we sat elbow to elbow at long tables and after much food had been eaten and cheap red wine drunk various people rose up from their seats to give us a turn. Bright-eyed and flush-cheeked, they stood on the small stage and warbled earnestly into the microphone, love songs mostly, accompanied by a woman with stout forearms who swung from the waist as she pumped away on a miniature organ. The audience applauded with hilarity and tossed coins and notes into the performer's little basket when it was passed around the tables afterwards. It was one way of airing your talent and offsetting the price of your lunch.

'Come on, Aimée!' cried Pascal. 'Your turn!'

Amy the performer could not resist. After a brief display of diffidence, she pushed back her chair and wended her way through the tables to the stage. She stepped up without looking down, her head held high. She took the microphone between her hands and began to sing *Mon homme* into it, with feeling. Each time she came to 'Je l'ai tellement dans la peau' (giving great emphasis to the 'peau' – she, like everyone else, had partaken of a fair amount of wine), her eyes swivelled

259

dramatically towards our table and rested on Pascal, and he gave a tiny nod of acknowledgement. The audience loved her, clapped lustily and bellowed for more. She gave them *Douce France* and then, for her grand finale, *Je suis seule ce soir*, which prompted offers to be called up from the floor. The songs were all unashamedly sentimental and romantic. 'Quand il dit viens, je suis comme un chien . . .' The men in the audience howled.

'She sounds just like Greco,' said a man in a checked suit opposite me. 'She should go on the stage.'

When we were walking back through the stalls to the Métro later, Pascal encountered a couple of people he knew. They were buying leather jackets. They had shoulder-length hair and looked like students. They greeted him in friendly fashion but Amy did not encourage him to stop. She told me later that he had a number of student friends she thought he would be better without. There was trouble brewing around the Sorbonne, and police were often out at night, batons at the ready, watchful for signs of dissent. 'Now that they haven't got the Algerians to pursue – at least, not in the same way as they had during the Crisis – they've got the students in their sightlines!'

I had promised to phone home and, when I did (knowing it would probably be a mistake), I learned that Vinca had a rash all over her chest. 'I'm hot,' she wailed into the receiver, 'boiling hot. I might even be going to die. Would you mind if I died?' I could also hear the youngest boy crying in the background. 'Don't worry,' said my husband, sounding harassed. 'I'll cope. Just you enjoy yourself.' Over dinner afterwards I wondered if I should return to Edinburgh. A rash! It could be chicken pox or measles. Or scarlet fever. Did one still get scarlet fever? I was unable to check; I'd left Spock at home. I recalled that I'd had scarlet fever as a child.

'I was off school for three weeks, in a darkened room. Or was that measles? But I do remember being pretty ill. You had it too, didn't you, Amy?'

'Have what?'

'Scarlet – '

'For crying out loud! That's what I'm going to do any minute now! Can't you ever put those children out of your mind?'

I considered that unfair. I *had* been putting them out of my mind for long stretches of time. Amy was becoming – had become – selfish, I decided, and self-centred.

Next morning, before she was awake, I slipped out to the café and phoned home again. Vinca herself answered as bright as a bee, pleased with herself for having beaten the others to the phone. An argument was going on in the background. *She always answers the phone! Why can't I? It's not fair!* The rash? I asked, what about the rash? Oh, *that*! Vinca was scornful. It had gone away in the night. But could she please have ten pee to go trampolining at Portobello with Mandy Miller? 'Ask your father!' 'Daddy won't give it me, he says he's broke. How can he be *broke*? Daddy's horrible.' I didn't phone Edinburgh again.

As I was coming out of the café I saw Pascal on the opposite side of the street. He did not see me. He was walking with his hands in his pockets and his head down. He looked unshaven and rather scruffy. He looked like a cat slinking home after a night out on the tiles.

That same evening, he was to come round and join us for dinner. Amy had decided to cook a cassoulet de Toulouse and had tended it all day. The smell was delicious. We opened a bottle of Burgundy while we were waiting for Pascal, and when we had finished it and he still had not come we decided to go ahead and eat.

'He forgets all about time!' said Amy. 'His head is in the clouds!'

After a while her indulgence turned to anger. She smoked one Gauloise after the other and told me how thoughtless he was. She was not the kind of woman to sit waiting for a man, nor did she come running like a lap-dog when he called her!

'Une chanson est une chanson,' she said. 'Mais ce n'est pas la réalité!'

As the minutes crept on towards eleven o'clock without any sign of Pascal, her anger was gradually nibbled away by an encroaching edge of anxiety. She paced up and down in the limited space, scattering cigarette ash. I didn't realize how dangerous it could be on the boulevards these days, she said, otherwise I would not be sitting there so complacently, looking dreamy. She worried that Pascal might get caught up in the middle of some student demonstration and be arrested. 'And he's not even a student! I mean, it would be a bit much if *he* were to be arrested! And you know what the police are like here, when they do get their hands on anyone!' I forbore to draw any parallel between her anxiety about the habits of the Parisian police and mine about measles. She was not in the mood to accept a teasing. When the student riots happened in May of the following year, I wondered if Pascal would be in amongst them, but decided probably not; I thought he would consider his own skin too precious to risk having it marked. But perhaps I was being uncharitable to him again. I never did manage to see him objectively.

At midnight he arrived with some long, garbled and obviously fabricated tale about a friend in need. Amy did not reproach him; she was too relieved to see him.

Amy and I made a Colette pilgrimage, going first to the rue Jacob, then on to the Palais-Royal, where we sat in the gardens on iron chairs. We were quiet; we each had our own recollections. As dusk crept in I fancied I saw the blue lamp glimmering behind the first-floor window. We were alone; the children had gone home, as had the nannies pushing prams.

A woman wearing a headscarf came through the archway from the rue de Beaujolais. She paused to put on her gloves.

Amy nudged me. 'Bel-Gazou.' Collette's daughter. We turned our heads to watch her walk though the gardens. She looked neither to right nor left and had soon vanished into the shadows. 'She's shy, so I've heard,' said Amy, 'though she does have good friends. But she's never been with another man – two months of marriage seemed to finish all that for her. She used to write herself but gave it up; she felt she couldn't match her mother. She puts all her energy into promoting her mother's work now.'

'Sad that they weren't closer when Colette was alive.'

'Did I tell you that Colette left half her royalties to Goudeket in her will? And stipulated that if Bel-Gazou were to contest it she was to receive nothing – no royalties, furniture, books, anything!'

Colette always put the interests of the man in her life before those of her daughter; this was an observation that I did not make to Amy. It would have cut too close to the bone. But it surprised me that Amy did not feel more sympathy for Colette de Jouvenel. Perhaps she could not afford to.

' "The lost child whom its mother abandons always finds a refuge in a secret place",' I murmured.

Amy started.

'*Claudine s'en va*,' I said. Colette uses this quote from a Burgundian folk song in the novel. I had noticed that Amy had underlined it in her own copy, and in the margin had pencilled a question mark.

'I know where it's from,' she said, a little irritably, and rose, adding that she was getting stiff.

As we were going through the galleries at the edge of the garden, two women glanced at Amy. Then one spoke.

'Colette!'

Amy stopped and turned.

'I saw you playing Colette, didn't I? You're Aimée Bussac!'

Amy was pleased to be recognized, both as herself and Colette. She spoke to the women for several minutes, becoming quite animated, and acceded to their request for autographs. 'Aimée Bussac alias Colette', she wrote, leaning against the wall. Over the years her handwriting grew steadily more and more like Colette's, until at the end it became natural for her to produce a perfect replica of the writer's signature.

*

We hired a car for a couple of days and went down to Burgundy. We stayed in a hotel in Auxerre (not the one on the Yonne; we picked a cheaper two-star in a side street), and drove over to Saint-Sauveur.

We called on Amy's only remaining relative in the village, Alphonse, the shoemaker, son of her Uncle Robert. He practised his trade in a small dark workshop that smelled overpoweringly of old shoe leather and strong dyes, and lived alone in a room above it. His father had died the previous year, his mother some time before that.

'You didn't come to Father's funeral,' he said.

'No, I'm sorry,' said Amy, who had not mourned her uncle's passing.

'Everyone is dead,' said Alphonse.

In the graveyard on the edge of the village we found the family plot where lay Berthe and André Bussac with their three sons and one daughter. In front of the black marble headstone reposed one of those dreadfully garish china-flower arrangements that the French are so keen on in their graveyards, particularly the provincial ones. The purple and pink flowers looked as if they had been stained with bad blood. We propped our fresh flowers in front of it.

Our eyes rested on the name of Eugénie.

'Just as well it's a double plot,' said Amy. 'There can't be much room left in there! There might just be a space for me. That's where I'd like to go when the time comes.'

She was trying to speak lightly but I saw that there were tears in her eyes. I put my arm around her shoulders and she leant against me; we stood in silence for a moment and I knew the bond between us to be strong and binding.

We returned to the village and went into the church on the corner of the rue des Vignes where Amy had received her second baptism. She lit a candle for Eugénie. I sat at the back and thought of Colette's mother Sido bringing her dog Moffino to mass and how he had raised his head and barked during elevation. I felt that I had been there to witness it myself.

*

Amy and I got on better when I stayed with her than when she did with me in Edinburgh, which was not surprising. She stayed with us one Festival when Jessie had a niece visiting. Amy was peeved. Jessie had known she would be coming, so why couldn't she have asked the girl to come at some other time? The girl wasn't interested in the Festival, was she? I said, 'Come and stay with us. I'll try to see the children don't bother you too much.' I gave her Vinca's room and put Vinca in with one of the boys, which did not please her at all. She was now aged ten. She said that she was too old to share a room with a boy. And he messed up her books, scribbled on her drawing-pad and so forth. Too bad, I said, she would just have to guard her possessions more carefully.

Amy was not a tidy person; within hours of installing herself, the floor of Vinca's room was covered with clothes and props, theatre fliers and piles of newspapers, and was to remain so for the rest of her stay. She also had the habit of taking mugs of coffee up to her room and forgetting to bring back down the mugs. After her departure I found four, behind chairs, under the bed, discoloured and with the remains of the coffee now viscid and scummy.

Vinca complained loudly to me. 'She's making a *revolting* mess of my room. It's like a pigsty.' This was how I frequently described the children's rooms myself. Each Saturday morning we'd insist that the chaos be at least reduced before we'd pay out pocket money. Sometimes I used to have the feeling that I was caught up in an Ionesco play, in which the objects in the house would grow and grow until I would be forced to retreat backwards out into the garden, whereupon they would relentlessly follow me down the path into the street. I shushed Vinca, who then demanded to know why it was all right for Amy to make a mess and not her. 'Is it because she's a grown-up?'

'Don't go out of your way to annoy me, I've got enough to do.'

'It's not fair!'

I then gave that well-worn stock response about life not

being fair, and added, 'I don't think it's fair that *I* should have to cook the dinner, clean up after you lot *and* finish a radio play by ten o'clock tomorrow morning.'

'You chose to be a mother! You didn't *have* to be one. I didn't *choose* to be a child. Especially with *three* brothers!'

As she flounced off, I called after her, 'Set the table! And don't ask me why someone else shouldn't do it.'

After a few days Amy was getting on my nerves, too, though I did not admit it to Vinca, only to my husband, whose ear was well bent once the door of our room was closed. He got fed up with me moaning.

'Why did you ask her to stay, then!'

'What else could I do? She had nowhere to go. She's family, isn't she? I feel a certain responsibility for her.'

Amy would come down (late) in the mornings, pour herself coffee from the pot on the stove, take the fresh toast I had made, spread it liberally with the whisky marmalade that someone had given me as a present (you see how petty one can become!) and proceed to read the *Scotsman*, which I had been about to read myself. When she'd finished she'd get up, saying, 'Thank you for a nice breakfast,' and off she'd go, leaving her dirty dishes on the table.

She'd come back after her show and go through it blow by blow, sparing me no detail of audience reaction, while I stood by the sink peeling potatoes. She'd eat dinner, frown when she was interrupted by a child (she would be telling my husband about the afternoon's performance) and then get up, saying, 'Thank you for a lovely dinner,' and off she'd go on her evening round of entertainment. A friend from Canada, who was over covering the Festival for the CBC, took Amy along with her so that she got into everything free. On her return she would keep me out of bed until the small hours, telling me about all the wonderful things I'd missed. Relations between us became decidedly strained.

We went to one Fringe performance together, on an afternoon when she herself was not playing, but even that outing was not entirely harmonious.

I had picked up a flyer about a one-woman show called *Gertrude Stein's Gertrude Stein*.

'It's by a woman called Nancy Cole.'

'Never heard of her.'

'She lives in Paris, too.'

'A lot of people do.'

'It says she was born in Chicago, and is an actress and painter. Perhaps we should go and see her show?'

'I don't care much for Gertrude Stein. She was a terribly unattractive woman. I'm surprised anyone would want to portray her.'

I didn't know if it was a genuine lack of interest in Stein, or the prospect of competition in the form of another one-woman show centred on Paris that made Amy react so negatively. The latter, possibly. Understandably. Giving performances, offering oneself to the public for approbation or condemnation, is a nerve-racking business. And she was normally generous about other people's work, after all. But perhaps this one-woman show was too close for comfort. I could see, though, that she was curious. She studied the flyer, then said, 'Okay, let's give it a whirl.'

Nancy Cole appeared on stage in a cream lace dress. She was a dark, dramatic-looking woman, then in her mid- to late-forties, with short black hair. She might have been Spanish; I was to learn later that she was part-Jewish, part-Hungarian. A single red rose sat in a slender vase. A rose is a rose is a . . . There was one on the programme, too. She had few props, as had Amy in her show. She played, I thought, with sincerity and intensity, building up a montage of Stein's life. There was more emotion in the whole show than I had expected, I commented to Amy afterwards. It seemed to me quite a feat to put emotion into some of Stein's words, not that I had known much about her before this afternoon. The 'rose' quotation was as far as I would have got, if pressed to reveal my knowledge of her work. Amy shrugged and said, 'One can put emotion into anything if one wishes to.' I had not meant

267

to imply that it was *easier* to put emotion into the work of Colette, but I realized quickly that anything I said would be taken personally by Amy, as if I were comparing them.

'Shall we go and speak to her?'

'If you want.'

We waited until the small crowd of people around the performer had ebbed away, then went up and introduced ourselves.

'How wonderful to meet some real Edinburghers! I've met so many lovely people this week – you can have no idea, I'm having an absolute ball! – but I'm especially thrilled when natives come to my show.' She was clearly still on a high following her performance.

I felt Amy stiffening beside me; I knew she would not care to be described as a 'real Edinburgher'. I had introduced her as 'my cousin Amy Balfour, alias Aimée Bussac, alias Colette', and added, 'She's performing at the Festival, too.'

I said now, 'Amy also lives in Paris.'

'Snap! Seems like we've got a number of things in common!'

'We'd better be going, hadn't we?' said Amy, turning to me. 'We've got to relieve Aunt Nan.' Her remark annoyed me, for this was the first time I could remember my domestic needs impinging on her consciousness. It was partly for this reason that I invited Nancy to supper. She accepted immediately, saying she would love to come.

Walking home, Amy said, 'As far as I know, Colette and Stein never met. I'm pretty sure they would not have been to one another's liking.'

Nancy Cole and I became friends on an intermittent basis, seeing each other two or three times during the course of a Festival and keeping loosely in touch in the times between with the occasional postcard. I seldom saw her and Amy together; they competed so strongly in personality that they tended to cancel each other out. They could both be very demanding: it was part of their intensity.

*

The day after that particular performance of *Gertrude Stein*, Amy and I had our row. It really began between Vinca and Amy. Vinca had gone into her room to fetch a sweater from her drawer and had disturbed Amy, who was resting before going out to do her show. (I would not like to put my hand on my heart and swear that Vinca did not do it deliberately, to be awkward.) Amy accused Vinca of being a thoughtless and inconsiderate little girl. Didn't she know that it was rude to burst into someone's room when they were in it? And without so much as knocking?

'I didn't know you were in. Anyway, it's *my* room!'

The row was happening on the top landing. I raced up the stairs.

'What's going on!' I demanded.

'She can be a cheeky little thing, this daughter of yours.'

There were times when I might have said so myself, but I was not prepared to hear anyone else say it. I informed Amy icily that she had not the faintest idea how to deal with or speak to children, that she didn't seem to realize or acknowledge that Vinca had *given up* her room for her – naturally I would not say that I'd had to twist her arm – and she was not used to grown-ups lying in their beds during the day. Out of the corner of my eye I could see Vinca's eyes gleaming.

'You can't stand anyone criticizing your children, can you?'

'Few mothers can. But you wouldn't know anything about that, would you?'

'You know what Colette said about motherhood? That it was a great banality.'

'I don't give a damn what Colette said! She's not God, you know.'

'I've never claimed that she was, but that doesn't mean I can't quote from her.'

'The trouble with quoting is that it's so easy to do it out of context, besides being a good cop-out, using someone else's words. *Printed* words, as if that gives them extra validity. It's time you stopped using Colette to hide behind.'

That stung, as I'd intended it to do; I had winded her. When she'd recovered she said, 'You're making it perfectly plain that you regret inviting me to stay here. Perhaps it would be better if I went.'

'Perhaps it would.'

I went back down the stairs. Amy began to pack.

'Where's she going to go?' asked my husband, who was washing the lunch dishes.

'I do not know, and, what is more, I do not care.'

'You can't let her go out on the street.'

'Can't I?'

She opened the door behind us, making us jump guiltily, and asked in an overly polite voice if she might use the telephone. She'd never asked before, not even when she'd made calls at peak times to Paris. She'd talked to Pascal daily, often for thirty or forty minutes. And, of course, she had never paid for any of the calls. I was ringing the amounts up furiously in my head as I seized a dishcloth and began to dry the dishes.

She made two calls now, one to a friend of mine who agreed to give her a room without being told the reason why, and another for a cab to take her there.

'Goodbye,' she said, 'and thank you for your hospitality.'

We didn't see each other for two weeks and then Jessie effected a meeting. 'You canne go on like this,' she said. 'You're like a couple of bairns, no better than Vinca and her friend Flora.' When I walked into Jessie's kitchen, there was Amy, drinking a cup of tea. We fell into each other's arms.

'I know I'm hopeless to live with,' she said.

'I know I'm paranoid about my children,' I said.

Amy didn't come to Edinburgh when my father died in 1974 – I told her on the phone that she should not: it would cost money, and she had recently been over for the Festival – but when Aunt Nan followed him a few months later she decided that this was a funeral she must attend.

It was a sad event for all of us. The children were virtually inconsolable. This was the first death to touch them. They'd been fond of my father, but Aunt Nan had been their very special friend. She had comforted them when they were sad, or when their parents were being horrible to them. They were too old now to shout, 'It's not fair!' but I could see it in their eyes. We were all agreed that Aunt Nan couldn't have gone on much longer. She'd been eighty-three, a good age. She hadn't been well recently and had come to the stage when she needed a rest. We said all the things one says at such times.

Amy, Jessie and I were the chief mourners, supported by my husband. The crematorium chapel was packed with friends and neighbours. The minister said that our dear friend Agnes had been much loved in the parish of St Stephen and would be sorely missed. Everyone had a good word to say for her afterwards when we stood at the door shaking hands. She'd been a real character in the neighbourhood. There didn't seem to be characters like her around nowadays.

My husband went off to reclaim the children from a friend and take them to the pictures. Jessie, Amy and I went to the steamie.

It had been turned into an Armenian restaurant. Gone were the tubs and big mangles, the pulleys and the scrubbing boards; gone was the smell of hot suds and steam. Gone were the women with bare red forearms, flapping white sheets in the air like sails in the wind. Gone were the beaten-up prams standing before the door. But, as I followed Amy and Jessie in, I had the sensation of there being someone at my back and I could swear I heard Granny Balfour's voice in my ear. 'Whit in the name's a' this! Plants in the steamie and folk frying in the steamie! And ye can hardly see yer finger in front o' ye, it's that dark. Candles in the steamie! *Armenian* food in the steamie! For crying out loud! I never thocht I'd see the day!' I expected to feel the wheels of her old pram dunt me in the back of the legs.

We were seated at a large round communal table. It was not possible to make out who was sitting on the other side; the faces were mere glimmers in the darkness. We were insubstantial beings at a ghostly banquet. Candles provided a flickering, shifting light and smoke issuing from the brazier at the back eddied into every corner of the room, to create a pall of blue-grey fog to hang over us. Our eyes watered profusely until they adjusted.

It was not a place to go if one was in a hurry. We were not. A death in the family seems to have the effect of slowing down time. We had to await the pleasures of the owner, who did all the cooking more or less single-handed. From time to time other black-outlined figures appeared around the fire, but it was not clear who they were or what they were doing. Making spells, perhaps, like the witches in *Macbeth*. Diners helped themselves to cheap red Bulgarian wine and at the end of the evening the number of bottles was totted up. We consumed a bottle among the three of us before food touched our lips, and when it did we were glad to eat without questioning what it was. One took what one was given.

The first course was some kind of meat pattie, which we demolished in two bites. I went to fetch another bottle.

'I'll be fleeing before I'm done,' said Jessie, holding out her glass. 'But I might as well be hanged for a sheep . . .'

'Here's to Aunt Nan, bless her soul!' said Amy.

'Aunt Nan,' we repeated, and drank to her.

I raised my glass again. 'And here's to Granny Balfour, too! May she not be turning in her grave!'

I had again the distinct feeling that she was doing nothing of the sort but was sitting right beside me, shifting her large bulk on the chair. And humphing. But enjoying herself, too, in her own way.

When my eyes began to see again, I recognized Amy's neighbour. He was a poet, and well under the influence of the Bulgarian wine. In spite of that he recognized me, and Amy, too.

'You play that Frenchwoman at the Festival, don't you?'

'Colette, yes.'

'What do you want to pretend to be someone else for?' He tried to poke Amy in the centre of her chest with two fingers but she drew back and he half-slumped on top of her. She had to push him back up. 'How do you know who you are?' he demanded, asking a question I would not have dared to ask anyone, let alone Amy. '*Do* you know?'

'I know perfectly well, thank you.' Her voice was tart. 'And I am well aware that I am not Colette except when I am on the stage.'

'But you can be on stage off.' (He was not all *that* drunk.)

'My life may be interwoven through hers, but it doesn't mean I'm confused about my own identity.' (Brave words of Amy's.)

He turned his attention to me. He pointed a finger. 'What about *her*? *Making up* folk? Hundreds, thousands of them? How many books have you written? Aren't there enough people in the world without having to invent them?'

'Ah, but I can control my people.'

'Think you're bloody God, do you?'

'You're darned right I do!'

'What about yourself?' said Amy.

'I only write about me.' He looked smug.

'And how can you be sure you're not inventing yourself?' I asked.

'That's enough of all that!' cried Jessie. 'Let's get on with the evening!'

Her voice was drowned out by a burst of Armenian music. From then on, one had to shout to communicate. The poet went to sleep, sprawled across the table, his head between his arms. Mine host left his fire to demonstrate an Armenian dance up the middle of the room; it resembled Russian Cossack dancing and involved much kicking and bending of the knees and flinging of the right arm upward. The clientèle obligingly stamped and clapped in time. Then Jessie rose and, lifting her arms above her head, more in the manner of a Spanish than a Russian dancer, went to join the proprietor. They twirled like two dervishes in the firelight. Amy and I clapped and chanted, our elbows moving in and out like bellows, and cheered loudly when the music ended and Jessie and her partner bowed low to one another.

'You didne ken I still had it in me, did you?' she said.

But we had always known: Jessie was game, ever ready for a laugh and a new experience. She brimmed with life.

We had arrived at the restaurant at eight o'clock; it was getting on for two in the morning by the time we went rolling home along Henderson Row, arms linked, singing a selection of songs from the Grand Picture House days. *Somewhere over the rainbow*, *Meet me in St Louis*, *Deep in the heart of Texas*. Aunt Nan had sung all these songs to my children.

But the Grand Picture House was no more; it had become a nightclub and traded its name for Tiffany's. We decided to go one evening, the three of us, before Amy returned to Paris. As part of our sentimental journey. It seemed like the end of an era.

So we went to Tiffany's and danced to the Band of Gold. It was an over-thirties night. 'I'll admit to being over thirty,' said Jessie as she settled herself at a table with a glass of tequila sunrise. She had had her hair tinted a new shade of strawberry-blonde and wore a shimmery lilac dress with a sequinned top. Her eyelids and lips matched her dress. She surveyed the room. 'First thing you've got to do at a dance is look over the talent. I must say, I wouldne mind a fella to rock with.' On cue, as if he'd overheard, up came an elderly gent nattily dressed in a blue blazer with gold buttons, fawn whipcord trousers and two-tone cream and tan shoes. He was not much of a rocker but he danced the waltz to perfection, as did Jessie herself. His two-tone feet blended beautifully with her silver ones. He was a retired servitor at the university. And a widower. They married four months later, a week before the Festival opened that year. Just a quiet family affair, with Amy and me acting as witnesses.

The marriage lasted for seven years, good ones, Jessie was able to say after Hughie's death. She was thrice a widow, and enough was enough, she said, so she decided to hang up her skates, at least as far as marriage was concerned.

*

Tiffany's was to remain a nightclub for some years, but in an effort to keep up with the times it changed its name again, to Cinderella's Rockafellas; then it closed, and for a while lay gloomy and silent until, one night, a flame caught and licked its way greedily along the roof's dry timbers, remorseless and insatiable. By the time it was quenched, it was too late. The roof had caved in, the walls were reduced to a shell. And so the street's landmark burned to the ground, leaving a huge gash in its side. Now one could see down across the wasteland to Henderson Row, but there was neither a steamie nor an Armenian restaurant to be sighted, for the building had been razed to the ground by bulldozers, and on its site had risen up an insurance company's posh offices masquerading as a French château. That surely must have caused Granny Balfour to turn in her grave! There are restless ghosts in Edinburgh as well as Paris.

When Amy returned to Paris after Aunt Nan's funeral, she found that Pascal had gone.

Twelve

'The big looking-glass in my room no
longer throws back the painted image of a
nomadic music-hall artiste. It reflects only
– myself. Behold me then, just as I am!'

La Vagabonde

'What do you mean he's gone?'

'*Gone* – just what I said. What does it usually mean when
you say that a person has gone? They've taken off. Vamoosed.'

Someone said something to her in the background, which
gave me a moment to gather my wits and adjust to the
situation. 'It's Chéri,' I mouthed to Jessie, who was sitting by
my fire drinking a cup of coffee and smoking a cigarette. 'He's
done a bunk.' She raised an eyebrow, but the news would not
have surprised her any more than it had me; it seemed as if
we had been waiting for it for years. We had discussed it often.
We couldn't expect him to stay with Amy for ever; he was so
young when he attached himself to her, he had been of a
romantic turn of mind, he was less young now, probably less
romantic . . . It was only the timing of the announcement that
had caught me off guard. We had seen Amy off twenty-four
hours before and we'd just been saying what good fettle she'd
been in during her visit, what a good time we'd all had in spite
of Aunt Nan's death, and how surprising life could be. And
now here was Amy on the line sounding frantic.

'Cinq minutes,' said Amy irritably to someone who was
pestering her. 'Are you still there?'

Yes, I was still here.

'When I came back, there was this note lying on the

table. As soon as I saw it, and his writing on the envelope, I knew!'

'Had he said anything before about going?'

'He had been drinking quite a lot of late. Avoiding me, I suppose. Damn, I'm about to run out of money!'

'I'll ring you back.' (This was following a pattern.)

'Wait five minutes. There's this imbecile who keeps trying to grab the receiver off me.'

To Jessie I said, 'He left a note.'

'A *note*?' She sniffed. 'Only cowards write notes.'

It meant that Amy had been deprived of playing out her last scene with Chéri. But what did surprise me was that Pascal had deprived himself of it; I had imagined he would be unable to resist it.

'Just as well, for her sake,' said Jessie. 'All that thinking he's going to change his mind and turn back! Yon scene always makes me want to greet. You writers fairly like to turn the screw.'

I leant on the fireplace and frowned down into the fire. 'I hope she's not going to ask me to come over.'

'You can't go, can you?'

I shook my head. I had a deadline to meet.

'Why is it that she always picks the wrong men?' I said

'Ach well, who can say?' said Jessie, cheering up. 'Chéri lasted a good long time. Think of it that way.'

'It must be sixteen years.'

'I count that long. What age will he be now?'

'Thirty-three, thirty-four.'

I glanced at the clock and saw that ten minutes had passed. I dialled the number of Amy's café; I knew it by heart. She answered on the first ring.

'I thought you'd forgotten!'

'I was giving the man time.'

'He was only calling a cab!'

'So where has Pascal gone? Did he say?'

'The Côte d'Azur!' She was sounding scornful now, even a little angry, which I considered a good sign. In a moment she might even be calling him a little rat. She had on an occasion in the past when he'd let her down; he'd turned up late for a show, a little drunk, without the flowers for the set. Some anger would be necessary to help burn out the pain. And I did not doubt that she would be feeling pain; I knew her attachment to Pascal was not superficial and her daily life was – had been – interwoven through his.

'Has he gone alone?'

'Can you imagine Pascal *alone*? He hates his own company.'

I suggested feebly that he might come back, that he might just be in need of a fling, but I could not convince myself let alone her. I allowed Amy to talk, to ramble on for almost an hour; she travelled back over the years with Pascal, remembering this incident and that, recalling the happy hours – for the present, the others were forgotten – until another man's voice broke through hers, demanding to know if she was going to be on the phone all bloody night.

'Un moment!' she said sharply. Then she sighed.

'I would come over,' I said, 'but – '

'I know, you've got your own life to lead.'

'Ring me tomorrow! Courage!'

She went back to her empty flat and wrote me a letter.

'I'm fifty now – a watershed. Another one! – doesn't seem long since I hurdled over forty. They get closer and closer together, like horse-jumps in a steeplchase; there's hardly room to loup over one before you're brought up short against the next. Bucking and rearing. But one must at least attempt to go up and over. Or else lie bleeding on the ground. Fifty is a difficult time, though, for a woman.'

More difficult for a woman who has no children, I reflected, knowing that there is no one coming behind, no younger hands to grasp the relay baton. Jessie being an exception. Though how do I know what Jessie feels deep down? She would never tell me. She's good for a laugh, is known in the street as a cheery soul: that is the way she wants to keep it. Perhaps I *can* take her at face value; I have never seen her other than basically content with her lot. I know that I cannot take Amy at face value; she has worn too many masks.

'Rejection is difficult at any age,' Amy's letter continued, 'for a man or a woman. So here I sit on top of the jolly old scrap-heap, rubbing shoulders with rusted car chassis, burst tyres and old refrigerators whose doors are hanging off their hinges. I am hanging off my hinge! All right, I won't give way to self-pity! It is too tedious for everybody.

'You could say I was a fool to take up with such a young man – I know that many would say it – but that is just the way the cards fell. And I did love him. I do, still. Goudeket was sixteen years younger than Colette and he stayed with her, but they met when they were the ages that Pascal and I are now. Perhaps that made a difference. Goudeket had his youth first. Pascal gave me his! What a gift! Should I be grateful, then, and resign myself? Je t'embrasse — Amy.'

'Plenty more fish in the sea,' said Jessie, who had just had her first date with Hughie. They'd danced the night away at a dinner dance at a hotel on Saturday night and had a date to go to the dogs the next day. 'She's a young woman yet.'

I went over to Paris a couple of months later. Amy's settee was lumpy and slightly too short for me; I got up in the morning with a stiff neck and I hated washing in cold water at the kitchen sink. My time for envying la vie bohème had passed. I missed my morning bath. I was soft, said Amy; I did not argue. We had to go round the corner to the flat of her friend Christiane for a bath, something one could not do every day. And Christiane had only a hip bath, so that one had to sit with one's knees up to one's chin. Christiane worked in advertising. She was one of a string of friends Amy had in Paris with whom she was intimate yet not close. She would see them constantly, for a while, talk about them, and then suddenly they would drop out of her life. When I'd ask, 'How's Christiane?' she'd say, 'Christiane? Oh, I haven't seen her for ages!' And I would never hear of her again. Amy still saw

Camille from time to time, either in Paris or Rouen (Camille went on to have five children, by her husband, as far as Amy knew, though could not be certain), and she was in touch with Paulette regularly, by letter and telephone. Paulette rang her once a month at the café, by prior arrangement.

'To keep me on the straight and narrow. While she grows fat! Look!' Amy showed me a picture of a plump middle-aged woman wearing butterfly-shaped spectacles. Beside her stood a handsome, silver-haired man looking a bit like Alistair Cooke. 'She's settled for domesticity. She says I have to live out her fantasies. Some fantasies!'

I lifted from the mat an envelope postmarked Saint-Tropez. The handwriting was curlicued and elegant. I laid it in front of Amy's place at the breakfast table and watched her open and read it.

'He is anxious to know if I'm all right.'

I sniffed, rather as Jessie might have done.

'He does care about me, I believe that. You can look as sceptical as you like! He's not heartless. But I suppose we'd come to the end of the road together and I have to accept that.'

I was realizing the full extent of Amy's loss: out of her life in one blow had gone lover, son, companion, stage manager and agent. She could not afford to employ anyone else to manage and organize her affairs; after all this time she had to start to do it again herself, and she was not finding it easy. It was Pascal who had had all the contacts, drunk in the bars, hung out with other theatre people. Her income began to decline. She had to take on more typing work. Her typewriter stood on the table, lopsided and battered-looking; the carriage return would work only in a downhill position and the letter 'b' had lost its back. On impulse I offered to buy her a new machine, an electronic one.

'Would you? That would be wonderful! Can you afford it? You're always saying the kids cost a fortune.'

'They do, but I'll buy it for you anyway!'

We bought it the next day. The purchase lifted her spirits. We put up fresh ads in a couple of bookshops on Saint-Germain. 'High-quality typing offered on brand-new electronic typewriter . . .' Then we went to a café and sat outside in the sun, drinking coffee and watching the people drift by, and Amy said that really she did like living in Paris very much still, in spite of everything. She hoped never to leave it.

'Perhaps even after a while I'll be able to be friends with Pascal.'

'Do you think that would be possible?'

'I wouldn't rule it out. Not yet, though. I'm too sore.'

'Wouldn't you be jealous of his other woman?'

'Oh, it's not a woman he's gone off with! That's why I could contemplate friendship.'

The following spring Amy went on a mini-provincial tour, starting again with Rouen, where Camille valiantly mustered an audience, though not one that could compare with the first time Amy played there, when they had arrived in their furs and jewels. Amy said she was becoming too familiar to them, she had lost her rarity value. 'I am too available,' she wrote on the back of a picture postcard of Rouen cathedral. From there she went on to Amiens, where Camille's sister lived. 'I am becoming a bore for other people's relatives! "Be kind to poor old Amy!" But everyone has been sweet here. And thirty people came to see my show. Suzanne's husband is a solicitor, so he is well known in the town. On now to Lille, where Camille has no relatives! I shall find a cheap room near the station, no doubt, where the light will be so poor I won't be able to see the shadows under my eyes in the mirror.'

'rue de Grenelle

'Just got in. Glad to be home. Touring alone is not a bundle of fun. Or perhaps I am getting a little old for it! I still enjoy the actual performances, that part is all right. Though I miss having Pascal to turn to in all sorts of ways. I miss him to chat to before I go on, to steady my nerve. I miss him at the end when I'm taking my bow. I look involuntarily to the back of the hall, and he is not there. I shall have to learn not to look, to keep my eyes on the audience.

'I have not made my fortune out there on the road, needless to say. I have done little more than cover expenses, as usual, and wouldn't have done that if it weren't for the hospitality of Camille and her family. Perhaps I should give up provincial touring and try to find a new location to play in here in Paris. But perhaps everyone who wants to see me has seen me. I can't go on reviving myself for ever!

'Je t'embrasse — Amy.

'PS A note from Pascal was waiting for me, by the way: he has gone travelling in Italy.'

'All right for him,' said Jessie. 'He must have struck it rich. But what's Amy going to do?'

Another letter arrived the following day: a chance meeting had brought her if not a shift in fortune, then the chance of playing again in Paris.

'I met two men, two nice men, at my friend Marianne's. Marcel and Maxim. Marcel is an interior designer, Maxim a poet. They live in a splendid apartment near the Luxembourg Garden and they have invited me to give my show in their salon!'

'Who's Marianne?' asked Jessie. 'I thought her friend was called Christiane?'

'That's someone different.'

When I spoke to Amy on the phone after the performance she sounded buoyant. It seemed that she had been a great success. About twenty people had come, and paid well for the privilege! And of course she had had no overheads. Maxim and Marcel had served champagne. They had enjoyed themselves; they had said they must do it again. So, you see, people still wanted her, and fresh opportunities kept coming up all the time!

'She's an optimist, I guess, in the end, wouldn't you say?' said Jessie. 'If she picked up a fiver in the street she'd think she was about to become rich.'

Amy would certainly never become rich giving one-woman shows on the Edinburgh Festival Fringe. I was having trouble finding a suitable venue for her that year. I had booked a small hall in the city centre originally, but there had been a mix-up over the reservation, some confusion about double-booking – or else someone had come in with a better offer – and so we had lost ours. After days of trailing around the city and numerous phone calls, I had been forced to take the only thing available: a church hall in the suburbs. Apart from the disadvantage of its location the hall was far too big, and far too high, and it smelt of dust and Presbyterian hymn books. Standing there in the chilly, echoing space, it was difficult to image oneself being transported to the Palais-Royal salon of Colette. We knew that Amy would not be pleased.

She was not. Oh well, she would just have to make the best of it, wouldn't she? As I had said, it would be a challenge, and she was aware that a good artist should be able to take an audience right out of its surroundings. 'You always do,' I said. 'Don't flatter me!' she said.

I phoned up everyone I could think of who had either not seen her 'Colette' or would like to see it again. I offered inducements. 'Come back for a drink afterwards! For supper!' Jessie talked Hughie into persuading some of the members of his bowling club to come; they would get in at a concessionary rate since they were senior citizens. I twisted the arm of a *Scotsman* reviewer. 'We have reviewed her before, you know, several times, and space is very limited at Festival-time. Do you know how many shows there are on the Fringe this year?' 'Just three lines,' I pleaded. 'A mention. She's had a difficult year.' 'So have I,' he said. But he did it.

At Amy's first performance Jessie and I awaited with trepidation the episode involving Chéri; it would come after Colette's marriage to Jouvenel and before she met Goudeket.

Jessie thought Amy would cut it. 'She would if she'd any sense!' I thought she might try to meet it head on, and she did; she played the scene with great intensity but unflinchingly. Watching her, I was confident she would not go to pieces. Jessie and I were not the only ones in the audience to be moved.

Attendances were down, overall, as we expected; who would want to trail out to a suburb for their entertainment? (Unless one was unfortunate enough to live there. Which is the way that Jessie and I, confirmed city-dwellers, see it). Then, too, the Fringe was burgeoning and had been for years, so that there was more choice. When we had a post-mortem at the end of Amy's run we came to the conclusion that she would have to try to bring something new next time.

Throughout the seventies and eighties, performances on the Festival Fringe mushroomed, their spores spreading further and further out from the city centre. It became increasingly difficult to find good central venues at moderate rents, attract audiences and reviews. The latter were essential for a successful run. For performers like Amy – and Nancy Cole – bringing back the same show year after year was especially difficult. They couldn't expect to go on being noticed, not with so many new events jostling for attention. The only answer was for them to bring new material themselves. Nancy Cole compiled a programme of Canadian writing, under the title *Ladiespeak*, which did not have the impact of her *Gertrude Stein*, and then a rather odd concoction entitled *With Love, John Lennon*, which she called 'a séance, a poetic surrealistic circus'. Victor Spinetti said, 'John would have loved it.' Others (including myself) didn't think it came off. *Stein* remained her triumph, just as *Colette* was to remain Amy's.

'You're right,' said Amy, 'I can't go on playing Colette for ever.'

'Went for a picnic in the Bois with my friends Marcel and Maxim. It was a perfect autumn day – warm, with a little

284

breeze. The colours were just beginning to turn. We sat under a tree and ate oeufs en gelée, chicken breasts scented with tarragon, fresh baguettes and some delicious cheeses, and drank chilled Vouvray. We got to reminiscing about Colette, of course, and how she used to walk her dogs here in the Bois, when she has lived on the boulevard Suchet in her role of Madame la Baronne. She walked them in the mornings and wrote in the afternoons from three to six. Maxim and Marcel say I should get a dog! Dogs are a tie, I told them.

'Je t'embrasse — Amy.'

'Like children,' said Jessie.

'Marcel and Maxim have presented me with a dog! An English bulldog. Called Toby-Chien. Surprise, surprise! They arrived with it at my door yesterday afternoon. The concierge's eyes were bulging, like the dog's. She took me aside to warn me that I should on no account allow it to crap in the courtyard. I could not pretend to be overjoyed by the gift. He sat on the rug in front of my fire and gazed at me sorrowfully. He knew he was not wanted. He looked as if he wanted to crap.

'Marcel and Maxim insisted that we all go for a walk in the Bois. They called a cab and we rode there with Toby-Chien sitting upright on my knee. I was then induced to promenade up and down one of the paths with the animal on a leash so that Marcel could take photographs. For publicity purposes, he said. It provided Marcel and Maxim with a great deal of amusement, at any rate. They were highly delighted with themselves. What was I to do with Toby-Chien when I went on tour? I asked them. When I went to Edinburgh? Such questions were inartistic, Maxim hinted.

'"To hell with art!" I told them, and walked off, leaving their present – and them – behind.

'Love to all — Amy.'

There was a time when Amy would have gone along with Maxim and Marcel's little joke; she would have been amused by it, would have been happy to *be* Madame la Baronne parading her dog in the Bois for all to see. I'd noticed, on her last visit to Edinburgh, that she no longer said 'I' when she was asked about Colette, and she used the past, not the present. *Yes, she was a great admirer of Balzac . . . Cocteau was her neighbour . . .* Jessie had noticed it too.

'It's as if she's trying to separate out the two sides of her life,' I said. 'On stage she's Colette, off stage herself – Amélie Bussac Balfour.'

But in shedding the protection of Colette's mantle Amy must now be having to face up more squarely to her own life. Was it simply because she was ageing that she was ready to do so? I wondered; or that her career was beginning to run down? I sensed that other thoughts were disturbing her. One night, when we'd been sitting up late, and there'd been a long silence between us, she twitched her neck as if a shiver had run up her spine, and she said, with a small, rueful smile, 'Restless ghosts . . .'

There was still the problem of a new show for her. I made various suggestions, amongst which was George Sand. Amy considered the idea and decided to go ahead. It would be a challenge! And keep her busy over the winter. Sand had written more than a hundred books and ten volumes of autobiography.

In the following months Amy's letters revolved almost exclusively around George Sand. Did I know that Turgenev had said, 'What a good man she was, and what a kind woman'? That Flaubert wept at her funeral? As did all the local country people who had come from round about, whilst they stood in the rain listening to a long letter from Victor Hugo being read out. Which they had not been able to make head nor tail of. 'Fascinating,' wrote Amy.

'Thank goodness!' I said to Jessie. 'It's what she needed. A new project to work on, to get her teeth into. To help her get over Pascal.'

He had remained in Italy but he still wrote weekly to Amy,

and she to him. He was settled in the hills above Florence, in some kind of palazzo, and was helping to organize art exhibitions.

'Living the life of Riley!' said Jessie. 'While Amy slogs away on her typewriter for a pittance.'

'Colette was right to call Sand the great bee,' wrote Amy. 'There is so much stuff! I'm probably doing too much research, but often it's difficult to know when to stop once you get started. And how do you know what you're going to need until you've done it? It's another lifetime's work, really.' And she must have known that she did not have much of hers left.

I was apprehensive about the undertaking as the time of the Festival drew nearer. Amy could not afford another failure in her life. She had been steeped in Colette from early childhood; there was no possibility of her getting into the skin of Sand in the same way.

'Does that matter?' asked my husband sensibly.

'Probably not,' I agreed; it would just be different.

'You wouldn't want to stick to one subject all your life, would you?'

The trouble was, I couldn't really see Amy as Sand. And it had been all my idea!

'Stop worrying yourself sick!' said Jessie. 'It'll be all right on the night. Isn't that what they say?'

Amy arrived full of enthusiasm. I had found a venue not too far from the centre, so she was happy about that. We had a dress rehearsal the day before. Jessie and I sat in the back row. After half an hour I felt Jessie stifling a yawn. Jessie was a good barometer: she demanded to be entertained, to have her attention held. A flow of ideas was not enough for her. I knew what was the matter: Amy was playing the part competently, she had done her homework well and arranged the material skilfully, but she had not worked her way emotionally into the part. She had forgotten Paulette and The Method. Watching her, I felt as if I were watching Colette trying to portray George Sand. To me the conflict of interest was obvious.

Amy had a fairly full house for her opening performance – composed largely of people we knew – and the response was warm. Next day there was a review in the *Scotsman*. 'A thoughtful, well-researched portrait with many illuminating moments, but not as convincing, it has to be said, as her "Colette" . . .'

Amy was furious. 'You try something new and they knock you for it!'

'They haven't *knocked* you. "Thoughtful, well-researched – "'

'"Not convincing"!'

'"Illuminating"!'

Two or three other reviews followed, saying much the same thing. None of them offered great praise, which of course was what Amy was looking for and what she needed to boost her ego. As always she seized on the negative parts of the reviews and churned them over in her mind, neglecting to take comfort from the praise. I did not reproach her for that: I understood it only too well.

'I hate critics,' she said. '*Reviewers*!'

She brought *George Sand* back the following year, then abandoned her in favour of the Russian painter and diarist Marya Bashkirtseva, who imbued her with fresh enthusiasm. She rang me from a telephone box at one in the morning (the café was shut) to tell me she'd 'discovered' her. 'Sorry, I didn't realize the time! Did I waken you?' She'd been sitting up reading Bashkirtseva's diaries. 'She died of TB when she was twenty-four, so although there's a lot of material – eighty-four volumes of autobiography – there aren't so many years to span.'

Amy's show based on Bashkirtseva survived for only one year; her treatment was too superficial and she had to play in a gloomy church hall in a far-flung suburb. She – we – lost money on that enterprise. On one occasion she had an audience of four, two of whom were Jessie and myself.

Amy missed a couple of Edinburgh Festivals in the mid-eighties and returned in 1987 with a revival of Colette, which went down well and played to good-sized houses. She needed a little success at this stage in her life; she tired more easily and her health was not particularly good, though she would not go and see a doctor. She coughed in the mornings and was breathless by the time she trudged up the steep incline from Stockbridge to Princes Street. She was also having a problem with allergies, which she attributed to the pollution in Paris.

'rue de Grenelle

'Returned from Edinburgh in stage of collapse. Continue to regret the passing of the Magic Bus. It's the lugging of luggage on and off buses and the ferry that's the killer. Have spent three days in bed, too tired even to read, listening to the radio. Radio 4 and the World Service are my lifelines at times like this: they bring words and voices into my room. I lie on my "raft" and let myself float. It would be nice to have a Maurice Goudeket to attend me! Have been reading his book again, *La Douceur de vieillir*, not because it is so very profound (it is not, and it's mostly about Colette, not about growing old), but because I would like to feel there is some delight in growing old! Right now I can't see much: the face that stares back at me from the mirror does not please me with its marks of pain and displeasure, and my body is running down like an old car. ("Not that again," you are going to say!) It was all right for Goudeket: he was probably of more sanguine temperament than I, and he also had the advantage of two good and stable marriages. Thirty years to an older woman, followed by nearly twenty to one much younger, both of whom were able to keep him in the comfort that he enjoyed. Does it all come down in the end to material security? Would hate to think so. — A.'

Jessie of course thought that Amy's salvation would have lain in finding another man. Amy had gone out occasionally with other men since Pascal's defection. One was called Simon, another, Pierre. She had had a couple of dates with each and written enthusiastic notes about their sensitivity and charm; she told us how much we would like them. Then they had gone the way of Christiane and many others, and we had never heard of them again. After Pascal, I thought that she had not had the heart to get involved with anyone else. I thought, too, that she wanted to be alone: it was a conscious choice.

'Rallying. Managed to go to church. I go most Sundays, either to Saint-Pierre du Gros Caillou in the rue Dominique or across the river to the Scots Kirk in the rue Bayard. Oh yes, I'm still having it both ways! Don't ask me if I believe! I don't know. I'm hanging on, in case. Perhaps that's belief enough. Can it all have been based on fiction? On lies? If it has, a mere story has had an amazing impact on the world! Surely there are at least grains of truth in there, at the heart. The soul must go somewhere after sloughing off its withered coil?

'Yesterday, I went to the Scots Kirk. Felt like talking to Scots people. Went home for lunch with my friend Madame Hamon. Have I told you about her? She was from Edinburgh originally, lived in Morningside, married a Parisian who is now dead, but she stayed on. She's been here fifty years.

'Did a little typing when I got back. Had to. Must keep the pot boiling, or at least simmering. Not much more work in sight, though. Too many damned word processors around. My friend Marcelle has suggested I buy one. Just like that! Do you know what they cost? I asked her. She is not a very sensitive person, Marcelle. She works for the government. She also suggested that I give up the idea of performing! "It doesn't make sense to go on," she said, "you're only beating your head against a stone wall. You don't make any money out of it, do you? You get all worked up for nothing." I asked her if she knew what it would mean to me if I had to give it up. It would be like putting out the light, I told her. She didn't understand. But you do, don't you?

'Je t'embrasse — Amy.'

'I'm wondering about Suzanne Valadon. What do you think? Would she be a suitable subject for me? Or Berthe Morisot? What thinkest thou? I'm reading a biog. of B.M. at present, see possibilities. Has to be an artist of some kind to turn me on, as you know.

'Met Maxim and Marcel outside the Orangerie yesterday. We stopped and talked and they have invited me to lunch. Was pleased to see my old friends again. How silly that one allows parts of one's life to fall away! How awful it is losing people – of all things! Especially over a dog. We laughed about that. (Toby-Chien went to someone who appreciated him more.)

'Je t'embrasse — Amy.'

'This stupid allergy of mine continues to bother me. It affects my breathing. Don't worry – I am still breathing! It's pollution that's the problem and no one's about to do anything about that. The guff from the exhausts gets worse every year. The cities of the world are being smothered, and their occupants along with them. I go about with a scarf over my mouth like a bandit! — A.'

My daughter Vinca went to stay with Amy for a few days. Vinca was now married and had a child of her own, as well as a full-time demanding job. Her husband thought she needed a break. He was to look after the child while she was gone.

Vinca did not mind the lumps in the sofa or washing in cold water; they took baths at the apartment of Amy's friend Sylvie in the avenue Bosquet. Sylvie was a freelance photographer. The few days in Paris brought a whiff of liberty to Vinca and she and Amy got on extremely well. They had had a great time, she reported on return; they'd been out to Clignancourt to the flea market, gone to museums, listened to jazz, sat at the cafés, talked to lots of interesting people.

'I have to confess that I do rather envy you your daughter,' wrote Amy.

*

She came to the Edinburgh Festival for the last time in 1991, and played Colette. She looked tired but was cheerful, even when audiences were small, which they mostly were. She would have to think up a new show for next year, she said. We batted ideas around. The Marquise de Sévigné? Not a big enough draw. Simone de Beauvoir? That would be a big undertaking! Berthe Morisot came round again, as did Suzanne Valadon, and Gwen John . . . Amy's mind darted about restlessly, tossing ideas up in the air like a juggler throwing balls, never keeping hold of any for long enough to test their weight. Maybe best to stick with Colette, I suggested. After all, new people came to the Festival every year. Amy had almost given up performing in France, apart from the occasional visit to Rouen or Amiens, where she played in the drawing rooms of Camille and Camille's sister; Edinburgh was the highlight of her year.

She wrote during the winter that Paris was beginning to get her down. 'I never thought I'd say that!' Tourists were crowding the galleries and pavements all year round, prices were rising weekly, muggers waited in the Métro. And typing work was getting more and more difficult to find. It was not like Amy to be so downbeat. I was worried. 'Perhaps I'm just getting too old to cope with a big city. Paris is best suited to the young.' Part of it, I thought, might be due to the fact that she didn't have as much energy to go out and about in the way she used to; even sitting on a hard chair in a café can be tiring. She must be spending longer hours in her little, ground-floor, sunless flat. She had her pretty coloured lamps, but lack of natural light, as is well known, can affect the spirits.

Soon it might be impossible for her to earn enough money to support herself in Paris. What then? She had no pension fund, no savings in the bank, no insurance policies ready to mature. She had lived her life a day, a week, at a time, without giving thought for the future.

Amy might have to think of returning to Scotland, to Edinburgh. Jessie and I discussed it but, being honest with each other, we admitted that we did not totally relish the idea, knowing how demanding Amy could be.

'She wouldne get a pension, would she?' said Jessie. 'She hasne worked here, has she, not since she was a young lassie? What would she live on?' Jessie sat with her feet on a stool sipping port, her favourite tipple. She was approaching eighty but would have no truck with the idea of sheltered housing, nor would I have thought of talking her into it. She liked her own place. She was an independent woman.

Amy might end up by having to be dependent. My heart quailed at the thought of having to support her materially and emotionally, if she were to come to Edinburgh. My children were grown up now and had left home; their rooms were vacant, but my husband and I had got used to being on our own. Jessie had a spare room, too, but she said it would drive her up the wall if she had to have Amy – or anyone, for that matter – living with her full-time.

Jessie had no feelings of guilt about not making Amy an offer; I did. And after she disappeared it was inevitable that I should reproach myself.

I was just about to go to Australia for a couple of months when Amy's letter, dated 31 May, arrived.

'Going away for a while. Don't worry if you don't hear for a week or two . . .'

Thirteen

'Restless ghosts, illrecovered from blows
received in the past.'

Le Pur et l'Impur

'Sorry to be so mysterious, but will explain everything when
I'm next in touch.'

I lower the piece of blue paper and look at Jessie. I have
read Amy's last message many times since returning from
Australia. 'She obviously didn't intend to leave us hanging.'

'I'm stumped,' says Jessie.

'There's a gap,' I say. 'A hole.'

'Like in a jigsaw puzzle? I always hated jigsaws when I was
a bairn. They put me in mind of wet afternoons. There was
aye a piece missing, and hunt all you would, underneath the
sideboard, down the sides of the chairs, every blinking place
you could imagine, still you'd never find it! It was usually a
man's face, something annoying like that.'

I find the image of a jigsaw too neat and tidy: each piece
clicking into place, no ragged ends left; whereas life is full of
raggedness. I prefer to see a life as a piece of tapestry woven
with threads of many textures and colours, some dark, some
light, some glowing, some sombre, some thick and knobbled,
some finely spun. I feel that a thread has been pulled out of
the fabric of Amy's life and has left a rip, a run, and has
puckered the material round about. I have some thoughts as
to the nature of that thread, but I keep them to myself.

*

The next day, I fly to Paris. I take with me the Baccarat paperweight that Colette gave to Eugénie, Amy's mother, on the occasion of her wedding. I check into a hotel on the rue Vaneau, in the seventh arrondissement, within walking distance of Amy's flat in the rue de Grenelle. I set the paperweight on the windowsill of my room, where it will catch the light. The white flower glows at the heart of it, on its midnight-blue ground.

It is September. The weather is fine, the crispness in the air invigorating, and the Parisians have returned to their city looking fit and bronzed. They throng the Métro steps in the mornings, crowd the small charcuteries and boulangeries of the neighbourhood after work. It reassures me a little to see the city working as normal.

My first port of call is Amy's corner café, where I am known to the patron.

'Any news of Aimée?' he asks. 'She's not been around for a long time.'

'Three months?'

'As long as that! What's she been up to? Not forsaken Paris, has she? She liked her little moan about the city but I didn't think she'd ever leave it, not for good.'

I tell him that Amy was last seen on the first of June driving off in a taxi, heading, as far as is known, for the Gare de l'Est.

'*Last* seen?'

'Yes.'

'Or heard of?'

I nod.

'Mon dieu!' He gives a whistle. 'The first of June, eh? So she never came back from that trip?'

'You *knew* she was going away?'

'I remember the last time she was in – yes! She came for her breakfast, same as usual. She was due to take off later that morning. Nice time of year for a trip, I said. June. Best month of the year. Take me with you, I said! We laughed.'

'Did she say where she was going?'

'Don't think so. She was always coming and going, wasn't she? I never could keep track.'

'Did you notice anything – well, *different* about her?'

He ponders. 'She seemed excited. And I'd say definitely a bit anxious.'

I ring the concierge's bell and wait. I can feel my heart bumping around. Perhaps Amy herself will open the door and stand back for a moment from the threshold regarding me, then she'll smile, say my name and come forward, and we'll embrace.

The door opens, and the concierge appears. She is clutching the top of a long-handled brush. I have disturbed her sweeping of the passage. 'Ah, Madame!' she says and props the brush against the wall. She wipes her hand on her overall, then offers it to me. She is not the concierge who glowered at the unfortunate Toby-Chien; that one is long gone into retirement. This madame is not so fierce, and is amenable to passing the time of day. She invites me into her room, her inner sanctum.

The little room is stuffy though she keeps the door standing open. A large television set, on which people are mouthing soundlessly, dominates the space. From time to time she glances over at it and frowns, as if she is trying to follow the action. She has already told me on the telephone all that she knows, which is little, but she has to go over it again – how Amy came out carrying two suitcases, a red one and a cream one, and what she said to the taxi driver – if only to emphasize that she is keeping nothing back. She commiserates with me. My poor cousin! I must be sick with worry. She knows how close we were.

Amy's apartment has been let again, of course; the landlord couldn't keep it for Amy just on the offchance, not when the rent wasn't being paid. There's a nice young man in there now, quiet, keeps himself to himself. No trouble. That's the kind the concierge quite naturally favours.

'Strange business, this, people disappearing,' she says. 'Some just do vanish, so one hears. The husband of a friend of mine did; he went one night. Right in the middle. Got up, said he had to go out, and was off, like that! Pouf! Never heard of again.'

'But he may have had a reason. To get away from his marriage maybe?'

'You have a point there! Your cousin must have had a reason too?'

I acknowledge that.

I ask if Amy left anything behind in the flat. A few bits and pieces, says the concierge, books mostly, she thinks. (She will know, she will have looked). She gets up. She opens a cupboard behind the television set and lifts out two large cardboard boxes.

I place the boxes on the bed. It is quiet in my blue-grey hotel room; the window is open and I can hear the birds in the Prime Minister's garden. There is no sign of him, there never is. I daresay he has no time to walk in gardens.

On top of the books there are two postcards from Pascal, both from Florence. One is dated 10 June of this year, and says: 'We are going off up to the mountains for a few weeks, where it will be cooler and quieter. Hope you can manage to get out of Paris during the summer. I know the heat bothers you. Je t'embrasse comme toujours, Pascal.' He must be about fifty now, I reflect. The second card, sent on 2 August, reads: 'Haven't heard from you for some time. Are you all right? Do write! Affectueusement — Pascal.'

Both cards were sent after Amy disappeared. I had been thinking that possibly she might have gone to Italy to see him, but obviously this was not so. There should have been other cards and letters which she received from him over the years and kept. Did she take them with her? Or, before leaving, did she burn all her journals and more personal correspondence? I look quickly through the box. There are some old theatre programmes, a menu or two, a few letters, short notes from people like Christiane and Pauline, saying, 'Come to lunch on

297

Sunday', or 'I'll meet you at the Flore at eight o'clock.' Items that she has overlooked because of their insignificance. The books are odds and ends of French and British writing which during their time made a stir but might not bear rereading. *Le Deuxième Sexe*. *La Nausée*. Durrell's Alexandrian quartet. All her Colette is missing.

None of her correspondents has signed a surname; one would not expect them to. This is part of my problem: that I know so few of Amy's friends by their second names. Christiane. Pauline. Camille. Paulette. Amy had many acquaintances in different parts of the world, acquired on tour. Chance acquaintances. She cultivated them, let few opportunities go by to get into casual conversation on buses, in cafés. She had accumulated dozens of little visiting cards. I have seen people passing them to her at the end of her performances in Edinburgh. *If you ever find yourself anywhere near us* . . . Whereas most of us would shove them away in a drawer and forget them, she would file them in a box under the headings of their towns and countries, so that if she were to land up in any of the places she would have a contact there, someone whose settee or floor might be slept on, who might help drum up an audience, lend a hundred francs, twenty dollars or ten pounds if need be. The box is not here.

I do know the telephone number of two friends, however: Marcel and Maxim. When I ring, they invite me to lunch the following day.

Their apartment is elegant, the walls are covered with fine paintings and the table is lovingly and artistically set. I recall that Marcel is an interior designer. It is all as I imagined, from Amy's telling, except for the occupants: I was expecting two dark, poetic-looking young men, and instead am greeted by two who are elderly and white-haired, one (Marcel) being tall and thin and going bald, the other small and round and bustly. Time has moved on for them as for all of us.

We discuss Amy over an excellent meal. How courageous

she was, they say, battling on against all the odds with no security, always so short of money.

'Have you tried her bank again?' asks Maxim.

I have, and have been told, as I had been previously, that there have been no transactions to her account since the end of May.

I ask Marcel and Maxim when they last saw her. Sometime in May, they are fairly sure about that; they have discussed it and they both remember the occasion.

'We were rather surprised, you see,' said Maxim.

They met Amy by chance in Printemps. She was buying presents.

'*Presents*?'

'Yes, quite a lot of presents. We wouldn't have thought Amy could afford to splurge out like that. "You'd think it was Christmas," we joked. She said she'd been saving up. She bought some beautiful scarves and a blue silk blouse and earrings and leather gloves and perfume — we helped her choose.'

'And toys!' adds Marcel. 'Don't forget the toys! She had books and a doll — '

I interrupt him. 'Who was she buying them for?'

' "Friends," she said.'

For want of other leads to follow, I spend a considerable amount of time hanging around Amy's café, drinking coffee and small glasses of marc and chatting to the patron. When I come in one lunchtime, he calls me over to the bar and introduces me to a middle-aged woman, a Madame Armand. She is receptionist at the doctor's surgery that Amy used to attend.

'I was just telling Madame Armand about your cousin.'

Madame Armand is sympathetic. We get into conversation and I end up joining her over her sandwich lunch. She didn't really know Amy, she said; she'd only seen her two or three times when she'd come into the surgery.

'But she did come in?'

'Oh yes.'

I ask if she could arrange for me to talk to the doctor and I accompany her back to the surgery. I sit in the waiting room, leafing through magazines, while she goes to consult with Doctor Barbaret. She comes back smiling, and beckons. He will see me.

A small, spare man, he receives me courteously, invites me to have a seat. He takes his time. He goes through the rigmarole of explaining that a doctor does not normally break confidentiality about a patient but, given the circumstances, and that I am a close relative, he will make an exception.

'You know she had a serious heart condition?'

I shake my head.

'I last saw her on 30 May.' He refers to a card. 'She told me she was going off on a long journey – no, she did not say where – and I had to warn her that that would be extremely unwise.'

On Sunday morning, I cross the river to the rue Bayard, off the avenue Montaigne, where the Scots Kirk is to be found. It is a small, modest-looking building, cream-washed, quite unlike the usual high, upstanding, grey stone Church of Scotland edifices to which I am accustomed. *The Scots Kirk* is written on its front in italic script, so that one cannot mistake it, and above is a large Gaelic cross. Inside, there are travel posters of Scotland on the walls to make the Scot abroad feel at home; one is of Craigievar Castle. On Sunday afternoons the Chinese community comes here to worship.

After the service I approach the minister, who introduces me to Amy's friend Madame Hamon. She is a little woman in her seventies, hatted and gloved. She might have stepped out of Jenners' store on Princes Street. She invites me to come back and have lunch with her in her apartment in the nearby place François Premier. I hear the Edinburgh in her voice – pure Morningside – even though she has been here for fifty years.

'Just a light lunch, dear, some salad and a little cold saumon en gelée. That's what Amy and I often used to have together.

300

I can't get over her disappearing. What a shock that's given me! I'd thought she might be in Scotland or even America and hadn't had time to write. It isn't like her not to write, not even a postcard. You say you've no idea where she might have gone?' Madame Hamon lays out the meal on a small table in front of the window in the sitting room. 'Would you mind?' She puts a half-bottle of white wine and a corkscrew into my hand. 'What about Budapest?' she says.

'*Budapest*?'

'Yes, she was married to a Hungarian once, was she not?'

'But what makes you think she would want to go there? To go after *him*?'

'Oh, I have no reason! I was just thinking of the Gare de l'Est.'

'You can go to lots of places from the Gare de l'Est.'

'That is very true. Do sit down, dear. A napkin? Of course, her marriage was pretty far back in the past.'

'The past is never quite past, though, is it?'

'How right you are! It tends to keep step with us into the present. I know I often feel as if my dear Eugène is still with me in the room.' She gives a little laugh. 'Sometimes I turn round and I think I'm going to see him! And it's ten years since he passed on. I don't think, however, that Amy was close to her husband in that way.'

I agree that she was not. 'Though after he left her she had a nervous breakdown.'

'She never really said much to me about that.'

I ask Madame Hamon if she knew any of Amy's friends.

'Only those at the church, dear. But none of them knew her well. Oh, and one year there was a very nice American couple who came over. From New York. I met them a couple of times. Amy brought them for drinks.'

'Luke and Paulette?'

'You know them?'

'Only *of* them. You wouldn't happen to remember their surname?'

'I don't, but I should be able to find it in my visitors' book.'

I have never liked visitors' books, find them pretentious (though Madame Hamon herself is not), and hate having to inscribe my name in them, but today I bless their existence, and will willingly sign in Madame Hamon's.

There, in front of me, in Paulette's sloping American handwriting (it looks like hers) is the entry: Paulette and Luke Nugent, and their address on W. 83rd Street. It should be easy enough to find their telephone number.

'Paulette Nugent speaking,' says a voice clearly in my ear. She might be in the next room. I tell her who I am and she says, 'Amy's cousin? Well, for goodness' sake! Hey, Luke, it's Amy's cousin from Edinburgh on the phone.'

'Calling from Paris,' I put in.

'We haven't heard from Amy in ages. We were starting to get a little worried. She's normally such a good correspondent. I called her café a while back but they said she hadn't been in. Has she been in Edinburgh? How is she?'

I repeat my story and give Paulette a few moments to absorb it. I hear her summarizing for Luke in the background.

'I'm trying to work out where she could have gone. Is there any chance it might have been Hungary?'

There is a brief silence at the other end and then Paulette's voice comes back a little guarded, no longer quite so open. 'It's hard to say.'

'You know she was married to a Hungarian?'

'Well, of course I know! I lived in the apartment beneath them.'

'He was called Janos, wasn't he? What was his surname?'

'Bakony.'

I write the name in my notebook. No doubt there will be dozens of Janos Bakony in Budapest. I know it will be a waste of time to start ringing up names plucked at random from a telephone book. For a start, I don't speak Hungarian.

'Amy was always fairly secretive about her marriage.' There is no response from the other end. I try again. 'You remember when she had her breakdown?'

'I'm hardly likely to forget it!'

302

'No, I realize that. She probably wouldn't have made it if it hadn't been for you.'

'I wouldn't say that,' says Paulette, but her voice is warmer again.

'I would. I've read her journal; I read it again this morning. And I keep feeling some factor is missing.'

Paulette sighs. 'Amy asked us never to talk about this, but I guess I'd better tell you.'

Amy had a daughter, born in 1953. I'd been beginning to suspect that there'd been a child in the picture, but if I'd voiced the idea to Jessie she would have said, 'Och, away ye go! You think everything revolves around kids in a woman's life.'

Both Amy and Janos adored the child; Paulette says she was the centre of their lives. It was when the little girl was six months old that Olivier Picard reappeared on the scene and Amy began to see him again.

'She was taking a big risk, she knew that. Janos was not the forgive-and-forget type. I shouldn't have aided and abetted her in any way – and I feel as guilty as hell that I did! – but she wasn't particularly happy with Janos and she was still in love with Olivier. And suddenly there he was, free! It just seemed too much to pass by, the chance of happiness. Most of us are seduced by that, or the idea of it, wouldn't you say?'

So Amy met Olivier in secret, but was watched covertly by Janos. Paulette even wonders if Janos might not have been pleased by Amy's defection. He had talked to Paulette about his growing desire to go back to his own country and how he knew Amy would never go with him. If he had good moral grounds to abandon her, as he would see it, he could talk himself into going, and taking the child with him. So when Amy went to the South of France with Olivier, Janos bought an old blue van, packed it up and left.

'There was no possible way Amy could go after them, she probably wouldn't have got a visa. And if she had, how could she have snatched her daughter and smuggled her out of the country? Especially a country like that, as it was then. Sealed off behind the Iron Curtain. The loss felled her. You can imagine, can't you? She blamed herself. She'd abandoned her daughter to go off with another man! It's a pretty big sin in most people's book. Well, she sure was punished for it! She did her best to wipe it from her memory. We were forbidden ever to speak of it. She went on with her life as if the child had never been. It seemed the only way she could stay sane.'

I think of the times I upbraided Amy for lacking sensitivity towards my children, when I told her, 'You wouldn't understand, not having had children yourself!' I confess to Paulette, whom I have never seen, yet feel I know. She says I shouldn't reproach myself for that, but I do, of course.

I then ask Paulette if she can remember the names of any of Amy's old Hungarian friends in Paris. She rakes her memory and comes up with a woman called Margarita. 'She was quite a bit older than Amy – she might be dead now. She lived in the rue du Bac. She was married to a Frenchman.' And her surname? Paulette thinks it might have been Boirot. 'I can't be sure. It was so long ago!'

I promise to stay in touch and let Paulette know what progress, if any, that I make. I have one more question before I ring off.

'What was her daughter called?'

'Oh, Gabrielle!'

I find a Boirot listed in the rue du Bac. A woman answers and it *is* Margarita. She invites me to come and see her.

She is widowed and arthritic, and walks with a stick, but her brown eyes shine out of her wrinkled face. She likes to sit by her window, which looks out on to the little square edged on one side by the rue de Commaille, where lived at one time Amy and Janos and Paulette.

'Amy and I used often to sit down there in the garden.'

'With her baby?'

Margarita nods.

'Did you have children, too?'

'Sadly, no. I had a problem, it wasn't possible. That was why I enjoyed Amy's baby. It was a sad business, that – Janos taking the child away. After that, Amy and I lost touch with each other. I expect she hated the sight of anyone Hungarian. I hadn't seen her for years until the spring.'

'You saw her *this* spring?'

'It was at a Hungarian get-together. I was so surprised to see her! She'd happened to bump into the friends who were holding it and they'd asked her to come along.'

Amongst the guests were a number of Hungarians who had come to Paris to visit relatives. 'There's been a steady flow since the opening up of Eastern Europe.' One of the visitors had known Janos Bakony back home.

'Is he still alive?'

'He died last year. She told us that.'

'Did Amy ask about her daughter?'

'She did. And was excited to get some news. She learned that Gabrielle was married and had two children.'

Not long afterwards, Amy took the decision to go to Hungary to see her daughter. She thought it best not to write before she went. She wasn't sure what Janos would have told the girl and was afraid that Gabrielle might write back and say she didn't want to see her.

Margarita does not know the married name of Gabrielle or her address.

'It would have been too much to hope,' I say to Jessie on the telephone. 'She gave me her friends' address – the ones who'd had the party. But they didn't know the woman who'd given Amy the information about her daughter – there'd been a lot of people there that night. They hadn't met her before. She'd come along in a crowd.'

'You wouldne think of going to Budapest yourself?'

'It'd be a bit of wild-goose chase.'

'Aye, you wouldn't know where to start, would you? Looking for a woman in her – what, late thirties? Called Gabrielle!'

305

I tell Jessie that I plan to stay on in Paris for a while. I have some research that I want to do for a book, and a friend, who is going abroad for a couple of months, has offered me the use of her small flat in the rue de Babylone, just around the corner from the rue Vaneau.

'Tomorrow, though, I'm going down to Saint-Sauveur.'

I look for a bell or a knocker on the door and, failing to find one, bang with my fist. Nothing happens for a while but I wait, listening, giving him time to make it to the door. I have to knock again before I hear shuffling steps and the slow tap of a stick on the other side of the splintered door. A voice asks, 'Who is there?'

'A cousin of Aimée Bussac's, her Scottish cousin.' Silence. Have I confused him? 'I am a cousin of the daughter of Eugénie Bussac. We met once, a long time ago.'

A key grates in the lock and the door opens a few inches. Through the slit I see one half of an elderly man's face, white-bearded, moustached, with a few wispy white hairs sprouting from the top of his brown-spotted skull. His buckled fingers keep hold of the edge of the door.

'I am from Edinburgh, Scotland.'

'Ah yes, Aimée. Come in, please.'

I wonder for a moment if Alphonse Bussac thinks I might *be* Amy (we do look somewhat alike, with the same thick, chestnut-coloured hair and triangular-shaped face), for his eyes, once I see them in the light, look almost opaque, and he mutters to himself as he turns to lead the way, leaning heavily on his stick. He is wearing slippers with a flapping sole, trousers held up with fraying string and a greyish shirt that may once have been another colour. The room smells uncleaned and unaired and is furnished with old, dark, heavy pieces – might some of it have come from the Grenot house in the rue des Gros Bonnets?

He asks me to sit down. I sink into a springless velour-upholstered chair. Dust rises and I sneeze silently into a handkerchief. I decline an offer of refreshment.

'I've come about Aimée,' I say.

'Ah, yes. Where is she? Is she still in Paris?'

'No. I was wondering if you might have seen her recently. In the last few months?'

'No, it's been a long time . . .'

I lean forward. 'Monsieur Bussac, Aimée had a daughter once – '

'A daughter? I never heard of a daughter.'

'She did have one, though, when she was married to a Hungarian. It is possible that this daughter may come here.'

'Why should she come?' He frowns, flustered.

'I cannot explain. But I just want to ask you: if she does, would you please get in touch with me?' I take a piece of paper from my bag and get up to give it to him. 'This is a telephone number in Paris where you can contact me, or, if I am not there, ring this number in Edinburgh.' Beside the paper I put a hundred-franc note. 'This will pay for the call. Could you do that? It's important.'

'But why should she come here to me?'

'You are the only living member of the family left here. If she comes at all to Saint-Sauveur, she will be directed to you.'

Back in Paris, I am restless, in spite of my research. I find it difficult to spend much time closeted in libraries or archives, away from the light. After two or three hours I go out and pound the pavements of the city. I inevitably revisit many of the old Colette haunts where Amy and I walked together. At Père Lachaise I see that another inscription has been added to the pink-and-black Burgundian granite: *Colette de Jouvenel, 1913–1981, Fille de Henry de Jouvenel des Ursins et de Sidonie-Gabrielle Colette.* So, at the end of the day, in death Colette lies alongside her daughter, to whom she was not close in life, and not with any of the men that she loved.

On another occasion, after wandering down the rue Jacob and arriving at its eastern end, I turn into the rue de Seine. The antiquarian bookshop is still there, with the name PICARD emblazoned in gold along the front. I open the door and step inside. The room smells of old, expensive books. Mozart is playing softly in the background.

The young man sitting at the leather-topped desk looks up as I enter and asks if he can help me.

'I'm looking for a first edition of *Le Blé en herbe*.'

'You're in luck! I bought one only an hour ago. Isn't that a coincidence? And it's signed.'

'Wonderful!'

He produces the book, which is in excellent condition; some pages have not been cut. I peep in at the flyleaf and smile at the sight of the familiar bold signature.

'This book is for my daughter Vinca.'

'Ah, how very apt!'

I pay and he slips the book into a crisp paper bag.

'I suppose Monsieur Picard is retired now?'

'Oh, indeed. He has just turned eighty-seven.'

'Is he still in good health?'

'Amazingly good. He has had few worries in life, you know! And Madame Picard, too, she is well also. Do you know them?'

'Not directly.'

We chat. I find out that he is Olivier's nephew. I tell him that my cousin used to work here a long time ago, before his time. 'Just after the war.'

He gesticulates apologetically. He was not born then. It is not something he should apologize for, I tell him, and we laugh, and I go on my way.

That night, I have my recurring dream.

A woman of advancing years, wearing a blue jacket, hair burnished by a chestnut tint, eyes concealed behind dark glass, emerges into a street. It is a divided street: on the sunny side, the graffiti, broken windowpanes, tin cans and spent cigarette packets are illuminated, as on a stage set, whilst on the other, the shady side, the scars of living merge with the grey stone. The sun is fierce. The woman does not like the sun. She resettles the bridge of her dark glasses over her nose. She looks left and then right. She sees nothing. She does not notice the man waiting in the shadows on the opposite side, his back pressed into a recessed doorway.

She crosses the street, taking her time. She gives a sigh of relief as she passes the line of demarcation and leaves the sun behind. She steps on up to the other kerb and pauses again to readjust the strap of her black shoulder bag. It appears to be heavy, this bag. It might contain money, passport, make-up, address book, old letters. Her personal effects. Her identification. She places the strap crosswise over her chest, in the way that women in big cities carry their shoulder bags these days, for extra protection. She moves on again, each step a conscious effort.

The man is waiting. He is not impatient. He does not fidget in the deep violet shadow. He knows she will come. He knows she will pass this way. I want to warn her, to cry out, but my mouth will not open, and my throat is locked. She is only a few steps from him . . . now three, two . . . He raises his arm. There is something in his hand, something thick and dark and rectangular. He brings it down. As it meets the crown of the woman's head, her eyes dilate and she screams . . .

I waken in grey light with a scream in my throat. My nightdress is twisted and damp with sweat. I struggle to sit up and gingerly feel my head. No blunt instrument appears to have struck it; my fingers encounter no lump. My heart is batting against my rib cage like a bird trying to escape. The woman in the dream was me and yet not me. I lean back against the pillows to allow my heart to subside and after a while sink back into sleep again, to be awakened by the telephone shrilling on the bedside table.

I lift the receiver. My head feels muzzy. The bedside clock blinks 9.03.

I hear a man's fumbling voice.

'Alphonse?'

'Yes, it's me. There's a young woman here. She says she's Aimée's daughter.'

*

I relay the news to Jessie in Edinburgh. Then I say that I have something to tell her, something else.

'Oh yes?'

'This is something I've carried with me for a long time.'

I can hear her lighting a cigarette at the other end of the line. Now she blows out smoke. 'And what would that be?'

'You remember when Granny Balfour found out about Amy's American airman?'

'Aye.'

'Someone betrayed her.' I pause, listen. 'Are you still there?'

'I'm still here.'

'It was me.'

'So?'

Is that all she can say? 'But don't you see, Jessie, it was because of that that Amy severed her link with the family and took off?'

'Dinne tell me you've been feeling responsible for all that's happened to her!'

Well, yes, I have, even though my rational side tells me that we cannot be responsible for another person's life. But guilt plays havoc with reason.

'You were only a bairn at the time!'

I know, I know.

'And we all kent it was you.'

'You did?'

'Of course! Who else could it have been?'

'Amy, too, did she know?'

'What do you think? But she decided not to raise it with you. We talked about it when she came to Edinburgh in '65. Water under the bridge, she said. She'd thought you'd probably forgotten all about it, anyway, with you being so young at the time. She bore you no ill will. Said it was her own fault for involving you, for putting such a load of responsibility on to your shoulders.'

I reach Saint-Sauveur in the late afternoon. The trees are turning; the stubble in the fields is golden under a mellow

310

sun. There is a smell of wood smoke. The village is quiet as I drive in. I pass only one woman, walking home, carrying her shopping. I walk calmly up the stairs to the flat of Alphonse Bussac. I am surprised by my calmness; I had expected to feel a tumult of emotion. Soon I shall know.

Alphonse admits me at once; he has been watching from the window. I saw his face when I looked up from the street. I saw the look of bewilderment on it. I follow him through the dark passage into the room.

A woman of middle height and slender to middling build is standing at the window with her back to the room. Her thick, springy hair is the colour of beech leaves in autumn. She is wearing a vivid blue silk shirt that looks as if it has been bought in Paris. She turns.

Amy! I almost cry out the name, then pull it back. For it is not Amy, not as she would have been now, in her late sixties, but as she was twenty-five years ago, when she came to her first Edinburgh Festival with the young Pascal. This is Amy's daughter.

'Gabrielle!'

She comes forward to meet me. I put out my arms and we hold on to one another. When we separate, I open my bag and bring out the Baccarat paperweight. 'This is yours,' I say.

She looks at me questioningly, as she lets her fingers close around it and her palm take the weight.

'I'll tell you the story, in due course.' Then I say, 'Let's go for a walk. I want to show you Saint-Sauveur.'

The shadows are deepening. C'est l'heure entre le chien et le loup. I tell Gabrielle that was how Colette described this time of day. We are talking in French; Gabrielle's father Janos Bakony taught her to speak the language when she was a young child. He told her that her mother was dead. But before he himself died he confessed that he had lied to her.

'He was sorry for that. He was not a bad man, my father. I loved him.'

'Amy is dead now, though, isn't she?' I say.

Gabrielle nods. 'That is why I am here.'

An elderly woman in a blue jacket arrives at a train station. She is carrying a large black leather handbag strung diagonally across her chest. All is hustle and bustle around her. Coming from the tannoy above her head is a voice speaking in a language that she cannot comprehend. Two suitcases stand on the platform in front of her, one carmine-red, the other a dirty cream. She dips at the knees to lift them up; the weight pulls her shoulders forward so that she looks as if she might topple over. She lurches forward, pushing her way through the crowd. Beads of sweat start around her hairline. She reaches a gap, a small oasis, a breathing space. She sets down the cases, then she opens the black bag that hugs her body and takes out a paper handkerchief. As she raises it to her forehead, a hand comes out and jerks the strap from her shoulder, wrenching it over her head, yanking her neck sideways, and then another hand comes up and punches her in the ribs and she goes down, issuing only one short piercing cry before she loses consciousness.

'There were two of them,' says Gabrielle, 'waiting for rich travellers arriving from the west! They took the cream suitcase, but the red one they had to abandon, on account of its weight. It was full of books.'

'The works of Colette?'

'Yes!'

'But how did the authorities connect her with you?'

'When they brought her into the hospital, they found a piece of paper in her jacket pocket.'

'With your name and address on it?'

She nodded. 'They phoned us and we went at once – my husband and I.'

When she stood beside the hospital bed, Gabrielle was not in doubt about the woman's identity. Her husband said, 'She looks like you.'

Amy recovered consciousness and rallied sufficiently for Gabrielle to be able to bring her home.

'We had a week together. She saw the children. I stayed with her all the time, I slept beside her. She'd be silent for long stretches then she'd talk a little ... in snatches ... disconnected ... moving backwards and forwards. She told us about you and a woman called Jessie and another, whose name I think was Paulette, and she spoke often about her mother Eugénie and her grandmother Berthe – *my* great-grandmother! – and her childhood friend, Gabrielle Colette. At times she seemed to be in the Colettes' garden, here in Saint-Sauveur.' We are walking now down the rue des Vignes, passing below the high wall that screens the secret garden. 'She'd ask me if the walnuts were ripe yet; had the big fir trees been cut down? When the priest came to see her she thought he was the curé from this church. This is it, isn't it? It is all familiar – I have been reading the books of Colette.'

We stand for a moment and look at the church on the corner, then we turn right, and right again, and come into the steep rue Colette, which was formerly the rue de l'Hospice.

At the end of the week with her daughter, Amy suffered a massive heart attack and died instantly. 'We couldn't contact anyone. We had no addresses.' But Amy had told them what she wanted. They had her cremated, and Gabrielle has now brought the ashes with her to Saint-Sauveur, to be placed in the Bussac family plot.

'She will lie beside her mother, then. I wasn't able to come before. First, I had to raise the money for the fare and then to get a visa and make arrangements.'

I slid my hand easily through the crook of Gabrielle's arm. She appears so familiar to me! We shall bury Amy's ashes together and ask the present curé to say a prayer over her grave.

We climb the hill to where the rue des Gros Bonnets meets the rue Colette. I point out the house where Berthe Grenot was born on the twenty-eighth of January, 1873.

'You're going to tell me all about the Grenots and the Bussacs aren't you?' says Gabrielle. 'I want to know everything!'

'There are the Balfours, too. You mustn't forget them! They're involved as well. You must come to Edinburgh and meet our side of the family. You must come and meet my daughter Vinca.'

We stand on the corner, at the intersection of the two streets. A little evening breeze skirmishes around our ankles. The streetlamps glimmer. The Colette house is dark. But as we keep watch, a light comes on in an upper window, in the room above the coach-house door, the room with the pearly-grey wallpaper sprinkled with cornflowers, where once upon a time slept the young Sidonie-Gabrielle Colette, her long, rippling, chestnut-coloured hair spread out on the white lace coverlet as in a fairytale. And watching from the doorway, listening for the sound of her rising and falling breath, stands the silhouetted figure of Sido, her mother.